Consumer Law
& Protection

Consumer Law & Protection

A Practical Approach for Paralegals and the Public

Neal R. Bevans

PROFESSOR
WESTERN PIEDMONT COMMUNITY COLLEGE

CAROLINA ACADEMIC PRESS
Durham, North Carolina

Library of Congress Cataloging-in-Publication Data

Bevans, Neal R., 1961-
  Consumer law and protection : protecting the rights of consumers / Neal R. Bevans.
      p. cm.
  ISBN 978-1-59460-837-7 (alk. paper)
  1. Consumer protection--Law and legislation--United States. I. Title.

    KF1609.B49 2010
    343.7307'1--dc22

                                          2010032007

Carolina Academic Press
700 Kent Street
Durham, North Carolina 27701
Telephone (919) 489-7486
Fax (919) 493-5668
www.cap-press.com

Printed in the United States of America

*To my niece, Katie Burnett, and
my nephew, Ben Burnett, with all my love.*

Contents

Preface   xv

Acknowledgments   xvii

About the Author   xix

Chapter 1 • Fraud and Misrepresentation   3
   Chapter Objectives   3
   I.   The Shareholders' Suit   3
   II. Introduction   3
   III. Fraud   4
      A. Proving Fraud   5
          1. Typical Sales Statements Don't Equal Fraud   6
      B. Alleging Fraud in the Complaint   6
      C. Limitations on Fraud Actions   7
      D. Fraud and Criminal Law   7
   IV. Negligent Misrepresentation   9
      A. Elements of Negligent Misrepresentation   9
      B. Awarding Monetary Damages in Negligent Misrepresentation Cases   10
      C. Opinions and Negligent Misrepresentation   12
      D. Negligent Misrepresentation vs. Mistake   13
      E. Pleading Negligent Misrepresentation   13
      F. Defenses to Negligent Misrepresentation   13
          1. Truth   13
          2. Opinion   14
          3. Statement Did Not Concern a Material Fact   14
          4. No Detrimental Reliance on the Statement   14
          5. No Damages   14
          6. Waiver   14
      G. Defenses That Are Not Available in Negligent Misrepresentation   15
          1. "No Knowledge"   15
          2. Good Faith   15
   Case Excerpt   15
   Case Questions   18
   V.   Follow-up on the Shareholders' Suit   18
   Chapter Summary   19
   Web Sites   20
   Key Terms   20
   Review Questions   20

Chapter 2 · Deceptive Practices   23
    Chapter Objectives   23
    I.   What Are Deceptive Practices?   23
        A. Examples of Unfair or Deceptive Trade Practices   23
        B. Common-law Remedies   25
    II. Federal Regulation of Unfair and Deceptive Trade Practices   26
        A. The Federal Trade Commission   26
            1. Enforcement and Investigation Powers of the FTC   27
            2. Role of the Federal Trade Commission in Modern Business Practices   27
            3. The Bureau of Consumer Protection   28
            4. The Expanded Role of the FTC in the Age of Cyber Commerce   28
            5. The Do Not Call Registry   28
    III. State Regulation   29
        A. What Is the UDTPA?   29
            1. Unlawful Actions under UDTPA   29
            2. Exceptions under UDTPA   30
            3. Remedies under the Uniform Deceptive Trade Practices Act   31
        B. Other State Limitations on Business Practices: The Uniform Commercial Code   32
        C. Role of State Agencies in Investigating Deceptive Trade Practices   33
        D. Other Consumer Protections   33
            1. Limitations on Commercial Advertisements   34
    Case Excerpt   34
    Case Questions   38
    Chapter Summary   38
    Web Sites   39
    Key Terms   39
    Review Questions   39

Chapter 3 · Product Liability   41
    Chapter Objectives   41
    I.   Product Liability   41
        A. A Short History of Product Liability in the U.S.   42
        B. Contract Law and the Privity Problem   43
        C. Suing for Breach of Warranty   45
        D. Contract Law and Product Liability Actions   45
        E. Bringing Suit under Traditional Negligence Theory   45
            1. Duty   46
            2. Breach of Duty   46
            3. Causation   47
            4. Damages   47
            5. Summarizing Karen's Case   48
    II. The Doctrine of Product Liability   49
        A. Product Liability Does Not Involve a Finding of Fault   50
        B. What Can Be the Basis of a Product Liability Lawsuit?   50
        C. Arguments For and Against Product Liability Cases   51
        D. Proving a Product Liability Case   51
            1. The Plaintiff Was Injured by a Product   52
            2. That the Injury Was the Result of a Defective Design   52
            3. That the Product Was Created or Manufactured by the Defendant   53

E. State Statutes on Product Liability 53
1. Different States/Different Theories of Product Liability 54
F. Model Uniform Products Liability Act 54
G. Federal Legislation Related to Product Liability 54
1. The Duty to Test and Inspect 55
2. The Duty to Comply with Health and Safety Regulations 56
3. Inherently Dangerous Objects 56
H. Tort Reform and Product Liability 56
Case Excerpt 57
Case Questions 59
Chapter Summary 59
Web Sites 60
Key Terms 60
Review Questions 61

Chapter 4 • Warranties 63
Chapter Objectives 63
I. What Are Warranties? 63
A. A Short History of the Law of Warranties 63
B. Express Warranties 65
1. Evidentiary Issues in Express Warranty Cases 66
C. Implied Warranties 67
1. Types of Implied Warranties 67
II. Federal Law Regarding Warranties 69
A. Magnuson-Moss Warranty Act 69
1. Jurisdiction of MMWA 69
2. Definitions under MMWA 70
3. Enforcement under the Act 71
4. Written Warranties under the Magnuson-Moss Warranty Act 71
5. Implied Warranties under the Magnuson-Moss Warranty Act 73
6. The Magnuson-Moss Warranty Act and Other Federal Law 73
7. What Is Required under the Magnuson-Moss Warranty Act? 73
III. State-Based Warranty Actions 75
A. "Lemon Laws" 75
Case Excerpt 76
Case Questions 79
IV. Disclaimers 79
Case Excerpt 79
Case Questions 85
Chapter Summary 85
Web Sites 85
Key Terms 86
Review Questions 86

Chapter 5 • Internet Scams, Forgery, Credit Card Fraud and Identity Theft 87
Chapter Objectives 87
I. Introduction 87
A. Internet Scams 89
1. Phishing 90

        2. Cramming   91
    B. Investigating Internet Fraud   91
        1. Jurisdictional Issues in Internet Fraud   92
 II. Forgery   93
    A. The Basic Elements of Forgery   93
        1. Make, Alter or Possess a Writing   94
        2. Without Authority   94
        3. Uttering and Delivering   94
 Case Excerpt   95
 Case Questions   96
 III. Credit Card Theft and Fraud   97
    A. Skimming   97
 IV. Identity Theft   98
 Case Excerpt   99
 Case Questions   102
 Chapter Summary   102
 Web Sites   102
 Key Terms   103
 Review Questions   103

Chapter 6 · Truth in Lending   105
 Chapter Objectives   105
 I. The Federal Truth in Lending Act   105
    A. Regulation Z   106
    B. Time of Disclosures   106
    C. Finance Charges under the Federal Truth in Lending Act 107
    D. Initial Disclosure Statements   107
    E. Continuous Obligation of Creditors   108
 II. Open-ended Credit   108
    A. Credit Cards   111
        1. Credit Card Applications and Solicitations   111
        2. Credit Card Disclosures   111
        3. Billing Errors on Credit Card Transactions   114
 III. Closed-end Credit Agreements   115
    A. Required Disclosures in Closed-end Credit Transactions 115
        1. Identification of Creditor   116
        2. The Amount Financed   116
        3. Itemization of Amount Financed   116
        4. Finance Charge   116
        5. Annual Percentage Rate   116
        6. Variable Rate   116
        7. Payment Schedule   117
        8. Total of Payments   117
        9. Demand Feature   117
        10. Total Sale Price   117
        11. Prepayment Provisions   117
        12. Late Payments   117
        13. Security Interest   117
        14. Insurance and Debt Cancellation Provisions   118
        15. Security Interest Charges   118

16. Contract Reference   118
17. Assumption Policy   119
18. Required Deposit   119
B. Right of Rescission   119
1. Notice of Rescission   119
IV. Enforcement of Federal Truth in Lending Act   120
A. Federal Trade Commission   120
B. Consumer Actions under TILA   120
1. Criminal Liability under TILA   121
2. Preemption of State Law   121
Case Excerpt   122
Case Questions   128
Chapter Summary   128
Web Sites   128
Key Terms   129
Review Questions   129

Chapter 7 · Predatory Lending & Other Questionable Lending Practices   131
Chapter Objectives   131
I.   Questionable Lending Practices   131
A. The Housing Market   131
II. Predatory Lending   132
A. Encouraging Borrowers to Lie About Their Income and Debts   132
1. Financing Fees   133
B. Charging High Interest Rates   133
C. Charging High Fees   133
D. Pre-payment Penalties   134
E. Stripping Equity   135
F. High Pressure Sales Tactics   136
G. Other Predatory Lending Practices   136
1. Yield Spread Premiums   137
H. Unreasonable Arbitration Clauses   137
I. Consequences of Predatory Lending   138
II. Other Questionable Lending Practices   138
A. Overdraft Loan Programs   139
B. Credit Repair   139
C. Loan Churning or "Loan Flipping"   140
D. Insurance Schemes   140
E. Payday Loans   141
F. Tax Refund Loans   141
G. Car Title Loans   141
H. Rent-to-own Contracts   142
I. Balloon Payments   142
Case Excerpt   143
Case Questions   148
Chapter Summary   149
Web Sites   149
Key Terms   149
Review Questions   149

Chapter 8 · Fair Credit Reporting   151
    Chapter Objectives   151
    I.   Introduction   151
        A. Importance of Good Credit   151
        B. Calculating a Credit Score   152
        C. Credit Reports   153
    II. Fair Credit Reporting Act   153
        A. Consumer Reports under FCRA   153
            1. Exclusions under FCRA   153
            2. Investigative Consumer Report   154
            3. Consumer Reporting Agencies under FCRA   154
        B. The Major Credit Reporting Agencies in the United States   154
            1. Equifax   155
            2. TransUnion   155
            3. Experian   155
    III. Purposes of Credit Reports Under FCRA   155
        A. Furnishing Credit Reports to Others   155
            1. Courts   156
            2. Creditors   156
            3. Employers   156
            4. Governmental Agencies   157
            5. Companies That Issue Offers of Credit or Insurance   158
        B. Consumer Disclosures   158
            1. Inquiries   159
            2. Denials of Credit   159
        C. Disclosing File Contents to Consumers   159
            1. Summary of Consumer Rights   159
        D. Disputing Credit Report Entries   160
            1. Frivolous or Irrelevant Disputes   161
            2. Notice of Reinvestigation   161
            3. Statement of Dispute   161
            4. Deleting Contested Information   161
        E. Items That May Not be Reported in Credit Reports   161
        F. Ensuring Accuracy of Credit Reports under FCRA   162
        G. Obtaining Copies of Credit Reports   162
            1. Free Reports   162
    IV. Enforcing the Provisions of FCRA   162
        A. Administrative Enforcement   163
        B. Civil Suits by Consumers   163
    Case Excerpt   164
    Case Questions   170
    Chapter Summary   170
    Web Sites   171
    Key Terms   171
    Review Questions   171

Chapter 9 · Fair Debt Collection Practices   173
    Chapter Objectives   173
    I.   The Fair Debt Collection Practices Act   173
    II. Jurisdiction under Fair Debt Collection Practices Act   174

A. Who Is Covered under Fair Debt Collection Practices Act? 174
1. Fair Debt Collection Practices Act Does Not Apply to
Actual Creditors 174
2. Defining "Debt Collectors" under the Act 175
3. Defining "Debt" under the Act 175
III. Communications between Debt Collectors and Consumers 176
A. Locating Consumers 176
1. Communicating with the Consumer 176
IV. Activities under Fair Debt Collection Practices Act 179
A. Permissible Actions under Fair Debt Collection Practices Act 179
B. Prohibited Actions under Fair Debt Collection Practices Act 179
1. Harassment 180
2. False Statements 180
3. Misrepresentations 181
4. Unfair Practices 182
V. Enforcing the Provisions of Fair Debt Collection Practices Act 183
Case Excerpt 184
Case Questions 188
Chapter Summary 188
Web Sites 188
Key Terms 189
Review Questions 189

Chapter 10 · Remedies Available to the Consumer 191
Chapter Objectives 191
I. Introduction to Consumer Remedies 191
II. An Overview of the American Legal System 191
A. Terminology in Civil Cases 192
B. Discovery 192
1. Depositions 193
2. Interrogatories 193
3. Requests for Production of Documents 193
4. The Significance of Completing the Discovery Process 194
C. Civil Trials 194
1. Verdicts in Civil Cases 195
D. Appeals in Civil Cases 195
E. Settlement 195
III. Arbitration & Mediation 195
A. Arbitration 196
B. Mediation 196
IV. Equitable Remedies 196
A. Injunction 197
B. Specific Performance 197
C. Rescission 198
D. Reformation 198
1. "Duty to Read" 198
V. Monetary Damages 199
A. Compensatory Damages 199
1. Calculating Monetary Damage Awards 199

2. Consequential Damages   201
3. Liquidated Damages   202
B. Punitive Damages   202
C. Nominal Damages   203
VI. Complaining to Federal, State and Private Organizations   204
A. Complaints to Local Better Business Bureau   204
B. Using the Media   204
1. TV and Newspaper "Crusaders"   204
Case Excerpt   204
Case Questions   209
Chapter Summary   209
Web Sites   210
Key Terms   210
Review Questions   210

Chapter 11 • When the Contract Is Invalid   213
Chapter Objectives   213
I.   Contracts That Are Invalid because of the Consumer's Status 213
A. Capacity   214
1. Minors   215
B. Intoxication   216
C. Mental Incompetence   217
D. Enforceable and Unenforceable Contracts   217
E. Legality   218
1. Public Policy   218
II. Mistake as Grounds to Void a Contract   218
A. Mistaken Description   219
B. Mistaken Existence   219
C. Mistaken Value   219
III. Canceling a Contract because of Duress, Coercion or Undue Influence 219
A. Duress   220
B. Coercion   221
C. Undue Influence   221
IV. Important Legal Doctrines for Consumer Contracts   222
A. Promissory Estoppel   222
B. Waiver   223
C. Accord and Satisfaction   223
D. Caveat Emptor   224
E. Laches   224
Case Excerpt   225
Case Questions   229
Chapter Summary   229
Web Sites   229
Key Terms   230
Review Questions   230

Glossary   231

Index   237

Preface

In recent years, the interest in consumer-related issues has grown tremendously, fueled by growing unemployment, high foreclosure rates, credit card interest rate increases and predatory lending practices. This book seeks to fill the need for a well-written text on consumer law and consumer protection. This is an area of law that will only grow in importance as Internet-based commerce continues to boom and as the ramifications of our economic recession spin out for years to come. Consumer law is a topic that will remain an important issue for everyone.

This book also addresses other issues, such as so-called "credit repair," foreclosures, Fair Debt Collections practices, scams, predatory lending and many other practices.

Key Characteristics of *Consumer Law & Protection: A Practical Approach for Paralegals and the Public*

1. Each chapter analyzes an important aspect of consumer law and protection, from fraud to warranties, identity theft to the Federal Truth in Lending Act.

2. Each chapter contains a relevant case and/or statute that illustrates the topics covered in that section.

3. Web sites for further research and/or discussion

4. Step-by-step analysis of problems as diverse as "bait and switch" schemes to Uniform Commercial Code applicability.

5. Extensive chapter discussion questions based on real cases and scenarios

6. Practical assignments, based on real world problems faced by consumers and their legal representatives.

7. Numerous sidebars addressing a wide variety of issues

8. End-of-chapter exercises, hands-on assignments, and practical applications of the concepts presented in each chapter

Description of the Key Characteristics and Features Found in *Consumer Law & Protection: A Practical Approach for Paralegals and the Public*

- Learning objectives stated at the beginning of each chapter
- Terms and legal vocabulary in **bold** and defined immediately for the student

- Figures and tables to illustrate crucial points, designed to capitalize on different student learning styles
- Scenarios to help students develop their understanding of the material
- Excerpts from seminal or otherwise noteworthy cases and important federal statutes, such as the Fair Credit Reporting Act and others.
- End-of-chapter questions, activities and assignments to increase student comprehension and retention of the concepts presented in the chapter
- Web site for further research, investigation and/or discussion, including a link to online legal research sources
- Glossary containing definitions of all terms used in the text

Acknowledgments

The author would like to thank the following people for their assistance in creating this book: Beth Hall, Lisa Burnett, Karen Johnston and Lisa McHugh.

About the Author

Neal Bevans is a former Assistant District Attorney and private attorney. A veteran of over 150 trials, Bevans has litigated every major felony from rape, murder, and narcotics to armed robbery. One of his cases was televised nationally on Court TV. He has a Juris Doctor degree from the University of Georgia (Order of the Barrister) and has been a college instructor for more than 10 years. A multiple-year honoree in *Who's Who Among America's Teachers*, Bevans is an instructor of both paralegal and criminal justice courses, and is the author of numerous textbooks and magazine articles. He received the Excellence in Teaching Award from Western Piedmont Community College in 2010.

Consumer Law
& Protection

Chapter 1

Fraud and Misrepresentation

Chapter Objectives

- Explain how a civil action for fraud is brought
- Define negligent misrepresentation
- Detail the elements required to prove fraud
- Explain how a consumer can bring a negligent misrepresentation action
- Demonstrate the defenses available in a negligent misrepresentation case

I. The Shareholders' Suit

In the 1990s and early 2000s, the End-Run Corporation was a high flyer. Its stock price, which had remained around $20 per share in the 1980s, rose to over $100 per share in the last few years. End-Run posted huge profits and proclaimed a rosy future. End-Run executives received huge, and apparently well-earned, seven figure salaries and a host of perquisites. Then, a reporter for the local newspaper broke a story claiming that the 'huge profits' of End-Run were actually part of a corporate scheme to fool stockholders and the public at large. In fact, End-Run was seriously in debt, but had disguised the fact by clever (and illegal) accounting practices. Tom, who owns one thousand End-Run shares wants to sue End-Run for what he says is outright fraud. Does he have a case? If so, what type of action can he file against End-Run? Before we can analyze his case, we must first have a solid understanding of the law of fraud, deceit and negligent misrepresentation.

II. Introduction

In this chapter, we will explore the various actions associated with fraud and negligent misrepresentation. We will examine how consumers are often defrauded and the types of actions that they can bring when they have been.

Everyone knows that lying is something to be avoided. However, when does a lie, or a knowing misrepresentation, become actionable under the law? Obviously not everyone who has told a lie has been sued. In fact, most lies are not actionable at all. However, under certain circumstances, a falsehood does give a person a cause of action against another person.

An outright lie can give rise to several possible actions. For instance, if the lie is in the context of a contractual agreement, this can provide the basis for a breach of contract suit. If the lie is unintentional, or made without concern for the actual truth, the plaintiff can sue for negligent misrepresentation. However, when and under what circumstances does a statement, or an action, become a misrepresentation? We will begin with the easier issue of fraud before moving into the more complex world of negligent misrepresentation.

Figure 1-1. "Totals and trends in civil suits." *Contract Trials and Verdicts in Large Counties, 2001*, Bureau of Justice Statistics, Selected Findings, January 2005, page 1.

Totals and Trends

- During 2001 an estimated 3,698 contract cases were disposed of by trial in State courts of general jurisdiction in the Nation's 75 largest counties. Contract cases represented nearly a third of all civil trials in these counties.

- Judges adjudicated 56% of contract cases, while juries decided the remaining 44%.

- The 3,698 contract trials disposed of in 2001 represented a 24% decline from the 4,850 contract trials disposed of in these counties in 1996.

- About half (54%) of the contract cases disposed of by trial in the Nation's 75 largest counties in 2001 involved failed agreements between buyers and sellers. In most contract trials, the litigants were either individuals suing businesses (33%) or non-individual such as businesses, hospital, or governments suing businesses (26%).

III. Fraud

The problem with words such as "fraud" and "deceit" is that they have been overused; their precise, legal meanings have been diluted over time to the point that they are almost incapable of an exact definition.

Fraud is a word that lends itself to many possible definitions. People have been lying, cheating and scamming each other for thousands of years. A basic definition of fraud could be: a deceitful action against another to gain some form of advantage.

> **Fraud:** A civil or criminal action based on the defendant's knowingly giving a false statement that an innocent party relied upon to his or her disadvantage.

Fraud includes outright lying, deceit, surprise, trickery, false claims and the whole panoply of treachery practiced by human beings. While it may be difficult to define what fraud is, we can certainly say what fraud is not. Fraud is an intentional action. There is no negligent fraud. We can certainly say that fraud is an intentional action, requiring an affirmative action on the part of the defendant. In order to prove fraud, a plaintiff must show that the defendant had knowledge that he was defrauding another. Later, we will see that negligent misrepresentation does not involve intentional action, but for fraud, the consumer must show the defendant's intent. Fraud can occur when a person knowingly makes a false statement or when a person conceals or withholds a fact.

> Example: One afternoon, Mary goes out shopping for antiques. She approaches John, who is standing beside a lovely 19th century armoire with a "For Sale" sign

taped to it. Mary asks, "How much?" John responds, "How much are you offering?" She looks the armoire over again and then offers $300. John says, "Okay." Mary has a friend help her load the armoire into her truck. Just as she is about to pull away, an irate man runs up to her and accuses her of theft. Mary explains that she bought the armoire from John, who has now disappeared. The irate man says that he is the rightful owner and that he did not intend to sell the armoire. Later, when Mary catches up with John and asks for her money back, John says, "I never told that you that I didn't own it." Can Mary sue John for fraud?

Answer: Yes. Although John did not make an actual statement claiming that he had the right to sell the armoire, he did withhold the fact that he did not have that right. Under these facts, withholding a fact is equivalent to making a false statement. Both are actionable.

Sidebar: "Fraud, actual and constructive, is so multiform as to admit of no rules or definitions. 'It is, indeed, a part of equity doctrine not to define it,' says Lord Hardwicke, 'lest the craft of men should find a way of committing fraud which might escape such a rule or definition.'"[1]

Getting to the Essentials:	Fraud involves any act (or omission) that conceals the breach of a legal duty or material fact. This act must cause injury to the plaintiff or give the defendant an unjustified or unconscionable advantage.

A. Proving Fraud

In order to prove fraud, a consumer must show the following:

1. The defendant made a representation of a material fact or concealed a fact

2. That the representation was false

3. That the defendant knew the representation was false

4. That the defendant made the representation with the intent that the plaintiff would rely on it

5. The plaintiff's reliance on the representation was reasonable under the circumstances

6. That the plaintiff suffered injury from his reliance on the representation.

One of the key elements involved in proof of fraud is that the representation involved a **material fact**. This is a fact that is crucial to the parties' understanding of the transaction or a key point of negotiation. In the example provided above, John's lack of ownership of the armoire was a material fact. It was a central point of the negotiations and an assumption that Mary made based on John's behavior. Many states have enacted statutes spelling out exactly what is a material fact. In fact, many refer to a misrepresentation of a "material past or present fact." A material *past fact* is simply a statement about a past fact, such as a statement detailing exactly where the armoire was manufactured and how it has been treated by previous owners. A material *present fact* refers to John's ownership of the armoire.

---

1. *Standard Oil Co. v. Hunt,* 121 S.E. 184 (1924).

1. Typical Sales Statements Don't Equal Fraud

It is not fraud to make the types of statements we commonly associate with selling techniques. For instance, it is not a material misrepresentation to claim that a car is "the best car in the world." On the other hand, it is a material misrepresentation to claim that the car has never been in an accident when it actually has been. 'Puffing' and other exaggerations are par for the course in a transaction and most buyers do not take such claims seriously.

> **Material fact:** A fact that is basic to a contract, one that the parties consider to be an essential ingredient of the negotiations.

It is difficult to come up with a solid definition of a material fact that will work in all situations. Suffice to say that a material fact is one of those facts that would make or break the deal between the parties.

> Example: John and Ted have decided to open up a craft store together. They have extensively negotiated the partnership deal between them. For instance, the partnership takes effect on January 1st of next year and each man will contribute $20,000 to the business. Both will work a minimum of 40 hours per week at the business. John prefers to work on Tuesdays and Thursday evenings, but he is flexible about other times. Ted is a morning person and plans on being at the store every morning at 8 a.m. Which of these facts is a material fact and which is not?
>
> Answer: All of the contractual details concerning monetary contribution, the date that the partnership takes effect and how many hours each man must work at the business are material facts. The non-material facts include each man's stated preference about when he will actually work. Their preferences are not essential components to the contract and therefore they are not material facts.

B. Alleging Fraud in the Complaint

When a complaint alleges fraud, the plaintiff must present enough detail in the complaint to show material facts, how these facts were untrue and specific instances (times, places and contents) of false representations.[2] Simply stating that the plaintiff was defrauded will not satisfy the requirements of notice pleading in most states.[3]

In most jurisdictions, fraud must be proven by "**clear and convincing**" evidence. This essentially means that someone alleging fraud has a higher standard to meet than allegations made in other types of civil cases (where preponderance of the evidence is usually enough).

> **Clear and convincing evidence:** A level of proof higher than mere preponderance of the evidence. In most civil trials preponderance of the evidence is sufficient.

> Sidebar: deceit is considered to be a lesser form of fraud. It is any false representation that misleads another person, but may not result in any harm. Although both terms are often used interchangeably, fraud is a recognized cause of action; deceit is not.

---

2. *Coley v. North Carolina National Bank*, 41 N.C.App. 121, 254 S.E.2d 217 (1979).
3. *Patuxent Development Co. v. Bearden*, 227 N.C. 124, 128, 41 S.E.2d 85 (1947).

Figure 1-2. Activities That Are Classified as Fraud.

- Any false statement that is reasonable and one which the plaintiff relies upon
- A willful, intentional misstatement that gives the defendant an unfair advantage over the plaintiff

C. Limitations on Fraud Actions

In some jurisdictions, omission of a material fact will not support a claim for fraud unless the defendant had a legal obligation to disclose it. Usually, the obligation to disclose a fact is limited to those with fiduciary responsibilities. A **fiduciary** is a person or corporation that has a legal and ethical duty to act in the best interests of another. An example of a fiduciary relationship is the attorney-client relationship. The attorney must be vigilant in protecting the interests of his or her client and certainly cannot use confidential information to enrich the attorney at the expense of the client. When a fiduciary fails to disclose a material fact, this failure can be the basis of a fraud claim. It can also be the basis for other actions, as well, including negligent misrepresentation.[4]

> **Fiduciary:** A person who enjoys a position of trust to another; a person who handles money or property for another.

D. Fraud and Criminal Law

Civil actions for fraud are complicated by the fact that what makes a particular situation actionable under civil law also makes it punishable under criminal law. Fraud is a form of theft under criminal law. As a form of theft, fraud involves proof by the prosecution that the defendant used trickery, deceit or deliberate falsehood to deprive the victim of his property. If these elements sound similar to the elements of a civil action for fraud, there is a specific reason. The criminal action for fraud developed from the same source as the civil action. In fact, several centuries ago, there was no clear distinction between civil and criminal actions. Fraud was fraud. Nowadays, that same confusion between civil and criminal actions still haunts any allegation of fraud. For instance, in the scenario we used to open the discussion of fraud, i.e., Mary's purchase of furniture she wrongfully believed was owned by John, are John's actions criminal or civil? Actually, they are both. Mary has a civil action against John for her monetary loss—the money she paid him believing that he was the owner—and the state also has an action against John for defrauding Mary of her property, namely, her money.

Civil actions and criminal actions can be based on the same facts, but the litigation in each case proceeds independently of one another. The same witnesses may testify about the same events, but the end result of the two cases will be different. In the criminal case, John faces jail time and a fine. In the civil case, he faces a court order forcing him to repay Mary for her out-of-pocket expenses (and any other damages the court deems proper). In order to clear up potential confusion, most police and prosecutors refer to criminal fraud as "computer-based" or "computer-related" crime, since nearly every type of modern fraud crime involves the use of a computer or other piece of advanced technology.

---

4. *AMPAT/Midwest, Inc. v. Illinois Tool Works, Inc.*, 896 F.2d 1035, 1040 (7th Cir. 1990).

Although the topic of fraud has a great deal of potential for both civil and criminal actions, negligent misrepresentation does not. That action is usually a civil action only.

> *Getting to the Essentials:*   Fraud can be both a civil action and a criminal action.

In what some have called the biggest fraud in U.S. history, Bernard Madoff pled guilty to running a Ponzi scheme for stock market investors. Sentenced to 150 years in prison for bilking investors, it remains the most severe sentence ever handed down for criminal fraud action. A Ponzi scheme is a multi-layer confidence game in which early investors are paid back staggering returns on money, but not from wise investments. Instead, the money the early investors make comes from the money later investors put into the scheme, believing that they will also receive such high returns. Madoff's scandal is noteworthy not only because of the highly sophisticated investors he conned, but for the amount of time he was able to keep the scheme going. Prosecutors in the case estimated that the scheme had been running for over twenty years and took in billions from investors. The estimates vary as to how much money that Mr. Madoff's victim's actually lost, but most put the figure over $10 billion and some much higher than that. That level of fraud is almost unimaginable.

Figure 1-3. "Computer-related crimes prosecuted by State prosecutors' offices, by type of crime." Prosecutors in States Courts, 2005, National Survey of Prosecutors, Bureau of Justice Statistics, July 2006, page 5.

Table 6. Computer-related crimes prosecuted by State prosecutors' offices, by type of crime and population served, 2005

| | Percent of prosecutors' offices | | | | |
| | | Full-time offices by population served | | | |
	All offices	Large (1 million or more)	Medium (250,000 to 999,999)	Medium (Under 250,000)	Part-time offices
Prosecuted cases under State's computer crime statute	60%	89%	90%	68%	26%
Type of computer-related crimes					
Credit card fraud	80%	91%	90%	77%	78%
Bank card fraud[a]	71	82	81	67	81
Identity theft[b]	69	97	85	66	63
Transmitting child pornography	67	82	90	69	22
Computer forgery[c]	40	56	38	40	37
Cyberstalking[d]	36	82	62	35	--
Unauthorized access[e]	23	53	40	21	--
Computer sabotage[f]	5	27	10	4	--
Theft of intellectual property	5	38	11	3	--
Unauthorized copying[g]	4	44	5	3	--
Other	11	15	11	12	4

Note: Data on prosecution of any computer-related crime under their State's computer statutes were available for 86% of prosecutors' offices.

Data were available on credit card fraud, bank card fraud, forgery, sabotage, unauthorized access to computer system, unauthorized copying or distribution of computer programs, cyberstalking, theft of intellectual property, transmitting child pornography, and identity theft for 52% of the offices.

--Less than 0.5%.

[a]Includes ATM or debit card.

^bDefined as unauthorized use or attempted use of credit cards, existing accounts, and or misuse of personal information to obtain new accounts, etc.

^cAlteration of computerized documents.

^dDefined as the sending of harassing or threatening e-mail to other users.

^eHacking.

^fDefined as any action hindering the normal function of a computer system through the introduction of worms, viruses, or logic bombs.

^gSoftware copyright infringement.

IV. Negligent Misrepresentation

In many ways, **negligent misrepresentation** resembles an action for fraud, with one important difference. In fraud, the plaintiff must show that the defendant's false statement was made knowingly. In negligent misrepresentation, the plaintiff may simply show that the defendant was reckless or negligent in representing the truth to the plaintiff.[5] The important distinction between negligent misrepresentation and fraud is intent. A fraudulent statement is made with full knowledge that it is false and in hopes that a person will rely on it. A statement that qualifies as negligent misrepresentation is one where the person making it does not know if it is true or not. The person may simply be making a statement with careless disregard for its truth. That person cannot be liable for fraud, but can be liable for negligent misrepresentation. In many ways, negligent misrepresentation allows a cause of action for a simple misstatement. As such, most courts impose a higher standard of proof on such cases. This higher standard places more emphasis on the consumer's allegations.

> **Negligent misrepresentation:** A statement made by a defendant that the defendant either does not know is truthful or does not care is truthful that induces a party to enter into an agreement

Although most negligence cases do not require any relationship between the parties, negligent misrepresentation cases often do. After all, the plaintiff/consumer must prove that he relied on a statement by the defendant and that this reliance was reasonable under the circumstances. Often this proof of reasonable reliance springs from the fact that the plaintiff and defendant knew one another. It also relies on the fact that they did business together, or that there was some other relationship between them that made the plaintiff's actions understandable.

> Sidebar: Although related to the general concept of negligence, negligent misrepresentation developed from the old common law tort of deceit.

A. Elements of Negligent Misrepresentation

Negligent misrepresentation consists of the following elements:

1. The defendant, in the course of his business or profession, makes a false statement
2. Believing that the statement is true

---

5. *Board of Ed. v. A,C and S, Inc.*, 546 N.E.2d 580 (1989).

3. But without reasonable grounds for his belief or in reckless disregard of the truth

4. The plaintiff suffered a financial loss because of his reasonable reliance on this false statement

The standard of care imposed on defendants in negligent misrepresentation cases is to use reasonable care in making statements. When a defendant has a business relationship with another person and supplies him with false information, either through incompetence or disregard of the truth, the defendant has violated his duty to the plaintiff. However, when the information is provided to another person with whom there is no business relationship, such as a favor to a friend, there is no duty to use reasonable care.

The plaintiff's reliance on the information provided by the defendant must be reasonable in order for the element of causation to be satisfied. If the plaintiff's actions are unreasonable, the defendant can claim that the plaintiff contributed to his own damages and is therefore, not entitled to any award from the court.

Figure 1-4. "Contract cases disposed of by trial in State Courts." *Contract Trials and Verdicts in Large Counties, 2001*, Bureau of Justice Statistics, Selected Findings, January 2005, page 3.

Table 1. Contract cases disposed of by trial in State courts in the Nation's 75 largest counties, 2001

Case type	All contract trials		Type of trial		
	Number	Percent	Jury	Bench	Other*
All contract trials	**3,698**	**100.0%**	**42.6%**	**55.8%**	**1.6%**
Fraud	625	16.9%	45.6%	52.0%	2.4%
Seller plaintiff	1,208	32.7	22.7	76.3	1.0
Buyer plaintiff	793	21.4	58.1	41.0	0.9
Mortgage foreclosure	22	0.6	--	100.0	--
Employment discrimination	166	4.5	86.7	10.2	3.0
Other employment dispute	287	7.8	57.5	38.7	3.8
Rental/lease	276	7.5	22.8	76.8	0.4
Tortious interference	138	3.7	55.8	42.0	2.2
Partnership dispute	40	1.1	55.0	45.0	--
Subrogation	69	1.9	68.1	27.5	4.3
Other or unknown contract	73	2.0	48.6	48.6	2.7

Note: Data for case and disposition type were available for 100.0% of the 3,698 contract trials. Detail may not sum to total because of rounding.

-- No cases recorded.

*Other trial cases include trials with a directed verdict, judgments notwithstanding the verdict, and jury trials for defaulted defendants.

Although these cases are typically placed in a separate category, they are a form of jury trial.

B. Awarding Monetary Damages in Negligent Misrepresentation Cases

In most jurisdictions, the plaintiff is entitled to any or all of the following types of damages:

- Fees associated with applications, licenses, permits, etc.

- Commission fees paid to real estate brokers, agents or others who are paid on a commission basis

- Monetary difference between a loan that the plaintiff thought he was going to receive and the loan he finally received

- Out-of-pocket expenses associated with the finding, obtaining, receiving a new service

- In some cases, the plaintiff is entitled to punitive damages, if the plaintiff can show malice on the part of the defendant.

- Attorney's fees for bringing an action against the defendant (when defendant acts with malice)

Figure 1-5. "Final damage awards for contract trials." *Contract Trials and Verdicts in Large Counties, 2001,* Bureau of Justice Statistics, Selected Findings, January 2005, page 5.

Table 5. Final damage awards for contract trials with plaintiff winners in State courts in the Nation's 75 largest counties, 2001

Case type	Contract trials damages awarded to plaintiff winners[a]	Final amount awarded to plaintiff winners		Percent of plaintiff winners with final awards —	
		Total	Median	Over $250,000	$1 million or more
All contract trials[b]	2,369*	$2,043,211,000	$45,000	17.7%	5.4%
Fraud	358	$768,506,000	$81,000	30.2%	12.0%
Seller plaintiff	925	165,3365,000	34,000	10.5	2.9
Buyer plaintiff	477	130,585,000	45,000	17.7	4.8
Mortgage foreclosure	13	2,731,000	70,000	13.6	13.6
Employment discrimination	73	44,913,000	166,000	39.4	14.4
Other employment dispute	162	265,939,000	78,000	23.8	4.8
Rental/lease	176	24,112,000	20,000	11.9	2.6
Tortious interference	83	580,211,000	94,000	30.7	6.9
Partnership dispute	19	52,462,000	97,000	41.8	12.8
Subrogation	44	2,047,000	8,000	4.1	--
Other or unknown contract	41	6,369,000	22,000	13.9	7.1

Note: Data for final awards were available for 98.9% of all sampled contract trials. Final amount awarded includes both compensatory (reduced for contributory negligence) and punitive damage awards. Detail may not sum to total because of rounding. Award data were rounded to the nearest thousand.

*The number of plaintiffs awarded damages may differ from the number calculated from the percentage of plaintiffs who successfully litigated the case (table 4). Missing award data, the fact that in some cases plaintiff winners receive nothing because of award reductions, and the inclusion of plaintiff winners in bifurcated damage trials (a group excluded from table 4) account for some of this difference.

-- No cases recorded.

[a]Excludes bifurcated trials where the plaintiff won on only the liability claim. Bifurcated trials involving only damage

Claims, however, have been included.

[b]Includes bench and jury trials, trials with a directed verdict, judgments notwithstanding the verdict, and jury trials for defaulted defendants.

C. Opinions and Negligent Misrepresentation

Under negligent misrepresentation, an opinion may be grounds for a cause of action, but only when the opinion is presented as based on some fact. For instance, many jurisdictions apply the rule that a statement from a loan officer that the loan can be obtained is a mere opinion and does not provide a basis for a cause of action in negligent misrepresentation.

> Example: Ted has applied for a loan at the local bank. Jack, the loan officer, looks over his paperwork and then tells Ted that the bank's underwriters must approve the loan. Ted asks, "How does it look?" Jack responds, "I think it looks pretty good."

> Ted goes on a buying spree, believing that he will soon have the loan proceeds to pay for the items. Jack calls him later in the week with some bad news. "I'm afraid your loan application was turned down." Ted is furious and wants to sue the bank, and Jack, for negligent misrepresentation. Does he have a case?

> Answer: No. Jack's statement to Ted was an opinion and was not apparently based on any fact. How could we change the scenario to give Ted a cause of action? Jack could make a statement such as, "I can tell you that they are going to approve this application. I've seen a dozen just like it this week and every one of them was approved." When a statement is expressed as though it were a fact, the statement becomes actionable under negligent misrepresentation.[6] (For a similar situation, see the Case Excerpt).

Negligent misrepresentation is also authorized in situations where the speaker has special knowledge or expertise in a certain area, and the speaker makes a statement that a reasonable person would rely on.

> *Getting to the Essentials:* Most opinions are not actionable as negligent misrepresentation. The only exception is when the person giving the opinion is in the business of offering opinions, such as financial advisors and attorneys.

> Example: Arthur is a Certified Public Accountant and has been asked to review the finances of XYZ Corporation. After several weeks, he issues a report stating that XYZ Corporation is in excellent financial health and poised for a major expansion. Myron, who is one of XYZ's employees, and owns a few shares of the company's stock, decides to use his life savings to purchase 1500 additional shares of XYZ stock as a way of beefing up his retirement holdings. Unfortunately, two days after Myron purchases the stock, the company announces that it is filing for bankruptcy. Arthur's report is filled with inaccuracies. Myron sues Arthur. Does he have a cause of action?

> Answer: Yes. Many jurisdictions are now allowing a cause of action in such a case for anyone who could foreseeably rely on a CPA's report on the financial health of a company. Myron is an employee and a stockholder. He falls into that category.[7]

---

6. Am. Jur. 2d, Fraud and Deceit § 143.
7. *Bily v. Arthur Young & Co.*, 11 Cal.Rptr.2d 51 (1992).

D. Negligent Misrepresentation vs. Mistake

Where do we draw the line between a simple mistake and an action that can be characterized as negligent misrepresentation? In some ways, they are very similar. "Mistake" as a defense is available when both parties have made some error about the contract. When only one party makes a mistake in the contract, the contract continues to have legal effect.[8] Negligent misrepresentation, on the other hand, is made by only one party and, when proven, gives the other party the right to void the contract.

E. Pleading Negligent Misrepresentation

On a practical level, proving negligent misrepresentation is easier than proving fraud. Having said that, however, the plaintiff must still set out a clear case of negligence. Often that is quite difficult. The plaintiff must present evidence of the specific false statement or information provided by the defendant, how the plaintiff relied on this information and that his reliance was reasonable. The plaintiff must also show proximate cause between that reliance and the monetary injury he suffered. Finally, the plaintiff must show a direct connection between a monetary loss and the defendant's actions.

F. Defenses to Negligent Misrepresentation

The defenses available in negligent misrepresentation cases are similar to the defenses available in most negligence cases. However, there are several other defenses that are more or less unique to this tort. They are:

- Truth
- Opinion
- Statement did not concern a material fact
- No detrimental reliance on the statement
- No damages
- Waiver

1. Truth

Perhaps the most obvious defense to negligent misrepresentation is that the statement was not false. After all, it is one of the essential elements of the claim that the plaintiff must prove that the statement was false or made in reckless disregard of the truth. If the statement is true, then the plaintiff's case is essentially destroyed.

> **Getting to the Essentials:** Truth is a defense to fraud and negligent misrepresentation.

---

8. *Baumann v. Florance*, 267 App.Div. 113, 114, 44 N.Y.S.2d 706, 707 (3d Dept. 1943).

2. Opinion

In most situations, an opinion is not actionable. An opinion is simply the defendant's belief or "feeling" about a particular event and lacks a solid grounding in fact. The exception is when the opinion is offered as though it were a fact. Another exception concerns people who are in the business of giving opinions about specific issues. An attorney, for example, is often called upon to give an opinion about the law. The client is entitled to rely on that opinion.

3. Statement Did Not Concern a Material Fact

The defendant can also raise the defense that his statement, even if false, was not about a material fact, and therefore cannot be the basis of a negligent misrepresentation claim. Essentially, the defendant is claiming that his statement did not concern any fact that would cause another person to change his behavior or to influence his conduct.

4. No Detrimental Reliance on the Statement

When the plaintiff hears a false statement, but takes no action based on that false statement, he has not relied on it. It is not enough that the plaintiff prove that the defendant's statement was false; the plaintiff must also show that he relied on it in some way. If the plaintiff did not rely on the statement to his detriment, he has failed to prove an essential element of negligent misrepresentation.

5. No Damages

Similar to the last defense, a defendant is entitled to raise the defense that even if the statement was false and the plaintiff relied on it, the plaintiff suffered no damages because of it. In almost all jurisdictions, monetary loss is an essential element of the claim. As far as this action is concerned, mental pain and anguish are not compensable. The plaintiff must show some form of monetary loss or he is not entitled to recover.

> *Getting to the Essentials:*   No matter how false the statement, if the consumer did not rely on it, there are no grounds for a suit.

6. Waiver

Finally, a defendant can claim that even if all of the elements are met, the plaintiff waived any right to pursue his action. A waiver occurs when the plaintiff signs a document officially relinquishing a legal right, or it can occur through conduct.

> *Getting to the Essentials:*   A waiver can be made orally, in writing or by behavior.

Example: During the course of Ted's business, Ted has made a statement that clearly constitutes a negligent misrepresentation. John, the person who received this false statement, acknowledges it and then continues to work with Ted anyway. Ted can now argue that because of John's **ratification**, he has waived any right to sue for the negligent misrepresentation.

Ratification: The process of confirming and accepting a previous action; a void contract can be ratified after the fact to make it legally enforceable.

G. Defenses That Are Not Available in Negligent Misrepresentation

It is not a defense to a claim of negligent misrepresentation that the defendant did not have a particular person in mind when he made his false statement. Any customer who could foreseeably have relied on his false statement has a potential claim against him. Other defenses that are not available to defendants in negligent misrepresentation cases are listed in Figure 1-6.

Figure 1-6. Defenses Not Available in Negligent Misrepresentation Cases.

- That the defendant had no knowledge of the veracity of the statement
- That the defendant acted in "good faith"

---

1. "No Knowledge"

Defendants are not permitted to raise the defense that they had no knowledge of the accuracy of their statements at the time that they made them. Since a negligent misrepresentation case is based on the theory that the defendant failed to use reasonable care and competence in making his statement, the fact that he failed to verify its accuracy actually helps the plaintiff prove one of his essential elements.[9] In fact, many jurisdictions allow a claim against the defendant precisely because he had no knowledge at the time that he made the statement to the plaintiff that it was true.[10]

2. Good Faith

In many jurisdictions, the defendant's "good faith" in making the statements is also not a defense.[11] The true test is whether the defendant has reasonable grounds for believing that his statement was true. Without that reasonable belief, his good faith is immaterial.[12]

Case Excerpt

Is it negligent misrepresentation for incorrectly telling a loan applicant that his loan had been approved?

---

9. *Riley v. Bell*, 95 N.W. 170 (1903).
10. *Wilson v. Murch*, 354 S.W.2d 332 (1962).
11. *National Bank of Pawnee v. Hamilton*, 202 Ill.App. 516 (1916).
12. *Vettleson v. Special School Dist. No. 1*, 361 N.W.2d 425 (1985).

Federal Land Bank Ass'n of Tyler v. Sloane, 825 S.W.2d 439 (1991)

OPINION

GONZALEZ, Justice.

The primary issues in this case are (1) whether the statute of frauds shields a bank from liability for negligently misrepresenting that it had approved a loan secured by real property; and (2) assuming that the statute of frauds does not apply, whether the prospective borrowers can recover damages for mental anguish attributable to the bank's alleged negligent misrepresentation. After a jury trial, the trial court rendered judgment for the prospective borrowers. The court of appeals affirmed in part and reversed and rendered in part. Specifically, the court of appeals held that the statute of frauds did not bar the claim, affirmed the part of the judgment awarding mental anguish damages, and reversed and rendered that part of the judgment awarding damages for lost profits. We reverse that part of the court of appeals' judgment with regard to the award of mental anguish damages and otherwise affirm. This cause is remanded to the trial court for rendition of a judgment that conforms to this opinion.

In early 1986, William, Lettie, and Robert Sloane had been out of the business of raising chickens for two years when they learned they could get a contract from Pilgrim's Pride to raise broilers for the company on the condition that they build new chicken houses on their farm. On March 7, 1986, the Sloanes applied for a $141,000 loan from the Federal Land Bank Association of Tyler. During the application process, the Sloanes obtained an estimate of $105,000 for the costs of necessary equipment and the construction of two chicken houses. They also obtained a letter from Pilgrim's Pride stating that the company agreed to "feed out broilers" for the Sloanes once the houses were constructed according to specifications provided by Pilgrim's Pride. The Sloanes subsequently sent the construction estimate and the letter from Pilgrim's Pride to their loan officer at the bank.

Approximately a month after the Sloanes had applied for the loan, the loan officer informed them that the bank's board had approved the loan, and that the Sloanes could go ahead with site preparation work. The contractor hired by the Sloanes to build the new chicken houses contacted the bank's loan officer to see if he should begin construction, notwithstanding the pending nature of the loan. The loan officer said that there was "no problem," and that "there was not any reason for them not to continue at that point." (The bank officer disputes these statements; however, the jury resolved this issue in the Sloanes' favor, and the bank subsequently did not challenge on appeal the legal or factual sufficiency of the evidence supporting the fact). In June 1986, the Sloanes had one of their old chicken houses demolished, and they paid approximately $9,000 for further site preparation. As the work progressed they supplied the bank with receipts. In August, 1986, the Sloanes received a letter from the bank denying their loan application, giving as reasons the fact that they failed to include two outstanding debts on their application, and that they incurred additional liability for a car purchase while the loan was being processed. The Sloanes subsequently failed to obtain other financing. They then sued the bank alleging that the loan officer had negligently misrepresented that the bank would approve their loan application. Their claims included the financial and property damages suffered in preparing to build the chicken houses, the loss of the Pilgrim's Pride contract, and the mental anguish caused by the bank's allegedly negligent conduct.

The case was tried before a jury, which found that: (1) the bank negligently misrepresented to the Sloanes that the bank had approved their loan application; (2) the Sloanes justifiably relied on such misrepresentation; and (3) reliance upon such misrepresentation caused the Sloanes pecuniary loss. The jury assessed damages against the bank amounting to $26,500 for past and future monetary losses other than lost profits, $28,500 for past and future lost profits, and $15,000 for mental anguish.

The trial court rendered an $81,974.48 judgment for the Sloanes, which included $11,974.48 in prejudgment interest. The court of appeals subsequently held that there was no evidence of lost profits and certain other expenditures, and thus the court affirmed the balance of the judgment after reformation. The bank now asserts that, as a matter of law, the statute of frauds bars the Sloanes' cause of action for all damages. The Sloanes counter that their cause of action sounds in tort, and thus the statute of frauds does not apply. They also assert that the court of appeals erred in reversing the trial court's award of damages for lost profits. The statute of frauds requires that certain specified classes of contracts be in writing to be enforceable. Tex.Bus. & Com.Code ' 26.01. The Sloanes do not claim that the bank agreed to loan them money and then breached that agreement; rather, they claim that the bank did not agree to loan them money, yet negligently misrepresented that it had made such an agreement. Moreover, the Sloanes do not seek damages for breach of the loan agreement never made, but for their reasonable reliance upon the bank's misrepresentation. Although a claim of negligent misrepresentation may not be used to circumvent the statute of frauds, under the circumstances of this case, the Sloanes' claim does not fall within the statute of frauds. To the contrary, the premise of the claim is that the Sloanes and the bank never reached an agreement, oral or written.

NEGLIGENT MISREPRESENTATION

The Sloanes claim that the bank has a duty to use reasonable care whenever it provides information to its customers or potential customers, and that the bank breached this duty when it allegedly encouraged the Sloanes to incur expenses in reliance on the information related to their loan application. The Sloanes further allege that the bank misrepresented an existing fact rather than a promise of future conduct. Both the bank and the Sloanes rely on Restatement (Second) of Torts § 552 (1977) to define the scope of this duty. We agree with the Restatement's definition, as have several courts of appeal that have previously considered this question.

The elements of a cause of action for the breach of this duty are: (1) the representation is made by a defendant in the course of his business, or in a transaction in which he has a pecuniary interest; (2) the defendant supplies "false information" for the guidance of others in their business; (3) the defendant did not exercise reasonable care or competence in obtaining or communicating the information; and (4) the plaintiff suffers pecuniary loss by justifiably relying on the representation. Issues substantially conforming to these elements were submitted to the jury, which returned a verdict favorable to the Sloanes. The bank makes no challenge to the sufficiency of the evidence of liability, so the remaining issue is what damages are available for this tort.

DAMAGES

The Restatement provides damages for this tort as follows: (1) The damages recoverable for a negligent misrepresentation are those necessary to compensate the plaintiff for the pecuniary loss to him of which the misrepresentation is legal cause, including (a) the difference between the value of what he has received in the transaction and its purchase price or other value given for it; and (b) pecuniary loss suffered otherwise as a consequence of the plaintiff's reliance upon the misrepresentation. (2) the damages recoverable for a negligent misrepresentation do not include the benefit of the plaintiff's contract with the defendant.

While the Sloanes adopt the Restatement's terminology to support the basic elements of their cause of action, they reject the language of Restatement section 552B, which limits damages to pecuniary loss alone. Specifically, the Sloanes argue that this court should allow them damages for mental anguish. The Restatement advances several policy reasons for limiting damages, including a lower degree of fault indicated by a less culpable mental state and the need to keep liability proportional to risk. There has been no trend to reject the pecuniary loss rule in what is essentially a commercial tort. We decline to extend damages beyond those limits provided in Restatement section 552B.

The Sloanes complain that they should receive damages for the profits they anticipated from the Pilgrim's Pride contract. As discussed above, Restatement (Second) section 552B allows for damages suffered in reliance upon negligent misrepresentation, but not for the failure to obtain the benefit of the bargain. The Sloanes would not have received the contract regardless of whether the misrepresentation was made. Under the legal theory of this section of the Restatement, they should not, therefore, receive the benefit of a bargain that would never have taken place. The sole reason the Sloanes did not get the Pilgrim's Pride contract is because the bank did not give them the loan money to build acceptable chicken houses. The Sloanes' claim to these damages is impermissibly predicated on giving them the benefit of the loan.

For the foregoing reasons, we reverse the judgment of the court of appeals insofar as it includes an award for mental anguish. In all other respects, the judgment of the court of appeals is affirmed. We remand this cause to the trial court for rendition of judgment for $11,427.03 for past pecuniary losses other than lost profits, plus prejudgment interest.

Case Questions

1. How soon after they had applied for the loan were the Sloanes informed that they had been approved for the bank loan?
2. What action did the Sloanes take based on this statement?
3. According to the court, what are the elements of negligent misrepresentation?
4. Why does the court refuse to allow the Sloanes damages they claim they suffered from the cancellation of the Pilgrim's Pride contract?

V. Follow-up on the Shareholders' Suit

We began this chapter with a hypothetical situation involving the End-Run Corporation and a shareholder with one thousand shares who wishes to sue the corporation for its false announcements and statements regarding the company's financial health. Now that we have reviewed the various types of suits that could be brought in this situation, are any of them appropriate to this situation?

First, let's review the basic facts. Tom, who already owns one thousand shares of End-Run stock, wants to sue the corporation for making false statements. Can he meet the essential elements of a fraud action? Remember that the elements for fraud consist of the following: 1) The defendant made a representation of a material fact or concealed a fact, 2) That the representation was false, 3) That the defendant knew the representation was false, 4) That the defendant made the representation with the intent that the plaintiff would rely on it, 5) The plaintiff's reliance on the representation was reasonable under the circumstances, and 6) That the plaintiff suffered injury from his reliance on the representation.

Assuming that Tom can present some proof to show that the company knew that it was making a false statement at the time it was made, elements 1–3 would seem fairly straightforward. What about the fourth element? There is no requirement that the plaintiff must show that the false statement was made with him in mind. If the plaintiff is in the group of people likely to be affected by the false statement, then this element is met. Tom is a shareholder and falls into this category. We begin to run into problems, though, with the fifth element. Tom must show that his reliance on the representation was reasonable. This presupposes that Tom took some action with respect to the false information. We know that Tom *already* owns one thousand shares. Unless we can show that Tom purchased more stock as a result, or took some other action, he cannot show any detrimental reliance on the information. We may also have some trouble with the last element. How does Tom show that he suffered economic injury? Surely the fact that he purchased the stock for a much higher price than it is worth now should be enough to prove damages, shouldn't it? In the pragmatic world of the courts, this may not be enough. The fact that Tom's stock was worth a lot more last year than it is worth this year may not be enough to prove an actual economic injury for Tom. There may be ways of dealing with this problem, but it is certainly an issue that the legal team must face.

Overall, Tom may not have a very strong case against End-Run, at least for fraud. His case for negligent misrepresentation also suffers from the same drawbacks.

Chapter Summary

In this chapter, we discussed two types of actions that are available to consumers. When a consumer believes that he has been the victim of fraud, he can present a civil case in which he alleges that the defendant made a false statement to him, knowing that it was false, on which the consumer relied and that the consumer suffered some type of monetary damage. When the defendant makes a statement without knowing that it is true, or in reckless disregard of the truth, he can be sued for negligent misrepresentation. The essential elements for an action for negligent misrepresentation include a false statement made by the defendant, in the course of the defendant's trade or occupation, to a consumer who justifiably relied on the statement. Another essential element of a negligent misrepresentation action is that the plaintiff suffered some type of monetary loss as a result of the false statement.

There are several defenses available to a claim for negligent misrepresentation including: truth of the statement made by the defendant, that the statement was an opinion, that the plaintiff did not actually rely on the statement to his detriment or that the plaintiff suffered no monetary loss because of the false information.

Web Sites

- Internet Fraud (FBI)
  http://www.fbi.gov/majcases/fraud/internetschemes.htm
- Federal Trade Commission
  http://www.ftc.gov/
- U.S. Business Advisor
  http://www.business.gov/

Key Terms

Fraud	Negligent Misrepresentation
Material Fact	Waiver
Clear and convincing evidence	Ratification

Review Questions

1. What is fraud and how does it differ from negligent misrepresentation?
2. Are there any factual changes that you could make to the "Shareholder's Suit" hypothetical that began this chapter that would give Tom a stronger case against End-Run?
3. Why did the Court in *Federal Land Bank Ass'n of Tyler v. Sloane*, [this chapter's Case Excerpt] refuse to allow the plaintiffs to receive damages for mental anguish? Why did the court allow some economic damages, but refuse the plaintiff's request for damages for future damages?
4. What are the elements of fraud?
5. Some have said that fraud is not something that can be done unknowingly. Why?
6. Courts have consistently refused to limit the definition of what acts constitute fraud. Why have they been reluctant to do so?
7. What is a material fact?
8. How do normal salesmanship statements differ from fraud?
9. What is "clear and convincing" evidence and how does this standard differ from "preponderance of the evidence?"
10. How does a fraud case change when the defendant is the plaintiff's fiduciary?

11. Actions that are classified as fraud can also be crimes. Explain the interplay between civil fraud and criminal fraud.

12. What are the elements of negligent misrepresentation?

13. Why is there a requirement of the plaintiff's "reasonable reliance" on the defendant's statement in a negligent misrepresentation case?

14. Opinions are usually not classified as negligent misrepresentations. Why? Are there situations in which an opinion can be actionable as a negligent misrepresentation? Explain.

15. Explain the defenses available in negligent misrepresentation cases.

Chapter 2

Deceptive Practices

Chapter Objectives

- Describe the typical common-law remedies available to consumers
- Define the federal legislation created as a response to consumer and business complaints about unfair and deceptive trade practices
- Explain the importance of the Federal Trade Commission
- Describe the importance of the Uniform Deceptive Trade Practices Act
- List and explain the role that the Uniform Commercial Code plays in protecting consumer interests

I. What Are Deceptive Practices?

As long as there have been businesses, there have been unscrupulous business practices. Whether these practices involved "passing off" one type of goods for another, "bait and switch" or outright fraud, courts were not overly concerned with deceptive trade practices. This was especially true in the United States, where **caveat emptor** was the general rule followed by most courts. Under caveat emptor, the buyer bore the brunt of the responsibility in determining the quality of the goods to be purchased and had few remedies when it turned out that they were not what the buyer had bargained for. In the early days of the United States and running through the end of the 1800s, courts usually declared caveat emptor the law of the land. Allowing buyers to bring suit against manufacturers and retailers was considered to be dangerous and might derail a fast-moving economy.[1]

Caveat emptor: (Latin) "let the buyer beware."

A. Examples of Unfair or Deceptive Trade Practices

There are, quite literally, hundreds of examples of unfair or deceptive trade practices that have been used by merchants over the years. We have already mentioned "bait and switch" and "passing off." However, these practices are merely the tip of the iceberg in the wide variety of scams and practices that consumers may fall victim to. The Federal Trade

---

1. *A History of American Law*, Lawrence Friedman, Simon and Schuster, 1973, New York.

Commission, discussed in detail later in this chapter, maintains an online service called Consumer Sentinel that tracks unfair and deceptive trade practices and provides a complaint service for consumers. As you can see in Figure 2-1, the top categories for unfair and deceptive trade practices are:

- Identity theft

- Internet auctions

- Shop at home in catalog sales

- General Internet and computer complaints

- Sweepstakes and lottery scams

- Advance fee loans, credit protection and credit repair, among others

Figure 2-1. 2008 Top Ten IC3 Complaint Categories. 2008 Internet Crime Report. Bureau of Justice Assistance, page 4.

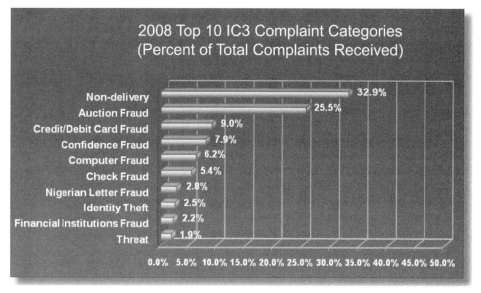

Chart 5
During 2008, non-delivered merchandise and/or payment was, by far, the most reported offense, comprising 32.9% of referred complaints. Internet auction fraud accounted for 25.5% of referred complaints. Credit/debit card fraud made up 9.0% of referred complaints. Confidence fraud, computer fraud, check fraud, and Nigerian letter fraud round out the top seven categories of complaints referred to law enforcement during the year.

Passing Off: Presenting inferior products as if they were quality or name brand products

Bait and Switch: A deceptive practice where a merchant lures a consumer with the promise of one type of goods but ultimately provides inferior goods

Identity theft has become such an important problem that an entire chapter of this book is devoted to it (Chapter 5). With the growing availability of Internet access, Internet-related complaints have risen dramatically in recent years. As you can see in Figure 2-2, in 2003 Internet-related fraud complaints surpassed other types of fraud complaints for the first time in history.

Figure 2-2. 2008 Yearly Dollar Loss (in millions). 2008 Internet Crime Report. Bureau of Justice Assistance, page 3.

Chart 3

Dollar loss of referred complaints was at an all time high in 2008, $264.59 million, exceeding last year's record breaking dollar loss of $239.09 million. On average, men lost more money than women.

B. Common-law Remedies

Of course, there were common-law remedies available. A buyer could always allege fraud and attempt to prove it in court. However, when the resources of a large manufacturer were pitted against a lone buyer, courts often sided with the manufacturer. There were other problems with common-law actions: it wasn't always easy, or even possible, for a buyer to prove who had been responsible for the substandard goods. Was it the fault of the manufacturer, the middleman, the retailer or the reseller? Faced with such daunting problems, most buyers simply tried to move on with business and absorbed the costs of substandard goods as a price of doing business. As we will see later in this chapter, the old common-law remedies discussed in Chapter 1 are still available for litigants on the state level. They include actions for:

- Fraud (Chapter 1)
- Negligent Misrepresentation (Chapter 1)
- Breach of contract (Chapter 11)
- Threats and coercion (Chapter 11)
- Bad faith (Chapter 11)
- Breach of warranty (Chapter 4)

Getting to the Essentials: Under the common law, the buyer had few remedies against an unscrupulous seller.

II. Federal Regulation of Unfair and Deceptive Trade Practices

In the early days of the 20th century, the complaints of buyers and consumers finally found the ears of politicians. Theodore Roosevelt, Woodrow Wilson and others focused their attention on corporations that routinely engaged in unfair competition, reckless manufacturing practices and questionable business dealings. There was also a gradual realization that allowing huge corporations to do as they pleased had not resulted in better goods, better business practices or fewer manufacturing-related fatalities. The Commerce Department's Bureau of Corporations, created in 1903 by Theodore Roosevelt, was the first federal agency to attempt to regulate large corporations. However, it lacked enforcement ability and eventually gave way to the much more powerful Federal Trade Commission.

However, before we examine the important role played by the Federal Trade Commission in modern business practices in the United States, it is important to note that federal legislation covers a diverse blend of businesses, from telemarketing to debt collection practices. Here is a list of the business categories currently regulated by federal law and that we will be discussing in future chapters:

- Telemarketing—The Do Not Call Registry (this chapter)
- Federal Truth in Lending (chapter 6)
- Real Estate Settlement Procedures (chapter 6)
- Predatory Lending Practices (chapter 7)
- Equal Credit Opportunity (chapter 8)
- Debt-Collection Practices (chapter 9)

A. The Federal Trade Commission

The Federal Trade Commission (FTC) came into existence in 1916 with the mandate to investigate and regulate national corporations. Although the focus of the Federal Trade Commission was to conduct investigations and gather information about corporations, the FTC has always played an important role in monitoring and regulating unfair business practices. Some of the Commission's early successes came in the meat packing industry, which in the early 20th century was engaged in a host of nauseating and dangerous practices. Meat packers routinely allowed rats to become caught up in the machinery and harvested animal parts from the floors of the slaughterhouses and resold this material for human consumption.

Over the decades, the role of the Federal Trade Commission has steadily expanded. New laws brought new responsibilities and greater powers. These days, the Federal Trade Commission focuses on a diverse menu of business practices, from mergers to identity theft. The Federal Trade Commission also has a heavy online presence. Its Web site gives consumers a wealth of information and a mechanism to register complaints through an online form. The Federal Trade Commission Web site, www.ftc.gov, provides a wealth of additional information for consumers and businesses.

Figure 2-3. The Federal Trade Commission has regional offices scattered across United States. The Southeast Region serves the residents of the following states:

Alabama, Florida, Georgia, Mississippi, North Carolina, South Carolina, and **Tennessee.**

The address is:

Southeast Region
Federal Trade Commission
Suite 1500
225 Peachtree Street., NE
Atlanta, GA 30303

1. Enforcement and Investigation Powers of the FTC

The Federal Trade Commission is empowered to investigate business practices throughout the United States. The FTC can initiate an investigation based on consumer or competitors' complaints. If the Federal Trade Commission believes that a business has violated the law, it can seek a voluntary consent with the violating company. The consent is not an admission of guilt, but it is the company's agreement to stop a particular practice. If the Federal Trade Commission cannot work out a consent order with the company, it is empowered to issue an administrative complaint and take the case to a hearing. The hearing does not occur in front of a jury. Instead, an administrative law judge hears the case and makes findings. Administrative law judges are empowered to issue cease and desist orders that force the company to stop engaging in certain practices. The judge has wide discretion to make other findings and to make additional findings. The company may appeal the administrative law judge's order to the full Commission. If the Commission rules against the company, the company can take the case up on appeal. The Federal Trade Commission handles thousands of such cases every year.

> *Getting to the Essentials:*   The Federal Trade Commission has a great deal of authority when it comes to investigating scams, cons and other deceptive trade practices.

2. Role of the Federal Trade Commission in Modern Business Practices

The Federal Trade Commission has, as its primary goal, the requirement to ensure that United States markets are "vigorous, efficient and free of restrictions that harm consumers."[2] The Federal Trade Commission is a feature of almost any type of business that you can imagine. The FTC works to enforce federal consumer protection statutes in areas as diverse as consumer labels inside the clothes that you purchase, the energy stickers on appliances and the National Do Not Call Registry. The Federal Trade Commission is broken down into various sub-bureaus, including:

- Bureau of Consumer Protection
- Bureau of Competition
- Bureau of Economics
- Antitrust Division

---

2. Guide to the Federal Trade Commission, available at www.ftc.gov.

3. *The Bureau of Consumer Protection*

The Bureau of Consumer Protection Division of the Federal Trade Commission is primarily responsible for protecting consumers against unfair and deceptive trade practices. The Bureau enforces federal statutes created by Congress as well as rules and regulations created by the Federal Trade Commission. The Division of Advertising Practices is a sub-agency of the Bureau of consumer protection and is primarily responsible for regulating claims made by food, vitamin and dietary supplement manufacturers, and the wide range of advertising claims made by businesses—from weight loss advertising to tobacco and alcohol advertising.

4. *The Expanded Role of the FTC in the Age of Cyber Commerce*

In the age of cyber commerce and the vast amount of transactions that occur over the World Wide Web, the Federal Trade Commission has taken a stronger hand in investigating and enforcing unfair and deceptive trade practices carried out in cyber commerce. The Federal Trade Commission has an online complaint form that consumers may complete and submit over the Web to complain about cyber commerce in the same way that a consumer would complain about a traditional brick-and-mortar business. (See Figure 2-4)

Figure 2-4. Consumer Information Complaint Form, Federal Trade Commission.[3]

The form can be accessed through the following Web site:

www.ftccomplaintassistant.gov/FTC_Wizard.aspx?Lang=en

---

5. *The Do Not Call Registry*

One of the most popular actions in recent years was the creation of the Federal Trade Commission's Do Not Call Registry. The Registry was created in compliance with a recent federal statute that gave the FTC the power to create a list of consumers who did not wish to receive telephone calls from telemarketers. In the past decade, the volume of these unsolicited calls, often coming late into the evening, had become a growing source of irritation for the public. Their clamors for action were finally heard by the U.S. Congress and put into action by the Federal Trade Commission.

The national Do Not Call Registry is a function of the Telemarketing Sales Rule created by the Federal Trade Commission. The rule requires telemarketers to search the registry every 90 days and to avoid calling people who have placed their telephone numbers in the registry.

a. *Exceptions to the Do Not Call Registry*

The Do Not Call Registry took effect on October 1, 2003. Although it does cover most telemarketers, the Do Not Call Registry does not apply to all types of telephone solicitations. Political organizations, charities and telephone pollsters are all permitted to call individuals who are listed on the Do Not Call Registry. All other organizations must abide by the terms of the Registry. If they fail to do so, the Federal Trade Commission may

---

3. American Family Publishing-Consumer Complaints on American Family Publishing Corp. (as of 05/02/02); http://www.ftc.gov/foia/americanfamilypublishing.pdf.

bring action against them and seek an injunction to prevent the company from contacting any other individuals listed on the Registry. The offending Company may also be subject to sanctions and fines.

As you can see, the FTC plays an important role in modern business practices and consumer protection. However, federal actions alone have never been sufficient to combat all types of deceptive trade practices. Individual states have also created their own statutes to penalize these actions.

III. State Regulation

All states have their own, separate laws on consumer protection and unfair trade practices. However, there was a wide disparity in the types of actions authorized under various state laws. One state might recognize negligent misrepresentation, while another would not. Given the example of the federal agencies, it made sense that states would eventually see the benefits of creating a more uniform system of regulating unfair and deceptive business practices, especially considering the fact that most modern businesses commonly engage in inter-state commerce. One attempt to achieve a level of uniformity among the states was the creation, in 1966, of the Uniform Deceptive Trade Practices Act (UDTPA).

A. What Is the UDTPA?

The Uniform Deceptive Trade Practices Act is a model for state legislation. It is not binding law in itself. Instead, like the Uniform Commercial Code and other uniform laws that have been proposed from time to time, the UDTPA was a creation of a panel that tried to anticipate problems and propose solutions to save individual state legislatures from having to do these actions for themselves. Unlike other uniform codes, such as the Uniform Commercial Code, the Uniform Deceptive Trade Practices Act does not seek to replace or eliminate previously existing common-law remedies. Instead, the UDPTA is a measure that gives consumers another avenue of attack. Consumers may bring actions under the UDTPA in addition to the actions such as fraud, negligent misrepresentation or interference with contract.

> *Getting to the Essentials:*   The Uniform Deceptive Trade Practices Act was designed to bring state law into greater uniformity and to provide a better infrastructure for litigants than was often available under current state law.

1. Unlawful Actions under UDTPA

In its wording, the Act does single out specific types of objectionable practices, but in general steers clear of specific limitations. Instead, the Act lists categories of transactions, not specific actions, which are unlawful. The Act prefers an approach that gives state courts broad discretion to fashion their own rules in the face of the continued creativity of those individuals and businesses that try to bend the rules. An example of the UDTPA is provided in Figure 2-5.

Figure 2-5. Delaware's Uniform Deceptive Trade Practices Act.[4]

(a) A person engages in a deceptive trade practice when, in the course of a business, vocation, or occupation, that person:

(1) Passes off goods or services as those of another;

(2) Causes likelihood of confusion or of misunderstanding as to the source, sponsorship, approval, or certification of goods or services;

(3) Causes likelihood of confusion or of misunderstanding as to affiliation, connection, or association with, or certification by, another;

(4) Uses deceptive representations or designations of geographic origin in connection with goods or services;

(5) Represents that goods or services have sponsorship, approval, characteristics, ingredients, uses, benefits, or quantities that they do not have, or that a person has a sponsorship, approval, status, affiliation, or connection that the person does not have;

(6) Represents that goods are original or new if they are deteriorated, altered, reconditioned, reclaimed, used, or secondhand;

(7) Represents that goods or services are of a particular standard, quality, or grade, or that goods are of a particular style or model, if they are of another;

(8) Disparages the goods, services, or business of another by false or misleading representation of fact;

(9) Advertises goods or services with intent not to sell them as advertised;

(10) Advertises goods or services with intent not to supply reasonably expectable public demand, unless the advertisement discloses a limitation of quantity;

(11) Makes false or misleading statements of fact concerning the reasons for, existence of, or amounts of price reductions; or

(12) Engages in any other conduct which similarly creates a likelihood of confusion or of misunderstanding.

(b) In order to prevail in an action under this chapter, a complainant need not prove competition between the parties or actual confusion or misunderstanding.

(c) This section does not affect unfair trade practices otherwise actionable at common law or under other statutes of this State.

2. Exceptions under UDTPA

The Uniform Deceptive Trade Practices Act does not cover all types of business transactions. For one thing, the Act requires that a person bringing a complaint must first qualify as a consumer.

a. Qualifying as a Consumer Under UDTPA

In order to qualify as a consumer under the UDTPA, a litigant must show two elements:

1. He or she must seek or acquire goods or services by lease or purchase; and[5]

2. The goods or services sought must form the basis of the party's complaint.[6]

---

4. 6 Del. C. 1953, §2532.

5. *Crown Life*, 22 S.W.3d at 386.

6. *Melody Home Mfg. Co. v. Barnes*, 741 S.W.2d 349, 351–52 (Tex.1987).

In addition to the requirement that a person must qualify as a consumer under UDTPA, there are other exceptions to the application of the UDTPA. For instance, the Act does not apply to orders or rules promulgated by federal, state or local governments. It also does not apply to publishers or media broadcasters who report on unfair and deceptive trade practices.

Figure 2-6. Exceptions to UDTPA.

(a) This chapter does not apply to:

(1) Conduct in compliance with the orders or rules of, or a statute administered by, a federal, state, or local governmental agency;

(2) Publishers, broadcasters, printers, or other persons engaged in the dissemination of information or reproduction of printed or pictorial matter who publish, broadcast, or reproduce material without knowledge of its deceptive character.[7]

---

3. Remedies under the Uniform Deceptive Trade Practices Act

The UDTPA provides for specific remedies if a consumer can prove a violation. Among these remedies are:

- Injunctions (no proof of monetary loss required)
- Attorneys' fees
- Treble damages

a. Injunctions

An injunction is a court order that compels a person or an organization to stop committing a particular action. Usually an injunction is for a limited period of time, such as 30 days. At the end of the 30-day period, both parties, the party who sought the injunction and the party who was bound by it, must appear in court for a hearing to determine if the injunction should be made permanent.

Injunction: A court order prohibiting a specific action.

b. Attorneys' Fees

When a litigant can show that the opposing party acted in bad faith, the party may be awarded attorneys' fees. This is an award that requires one party to pay for the services of the attorney for the other side. In most types of civil cases, the parties must pay their own attorneys for services that they provide. Most attorneys bill by the hour and over the course of an extended lawsuit, the attorney's fee could be substantial. However, in cases where the court determines that a party has acted in bad faith, the judge may order one party to pay not only his or her own attorney, but also the other side's attorney as well. This is often seen as a punitive action.

Attorneys' fees: A court award that requires the losing party to a lawsuit to pay the winning party's legal expenses.

---

7. 6 Del. C. 1953, §2534.

c. Treble Damages

Because the UDTPA is an action that can be brought in addition to other common-law actions, treble damages are awarded. Under treble damages, a judge can award an amount to the winning party that is three times the total, actual damages suffered by the party. Such an award is often seen as a form of punitive damages and a way of sending a message to the commercial community that deceptive business practices can result in a huge monetary loss. The idea behind treble damages is to discourage other businesses from engaging in the same practices that required the offending party in the current case to pay such a high damage award to the plaintiff.

Treble damages: An award of damages three times the amount of the actual damages incurred by a party.

Figure 2-7. Remedies under UDTPA.

(a) A person likely to be damaged by a deceptive trade practice of another may be granted an injunction against it under the principles of equity and on terms that the court considers reasonable. Proof of monetary damage, loss of profits, or intent to deceive is not required. Relief granted for the copying of an article shall be limited to the prevention of confusion or misunderstanding as to source.

(b) The court in exceptional cases may award reasonable attorneys' fees to the prevailing party. Costs or attorneys' fees may be assessed against a defendant only if the court finds that defendant has wilfully [sic] engaged in a deceptive trade practice.

(c) The relief provided in this section is in addition to remedies otherwise available against the same conduct under the common law or other statutes of this State. If damages are awarded to the aggrieved party under the common law or other statutes of this State, such damages awarded shall be treble the amount of the actual damages proved.[8]

Sidebar: UDPTA does not authorize actions under warranty theory. Warranties are a creature of common law and other legislative provisions. For this reason, we will deal with warranties in a different chapter. (Chapter 4)

B. Other State Limitations on Business Practices: The Uniform Commercial Code

The Uniform Commercial Code is another suggested or pattern act designed to create a uniform system. In this case, the uniform system is designed to ease commercial transactions by people in different states. Like the uniform deceptive trade practices act, the UCC was created by a panel that attempted to anticipate all the problems and to provide solutions for commercial transactions. The UCC was adopted by most states with few changes to the text. Although the Uniform Commercial Code spends a great deal of time addressing issues such as sales, bills of lading and warehousing, the UCC does provide remedies for consumers and buyers. For instance, in Article 2 of the Uniform Commercial Code, both sellers and buyers have specific remedies against one another. Section 2–703 provides that the seller has the following remedies against the buyer in the event of a wrongful rejection or breach of the sales contract:

---

8. Delaware Statute § 2533.

- Withhold delivery of the goods
- Stop delivery of the goods
- Reclaim the goods
- Cancel the contract
- Resell the goods and seek damages against the buyer
- The UCC also provides buyers with remedies against sellers who provide defective goods. The buyer's remedies include:
- Recover the purchase price
- Deduct damages from any part of the price that is still unpaid
- Cancel the contract
- Recover damages for non-delivery
- Recover any other reasonable damages[9]

> *Getting to the Essentials:*   The Uniform Commercial Code provides several extremely effective remedies against buyers or sellers who engage in questionable practices.

C. Role of State Agencies in Investigating Deceptive Trade Practices

Many states also provide agencies to investigate consumer fraud and deceptive trade practices. In some states such as New York, this responsibility falls to the State Attorney General. Eliot Spitzer, the former New York State Attorney General, generated a lot of media attention by taking an activist stand on consumer issues ranging from improper accounting to outright fraud by major companies based in New York. His strong stand on these issues no doubt helped him gain the governorship of the state, which he kept until a spectacular sex scandal necessitated his resignation. The Attorney General's Bureau of Consumer Fraud Protection is responsible for investigating and prosecuting businesses and individuals who violate New York law by engaging in fraudulent, misleading or deceptive trade practices. In other states the responsibility for investigating these types of claims falls to the State Secretary of State's office. Behavior that violates state criminal statutes may also be investigated by state and local law enforcement.

D. Other Consumer Protections

In future chapters, we will examine many other types of consumer protection statutes, agencies and common-law actions all of which are designed to protect consumers and others from unfair or fraudulent business practices. As you can see, the area of consumer law is rapidly expanding and covers a diverse spectrum of business practices.

---

9. U.C.C. § 2-711.

1. Limitations on Commercial Advertisements

Several different layers of both federal and state statutes govern commercial advertisements. Interestingly enough, we return to the jurisdiction of the Federal Trade Commission when it comes to application on Federal truth in advertising requirements. The FTC has three general requirements on all commercial advertisements:

1. They must be truthful.
2. Advertisers must have evidence to back up the claims that they make in their ads.
3. The advertisements must be fair.

In addition, another federal agency, the Federal Communications Commission, also has limitations on what can and cannot be said in commercial advertisements that are broadcast.

Case Excerpt

Is it unfair trade practice to commit "cyber piracy?"

Diller v. Steurken[10]

CHARLES EDWARD RAMOS, J.

Plaintiffs Barry Diller and USA Networks, Inc. ("USAi") request a permanent injunction and award of attorneys' fees and costs after obtaining a default judgment against defendants, Eric M. Steurken, Rich A. Preisig, Jr., Thoughts, and Cybermultimedia, Inc.

BACKGROUND

Barry Diller is the Chairman and Chief Executive Officer of USAi, a diversified media and e-commerce company. On January 19, 1999, defendants Steurken and Preisig, using "Thoughts," an assumed business name, registered the Internet domain name "barrydiller.com." They then registered their own domain, "cybermultimedia.com," using another assumed business name, "Cybermultimedia, Inc." ("CMM"), and started designing a Web site. On January 27, defendants incorporated CMM and began to publicize their Web site one month later.

Defendants essentially established cybermultimedia.com as a domain name brokerage site. They would collect the names of celebrities, register their names as Internet domains, and then attempt to sell them to the celebrities at a substantial profit. From June 1, 1999, until June 22, CMM's site contained numerous uses of Barry Diller's name, one use of his picture, and one use of the name "USA Networks." Defendants never asked Diller for permission to use his name, his picture, or the name "USA Networks" in any manner on the CMM Web site. On June 10, plaintiffs wrote a letter to defendants demanding removal from the CMM Web site of all references

---

10. 185 Misc.2d 274, 712 N.Y.S.2d 311 (N.Y. Sup., 2000).

to Barry Diller and USAi. Plaintiffs also demanded, inter alia, that defendants transfer "barrydiller.com" to their control. In response to this letter, on June 22, defendants removed Diller's picture and the reference to USAi from the site. However, they did not remove Diller's name and continued to offer the sale of "barrydiller.com" for $10,000,000.

Plaintiffs immediately filed suit against defendants alleging violation of Barry Diller's civil rights under § 51 of the New York Civil Rights Law, trademark infringement under § 360-k of the New York General Business Law ("GBL"), and unfair trade practice and unfair competition under §§ 349 and 350 of the GBL. In mid-July of 1999, defendants removed all references to Diller's name from their site and discontinued offering " barrydiller.com" for sale. However, they did not transfer "barrydiller.com" to the plaintiffs. Consequently, plaintiffs did not withdraw their suit and obtained a default judgment on November 15, 1999. Plaintiffs now ask the court to enjoin defendants from using "barrydiller.com" and to order a transfer of ownership of the domain name. Plaintiffs also request attorneys' fees and disbursements as damages in the amount of $68,615.20 and costs in the amount of $200. Plaintiffs do not claim any other damages.

ENTITLEMENT TO INJUNCTION

On the issue of injunctive relief, defendants have conceded liability for violation of § 51 of the Civil Rights Law and §§ 349, 350, and 360-k of the GBL by defaulting (see, Conteh v. Hand, 234 A.D.2d 96, 650 N.Y.S.2d 723 (1st Dept. 1996) (stating "it is well settled that by defaulting a defendant admits all traversable allegations in the complaint, including the basic allegation of liability.")). Section 51 of the Civil Rights Law provides:

Any person whose name, portrait, picture or voice is used within this state for advertising purposes or for the purposes of trade without … written consent … may maintain an equitable action in the supreme court of this state against the person, firm or corporation so using his name, portrait, picture or voice, to prevent and restrain the use thereof.

(Civil Rights Law § 51) (emphasis added). Similarly, GBL § 349(h), which applies to deceptive trade practices, provides that "any person who has been injured by reason of any violation of this section may bring an action … to enjoin such unlawful act or practice." The language of GBL § 350-e(3), which applies to false advertising, is identical. Furthermore, GBL § 360-l provides that "likelihood of injury to business reputation or of dilution of the distinctive quality of a mark or trade name shall be a ground for injunctive relief in cases of infringement of a mark registered or not registered or in cases of unfair competition." Consequently, defendants are to be enjoined as a matter of law from using the domain name "barrydiller.com."

In addition to provisions of State law providing plaintiffs with support for an injunction, the recently enacted Anticybersquatting Consumer Protection Act ("ACPA") (15 USC § 1051 et seq., added by Pub. L. 106–113, 113 U.S. Stat. 1501) provides for "injunctive relief, including the forfeiture or cancellation of the domain name or the transfer of the domain name to the plaintiff " (15 USC § 1129(2)) (emphasis added). While the ACPA was not in effect when defendants registered "barrydiller.com" (see, 15 USC § 1129(4)), the Second Circuit has ruled that the ACPA applies retroactively where prospective or injunctive relief is at issue (See, Sporty's Farm v. Sportsman's Market, 202 F.3d 489). Moreover, domain name transfer is a remedy of choice in anti-cybersquatting actions (See, Toys "R" Us v. Abir, 1999 WL 61817, 1999 U.S.Dist. LEXIS 1275, (S.D. N.Y.) (referring to previous order directing a domain name transfer); Green Products Co. v. Independence Corn By-Products, 992 F. Supp. 1070, 1079–1080 (N.D. Iowa 1997) (ordering domain name transfer as part of a preliminary injunction)). Given the provisions of state law, supra, the Second Circuit's construction of the ACPA, judicial recognition of domain name transfer as a recognized remedy in anti-cybersquatting actions, and the fact that defendants have indicated a willingness to consent to an injunction in their opposition papers, the court grants plaintiffs' request for injunctive relief and compels defendants to transfer ownership of "barrydiller.com" to the plaintiffs.

ENTITLEMENT TO ATTORNEYS' FEES AND COSTS

The general rule of law in New York is that attorneys' fees are "merely incidents of litigation and thus are not compensable in the absence of statutory authority providing for such" (City of Buffalo v. J.W. Clement Co., 28 N.Y.2d 241, 262–263, 321 N.Y.S.2d 345, 269 N.E.2d 895). Plaintiffs rely upon GBL §§ 349(h) and 350-e(3) for their statutory authority. These sections provide for an award of reasonable attorneys' fees at the discretion of the court (See also Independent Living Aids v. Maxi-Aids, Inc., 25 F.Supp.2d 127, 131 E.D. N.Y.1998) (noting that an award of attorneys' fees is generally a matter of judicial discretion).

However, plaintiffs' reliance upon these statutes for an award of attorneys' fees is misplaced. "The goals of GBL §§ 349–350 were major assaults upon fraud against consumers, particularly the disadvantaged ... not adventitious intervention in commercial or trade identification cases brought by one business against another. This reality may properly guide their interpretation" (Givens, Practice Commentaries, McKinney's Cons. Laws of N.Y., Book 19, General Business Law § 349, at 574–575; see also Genesco Entertainment v. Koch, 593 F. Supp. 743, 752 (S.D. N.Y.1984) (noting that § 349 claims must concern the public interest); Independent Living Aids v. Maxi-Aids, supra, at 132 (applying the interpretation of the practice commentaries to § 350 as well)). Plaintiffs did not bring their suit as consumers but rather as defendants' competitors alleging unfair trade practices and unfair competition as the basis of their GBL claim. Furthermore, "a prima facie case under § 349 requires ... a showing that defendant is engaging in an act or practice that is deceptive or misleading in a material way and that plaintiff has been injured by reason thereof" (Oswego Laborers' Local 214 Pension Fund v. Marine Midland Bank, 85 N.Y.2d 20, 25, 623 N.Y.S.2d 529, 647 N.E.2d 741 (1995). An improper act or practice on the part of a defendant does not in and of itself constitute a deceptive act or practice (See, Varela v. Investors Ins. Holding Corp., 81 N.Y.2d 958, 961, 598 N.Y.S.2d 761, 615 N.E.2d 218). To be sure, the initial posting of "barrydiller.com" on the Internet constituted trademark dilution and infringement upon Barry Diller's civil rights. However, plaintiffs have not proven to the court's satisfaction that defendants engaged in significant deceptive or misleading practices through their offer of "barrydiller.com." In contrast stand the corporate cases cited by the plaintiffs, Centaur Communications v. A/S/M Communications, 652 F. Supp. 1105, 1114–15 (S.D. N.Y.1987), aff'd. 830 F.2d 1217 2d Cir.1987 and Vitabiotics Ltd. v. Krupka, 606 F. Supp. 779, 786 (E.D. N.Y.1984), where the defendants engaged in deliberate and deceptive practices. In conclusion, although defendants' default has established their general liability, the court will not award attorneys' fees when plaintiffs have failed to establish that they are entitled to them as a matter of law.

In addition to their argument for attorneys' fees under the GBL, plaintiffs argue that they are entitled to attorneys' fees based upon Congress' intent in passing the ACPA. Plaintiffs do not argue that the ACPA is directly applicable since the act limits its applicability to "domain names registered on or after November 29, 1999" (15 USC § 1129(4)). While plaintiffs correctly observe that the plain language of the ACPA provides for remedies of costs and attorneys' fees, see 15 USC § 1129(2), they incorrectly assert that Congress would condone a state court's use of the remedies provision of the ACPA as a rationale for awarding attorneys' fees in this case. Congress provided that "damages under subsection (a) or (d) of section 35 of the Trademark Act of 1946 (15 USC 1117) ... shall not be available with respect to the registration, trafficking, or use of a domain name that occurs before the date of the enactment of this Act (Nov. 29, 1999)." Subdivision (a) of 15 USC § 1117 provides for, inter alia, an award of attorneys' fees as damages. Since Congress explicitly excluded from retroactive effect awards of attorneys' fees under the ACPA, plaintiffs cannot claim that Congress intended for a state court to use the ACPA as persuasive authority for awarding attorneys' fees in a pre-ACPA case (See, McKinney's Cons. Laws of N.Y., Book 1, Statutes § 76. "Where words of a statute ... express plainly, clearly and distinctly the legislative intent, resort may not be had to other means of interpretation."). Therefore, plaintiffs may only use New York law to advance their case for attorneys' fees. Since plaintiffs fail to demonstrate that they are entitled to attorneys' fees under the New York GBL, the court denies any such award to plaintiffs.

The court next turns its attention to the issue of costs and disbursements. Having received no argument from defendants as to why the court should not grant plaintiffs costs in the amount of $200 under CPLR § 8201, the court grants this request. However, the plaintiffs are not entitled to any further sum for disbursements or out-of-pocket expenses. "GBL §§ 349 and 350 do not mention, and hence do not provide for, a recovery of costs" (Independent Living Aids v. Maxi-Aids, supra, at 134). Finally, defendants contend that any attorneys' fees or costs that the court would impose would be appropriate only against CMM because only CMM listed "barrydiller.com" for sale on its site. The court finds this contention void of merit. Defendants had a fair opportunity to litigate the issue of liability and chose to default instead of mounting a defense. Consequently, the court finds all defendants liable.

Accordingly, it is ordered that defendants, their agents, servants, employees, representatives, attorneys, related companies, successors, assigns, and all others in active concert or participation with defendants are hereby permanently enjoined and restrained:

1. From retaining ownership of or using the name "barrydiller.com" or any form of the name Barry Diller, any colorable imitation of the name, or any thing, symbol or name confusingly similar thereto or likely to cause injury to Barry Diller and USAi's business reputation;

2. From using any form of the trademarks of plaintiff USA Networks, Inc., any colorable imitation of those marks, or any thing, symbol or name confusingly similar thereto or likely to cause injury to Barry Diller and USAi's business reputation;

3. From representing by any means whatsoever, directly or indirectly, that defendants, any products or services offered by defendants, including information services on the Internet, are associated in any way with Barry Diller and USAi or their products or services, and from otherwise taking any other action likely to cause confusion, mistake, or deception on the part of purchasers or consumers;

4. From doing any other acts or things calculated or likely to cause confusion or mistake in the mind of the public or to lead purchasers or consumers into the belief that Defendants' products or services come from or are the products or services of Barry Diller or USAi, or are somehow sponsored or underwritten by, or affiliated with, Barry Diller or USAi, and from otherwise unfairly competing with Barry Diller or USAi; ordered that defendants shall transfer ownership of the domain name "barrydiller.com" to Barry Diller by July 20, 2000, and it is further ordered that the clerk shall enter judgment against defendants for costs in the amount of $200.00.

Case Questions

1.   What scheme did the defendants dream up that became the subject of this lawsuit?
2.   What are the plaintiffs seeking in this case?
3.   What position do the defendants take on the issue of the injunction?
4.   Why does the court refuse to award attorneys' fees to the plaintiffs?

Chapter Summary

In this chapter we explored both federal and state legal actions that can be brought against businesses that engage in deceptive or unfair trade practices. Under the common law, consumers can bring actions against companies based on fraud or negligent misrepresentation, but many of these actions have serious shortcomings. In the early 1900s, the federal government responded to the lack of regulation of national corporations by creating the Federal Trade Commission. The focus of the Federal Trade Commission is to level the playing field and ensure that companies are engaging in fair practices. The Federal Trade Commission regulates a wide variety of business practices, from commercial advertisements to clothes labels and the national Do Not Call Registry. On the state level, in addition to the common-law remedies that have been available to consumers for decades, most states have adopted the Uniform Deceptive Trade Practices Act that expands on the common-law remedies and provides additional legal infrastructure for consumers to challenge a wide variety of unfair and deceptive practices. Under this act, consumers can challenge business practices such as "passing off," misrepresentation of brand names, and a wide variety of other business practices that may or may not have been actionable under the common law. The Uniform Deceptive Trade Practices Act also gives consumers three possible remedies: injunctions, attorney's fees and treble damages. An injunction is a court order preventing a company from taking a specific action. An award of attorney's fees forces the losing party in a civil case to pay the winning party's bill for legal services. Treble damages allow the winning party in a civil case to receive three times the actual damages incurred. In addition to the Uniform Deceptive Trade Practices Act, the Uniform Commercial Code, adopted by all states, also provides a framework for remedies for consumers and buyers against merchants and manufacturers who engage in unfair or deceptive practices.

Web Sites

- Consumer Information from the federal government
  http://www.consumer.gov/
- Federal Trade Commission
  www.ftc.gov
- Consumer Sentinel
  www.consumer.gov/sentinel/

Key Terms

Caveat emptor	Injunction
Passing off	Attorneys' fees
Bait and switch	Treble damages

Review Questions

1. What types of common-law remedies are available under state law for consumers who claim that they have been the victims of unfair or deceptive trade practices?

2. What is "bait and switch?"

3. What is caveat emptor?

4. When did the push to create consumer protection of the federal level originate?

5. What is the Federal Trade Commission?

6. What powers has the Federal Trade Commission been granted?

7. What is the Federal Trade Commission's Bureau of Consumer Protection?

8. What is the national Do Not Call Registry?

9. What types of organizations are exempt from coverage in the Do Not Call Registry?

10. What is the Uniform Deceptive Trade Practices Act?

11. What are some examples of deceptive trade practices under the Uniform Deceptive Trade Practices Act?

12. How does someone qualify as a consumer under Uniform Deceptive Trade Practices Act?

13. What is "passing off?"

14. What types of organizations are exempt from coverage under Uniform Deceptive Trade Practices Act?

15. What remedies are available to consumers under Uniform Deceptive Trade Practices Act?

16. What protections does the Uniform Commercial Code offer to consumers?

17. What are some of the remedies available to buyers and sellers under the Uniform Commercial Code?

18. What are some examples of state agencies that may regulate unfair or deceptive trade practices?

19. How does the Federal Trade Commission govern commercial advertisements?

Chapter 3

Product Liability

Chapter Objectives

- Describe the development of product liability doctrine
- Explain the problem of proving a product liability lawsuit under traditional contract law principles
- Define the difficulties involved in bringing a product liability lawsuit under traditional negligence law
- Describe how product liability doctrine developed in various states
- Explain the elements of a product liability lawsuit

I. Product Liability

Product liability is an area of law that assesses legal responsibility against manufacturers, designers, producers and marketers of products that cause harm to individuals. In a common scenario, a consumer purchases a product and then is harmed by it. The option of suing the manufacturer seems obvious to us, but this area of law has developed slowly and the possibility of recovering damages from the manufacturer has only been a realistic option since the mid 20th century. Prior to that, the law favored manufacturers and producers and the chance of a consumer receiving compensation for any type of injury was essentially zero.

In this chapter, we will explore the development of product liability law, first by discussing the societal pressures that created it and then by exploring the options available to consumers before it was created. After that, we will examine the current state of product liability law on both the state and federal levels and discuss the options currently available to consumers.

Product Liability: A claim brought by a consumer for the harm caused by the manufacture, design, production and marketing of a product without regard to fault.

Getting to the Essentials	There are two names for this area of law. Some legal authorities refer to it as "Products liability," while others prefer "product liability." We will use product liability simply to remain consistent throughout the chapter.

A. A Short History of Product Liability in the U.S.

As far as the law is concerned, product liability lawsuits are a relatively recent phenomenon. In the early 20th century, consumers had very few options if defective products injured them. Traditional common-law remedies, such as lawsuits based on violation of contract law or as negligence cases were not fertile ground for injured consumers. In the next section, we will see why.

Besides the fact that traditional legal approaches provide very little assistance to consumers, these types of cases faced a practical hurdle: how does a plaintiff prove that a product is defective when the process to create it is protected by trade secrets? A business could easily claim protection of various manufacturing processes, thus making it virtually impossible for a plaintiff to prove that the process was faulty.

Figure 3-1.

Table 1
Estimated Non-Fire Carbon Monoxide Poisoning Deaths
by Associated Fuel-Burning Consumer Product, 1999–2006

| Consumer Product | 2004–2006+ | | Annual Estimate | | | | | | | |
	Average Estimate	Average Percent	1999	2000	2001	2002	2003	2004	2005+	2006+
Total Deaths	181	100%	109	137	122	181	154	167	197	180
Heating Systems	63	35%	50	81	72	97	66	87	53	50
Unspecified Gas Heating	8	4%	5	1	5	2	4	14	6	3
LP Gas Heating	22	12%	22	28	24	41	22	28	20	19
Natural Gas Heating	20	11%	20	42	28	32	27	30	8	23
Coal/Wood Heating	2	1%	*	2	6	4	2	4	3	*
Kerosene/Oil Heating	4	2%	2	8	6	8	6	4	4	3
Diesel Fuel Heating	*	*	*	*	*	1	*	*	*	*
Heating Systems, Not Specified	6	3%	1	*	3	9	5	6	12	1
Charcoal Grills or Charcoal	6	3%	17	8	10	11	8	3	6	10
Gas Water Heaters	4	2%	1	3	1	1	7	2	6	4
Gas Grills, Camp Stoves, Lanterns	6	3%	14	4	1	5	2	8	6	4
Gas Ranges/ Ovens	3	2%	6	12	9	3	3	4	6	*
Other Appliances	1	1	1	*	*	*	2	1	2	1
Multiple Appliances	7	4%	6	2	7	12	8	4	9	7
Engine-Driven Tools	90	50%	13	27	22	51	57	57	111	104
Generators	75	41%	7	19	21	41	50	42	97	85
Other Engine-Driven Tools	16	9%	6	8	1	10	7	15	13	18

+ Data collection for 2005 and 2006 is nearly complete. Italicized estimates may change in the future if more reports of fatalities are received.

* No reports received by CPSC staff.

Source: U.S. Consumer Product Safety Commission/EPHA.
CPSC Death Certificate File, CPSC Injury or Potential Injury Incident File, CPSC In-Depth Investigation File, National Center for Health Statistics Mortality File, 1999–2006.

Note: Reported annual estimates and estimated averages and percentages may not add to subtotals due to rounding.

Non–Fire Carbon Monoxide Deaths Associated with the Use of Consumer Products.[1]

Added to the difficulties of gathering evidence to prove a case at trial, plaintiff-consumers faced another problem. Courts in the 1800s and early 1900s were notoriously business-friendly when it came to such cases. The basic idea behind court philosophy seemed to be that if manufacturers and large, multi-national corporations were given the opportunity to develop their businesses without the possibility of having to pay out large monetary damages, then the overall economy of the United States would improve and the benefits of a robust economy would find its way to the lowest members of society. In practice, however, the opposite result usually occurred. Manufacturers, with no threat of legal liability for producing products, had no incentive to make their products safer. Consumers were injured, and although manufacturers did not have to absorb the cost of these injuries by paying out large monetary damages, society as a whole was forced to absorb the cost of individuals who could no longer produce at the same level, borrowers who could no longer meet their financial obligations because of injuries, and individuals who had to seek medical treatment, often without being able to pay for it.

Before the creation of product liability doctrine, there were only two approaches that an injured consumer could take to seek compensation for an injury caused by a defective product. One approach involved contract theory, while the other was based in tort law.

Getting to the Essentials	"Product liability" or "products liability" refers to a broad category of civil actions where consumers seek monetary damages against manufacturers, producers or others to create products that cause them injury

B. Contract Law and the Privity Problem

Before the advent of product liability theory, one of the two possibilities that a plaintiff had in such cases was to sue under contract law. The idea was that the consumer-manufacturer relationship was like any other contract and when one party produced goods that failed to live up to the agreed-upon terms, the party could sue. Obviously, if the product actually injured a party, this would qualify as contract violation. However, there was one problem: **privity**.

Part of the evidence that an injured plaintiff would have to prove under contract law theory was that privity existed in the relationship between the plaintiff and the manufacturer. Privity is an ancient contract law concept. The idea behind privity is very simple: before a party can sue under a contract, he or she must show that there is a legally

---

1. Non-Fire Carbon Monoxide Deaths Associated with the Use of Consumer Products 2006 Annual Estimates. Consumer Product Safety Commission, September, 2009.

recognized relationship between the parties. In most contract cases, this is a relatively simple matter. The plaintiff can produce a contract that shows a clearly defined, contractual obligation between the parties. Once proven, the plaintiff could then proceed on the real issues in the case: how the other party had failed to live up to the contract's terms.

Privity: A relationship between two parties that is sufficiently close to establish that each was aware of the legal ramifications of entering into a contractual relationship with one another.

However, privity presented a real obstacle in early product liability cases. Where was the contractual agreement between the end-consumer and the original product manufacturer? Before the days of mass-produced goods, consumers and producers dealt directly with one another. If Bill Buyer wanted a new plow to till his fields, he would contact a manufacturer and directly negotiate the details. However, the Industrial Revolution changed the nature of the consumer-manufacturer relationship forever. In modern times, what individual consumer ever negotiates directly with a manufacturer about the dimensions of his television screen or the type of metal used in the chassis of his new car?

Figure 3-2.

Selected Consumer Product Categories for Persons 65 and Older
Injury, Death and Cost Estimates[2]

Title	ER-treated injuries 2002	Medically-treated injuries 2002	% Hospitalized 2002	Deaths 2000	Injury Cost ($Million)	Death Cost ($Million)	Total Cost ($Million)
Home workshop tools and attachments	38,210	86,830	6.8%	20	$1,363.0	$100.0	$1,463.0
Yard and garden equipment	41,780	108,710	12.6%	51	$1,971.6	$255.0	$2,226.6
Housewares	52,990	122,410	5.5%	17	$1,588.9	$85.0	$1,673.9
Ladders and step stools	28,510	76,890	26.0%	79	$2,286.7	$395.0	$2,681.7
Sports	57,120	168,890	11.8%	128	$3,164.2	$640.0	$3,804.2
Personal use items	58,220	149,660	16.5%	174	$3,046.5	$870.0	$3,916.5
Household chemicals	7,880	20,100	13.2%	24	$315.9	$120.0	$435.9
General household appliances	8,700	22,660	12.8%	12	$448.8	$60.0	$508.8
Kitchen appliances	12,790	32,270	15.3%	56	$747.3	$280.0	$1,027.3
Packaging and containers for household products	35,020	97,850	9.2%	14	$1,399.5	$70.0	$1,469.5
Children's products	18,630	19,000	18.2%	106	$1,321.4	$530	$1,851.4
Bathrooms	85,630	220,630	27.5%	194	$6,039.8	$970	$7,009.8
Home communication	11,930	31,230	22.5%	4	$610.4	$20	$630.4
Miscellaneous products	13,060	33,090	10.6%	20	$728.3	$100	$828.3

Table 1

---

2. Special Report: Emergency Room Injuries Adults 65 and Older. U.S. Consumer Product Safety Commission, 1991–2002.

C. Suing for Breach of Warranty

Another approach used by injured consumers was to sue under the theory of breach of warranty. A breach of warranty claim is based on a different form of contract law theory that states that the manufacturer has made express and implied promises about the safety of a product that it manufactures and sells. When the product fails to live up to these warranties, it is essentially a breach of that expressed or implied promise. In recent decades, this has become an area of law that offers some potential for injured consumers. For that reason, we will examine the law of warranty in the next chapter.

D. Contract Law and Product Liability Actions

Even though the Industrial Revolution changed business practices, it did not change the state of the law. Privity remained a required element in all such cases and was often used by manufacturers to defeat such cases before they could even begin. Most consumers deal directly with retailers or other merchants, and these merchants in turn deal with middlemen or other transport agents who then have contractual relationships with manufacturers. This arrangement was considered to be too tenuous to establish privity of contract between the end-consumer and the original manufacturer. Therefore, most of these cases ended with a verdict for the manufacturer. However, over time, courts and other legal commentators noted that this was causing serious injustice. Defective products were injuring consumers, sometimes seriously, and consumers had no recourse. Many turned to tort law for redress.

E. Bringing Suit under Traditional Negligence Theory

When a person sues another for a personal injury, the suit falls under tort law. Tort law is a branch of law that governs civil actions brought between parties who allege personal, financial or property injury. Consumers who were injured by products and who did not fancy their chances under contract law theory might be attracted by the prospects of suing under negligence theory.

Negligence is a tort action where one party alleges that another caused injury through inaction, inattention to detail or by reckless disregard for the consequences of his actions. This is not a book designed to introduce tort law concepts. Entire books have been written about negligence theory itself. However, it is important to understand the elements of a tort case, if for no other reason than to distinguish it from a product liability action. Negligence cases have existed in one form or another for centuries. Product liability lawsuits originated out of this branch of law, but have developed into their own subspecialty. As a result, there is a great deal of similarity between traditional negligence cases and product liability lawsuits. We will explore the similarities and differences between these two areas of law. First, we will discuss the four traditional elements of a negligence case and then show how a product liability lawsuit differs from a traditional negligence case.

Under traditional negligence–tort analysis, a defendant can be liable for the injuries to a plaintiff if the plaintiff can prove four elements. The elements are:

- Duty
- Breach of duty

- Proximate cause between breach of the duty and injuries to the plaintiff
- Damages suffered by the plaintiff

1. Duty

Under traditional negligence theory, a plaintiff must prove that a defendant owed a duty either to the plaintiff or to society as a whole. The most common example of a negligence case involves personal injury sustained in a car wreck. People who drive on the public roads owe a duty to all other drivers. They must drive safely. Do manufacturers owe a duty to consumers? Although our initial inclination is to answer yes, the law on this topic is complicated. We obviously owe duties to people with whom we are in a contractual relationship, and we owe duties to individuals in other contexts as well. However, if a consumer cannot show a contractual relationship with the manufacturer or a personal obligation between the consumer and the manufacturer, establishing duty, at least under traditional negligence theory, may be quite difficult. In many ways, establishing duty between the parties in a negligence case suffered from the same limitation that a party faced in bringing a contract law case. Without a showing of a general duty to all consumers, the plaintiff was forced to show a specific duty by the manufacturer to the plaintiff and that usually required some recognized relationship between the parties.

Each of the elements in a traditional negligence case builds on the other. If one element is missing, the case falls apart. Traditional negligence theory as the basis for a product liability suit runs into trouble on the very first element. However, there are other difficulties faced by injured consumers. For instance, there is the issue of breach of duty.

2. Breach of Duty

Under traditional tort analysis, the second element that a plaintiff must prove is that the defendant breached a duty to the plaintiff. We have already seen that it may be difficult for a consumer to establish a duty owed by the manufacturer to the consumer, but once the duty is established, shouldn't it be relatively straightforward to prove a breach of the duty? Here, again, we run into difficulties. Consider Example 3–1.

Example 3-1

Karen is at the store one afternoon doing some grocery shopping. She has almost completed her purchases and needs a bottle of soda. As she reaches for the bottle, it explodes. Karen's hand is severely injured, and she wishes to bring suit. Assuming that she can establish duty on the part of the soda manufacturer, can she establish breach of duty?

How would Karen prove breach of duty? It would seem rather obvious that a soda bottle that explodes would be a clear breach of some kind of duty, but how does Karen prove that the manufacturer created a faulty bottle? The manufacturer might easily claim that the bottle was perfectly safe when it left its manufacturing plant, but was mishandled in some way between the plant and the time it was placed on the store shelf. If the burden is on Karen to prove breach of duty, how can she prove at what point the bottle was damaged?

Answer: Under traditional negligence theory, Karen might not be able to prove breach of duty and would therefore lose her lawsuit and not receive any compensation for her injured hand.

Suppose that the soda bottle manufacturer can point to the fact that it followed all applicable safety codes in fabricating the bottle? Wouldn't that negate Karen's claim that the company breached its duty? It would, at least, raise a question about Karen's claim. Because Karen is not in the soda bottle manufacturing business, she may have difficulty showing exactly how, or why, the bottle exploded. Without such proof, a court might easily conclude that Karen has failed to meet the burden of proof on this element.

3. Causation

The third and fourth elements of a traditional negligence case would not pose any problems for injured consumers. **Causation**, or **proximate cause**, is the requirement that the plaintiff prove a direct factual connection between the negligence of the defendant and the plaintiff's resulting injuries. Although proximate causation can be a difficult question, in this example there doesn't appear to be any real question about Karen's injuries and the source of those injuries. There is certainly no claim about an intervening cause, something that occurred immediately before or after the bottle explosion that exacerbated Karen's injuries. However, as we have previously stated, all four elements of a negligence case must be proven, or the case will be dismissed. The fact that Karen can prove causation in this case does not alter the fact that the first two elements in the case are difficult if not impossible to prove.

Causation: A direct connection between one party's actions and the resulting injury to the other party.

Proximate Cause: An event that immediately precedes the injury and is the natural and direct cause of the injury.

4. Damages

The fourth and final element of a traditional negligence case is that the plaintiff must suffer some compensable injury. Here, the law creates the requirement that a plaintiff suffer some form of physical, economic or property interest that is compensable under the law. This requirement was created in order to prevent people from bringing suits for innocuous or wholly subjective injuries. Consider Example 3-2.

Example 3-2

In this scenario, Karen is walking through the grocery store and passes close to the display where the soda bottles are kept. One of the bottles explodes. Karen is not injured. She suffers no economic or property loss. However, that night she has a nightmare that bottles are exploding all around her. The following day, she goes to a law firm requesting to bring suit against the soda bottle manufacturer for causing her psychic distress. Can Karen establish element number four of a negligence case?

Answer: No. The requirement of damages in a negligence case was specifically designed to weed out claims that are not compensable under the law. Although some forms of mental distress are compensable in some states, no court would award Karen damages based on the fact that she has had a nightmare about an exploding soda bottle. Karen must establish a more conclusive case of damages before she will be allowed to receive any money.

In our original scenario, Karen's hand has been severely injured. Physical injury is a compensable loss under traditional negligence theory and if Karen can establish the other three elements in her suit, she would be entitled to compensation under tort law.

5. Summarizing Karen's Case

If Karen were to sue under traditional tort law, she would almost certainly lose. Here is a summary of the problems with Karen's case:

1. Duty: She may have trouble establishing the manufacturer's duty, under the theory that she has no legal relationship with the manufacturer.

2. Breach of duty: She will have difficulty proving that the manufacturer breached that duty or that the manufacturer did something wrong in fabricating the bottle.

3. Causation: If the manufacturer can show compliance with all applicable safety standards and practices, this would tend to negate Karen's proof that the manufacturer was negligent.

As you can see, traditional negligence theory analysis almost always results in a verdict for the manufacturer. Although most plaintiffs who have been injured by defective products can prove the third and fourth elements of a tort case, proof of elements one and two are difficult, if not impossible. Prior to the creation of product liability doctrine, plaintiffs who sued under traditional negligence theory almost always lost their cases and received no compensation for what were often horrible injuries.

Figure 3-3.

Table 1: Reported Toy-Related Deaths Among Children Less Than 15 Years of Age 2006–2008

Type of Toy (Hazard)	2006*	2007*	2008
TOTAL	28	22	19
Tricycles (drowning, motor vehicle involvement, fall)	5	5	4
Rubber balls (airway obstruction, aspiration, suffocation, choking)	4	4	1
Balloons (airway obstruction, aspiration)	3	4	1
Non-motorized scooters (motor vehicle involvement)	3	2	1
Powered riding toys (drowning, strangulation, motor vehicle involvement)	3	1	
Non-motorized riding toys/unspecified riding toys (fall, motor vehicle involvement, drowning)			4
Toy nails/pegs (airway obstruction, aspiration)	3		
Rubber darts (aspiration)	1	2	

Stuffed toys (suffocation)	2	1	
Balls, other (motor vehicle involvement, blunt force, drowning)	2		2
Other toy with a single reported fatality in the year (airway obstruction, drowning, hanging, toy pierced eye/brain)	2	3	6

Source: In-Depth Investigations (INDP), Injury and Potential Injury Incidents (IPII), Death Certificates (DTHS), and the National Electronic Injury Surveillance System (NEISS) from 1/1/2008 to 12/31/2008; CPSC. Data was extracted July 2009.

* One new toy-related fatality was reported to CPSC staff occurring in the 2006 calendar year, and four new toy-related fatalities were reported occurring in the 2007 calendar year, increasing the number of reported deaths in these years to 28 and 22.

The state of the law prior to the creation of product liability doctrine heavily favored the manufacturer. Whether a consumer sued under contract theory or negligence theory, the chances that the consumer would win were virtually non-existent. Whether suing under traditional contract or tort law, an injured consumer had little chance of succeeding on a claim. Courts and legislators began to see that a change in the law was necessary. They began to shift their emphasis from protecting manufacturers to ensuring that injured consumers had some form of redress. Product liability doctrine was the answer.

II. The Doctrine of Product Liability

Beginning in the 1920s, courts and legislatures began taking a hard look at the current state of law regarding defective products. They began casting around for an alternative that would create a more rational system. The limitations of contract and tort law approaches to these cases were obvious for all to see. How could they create a branch of law that creates a level playing field for both manufacturers and consumers? Fortunately, there was already an example ready at hand. The doctrine of **strict liability** places liability on a party without regard to fault in certain specific actions. Dynamite manufacturers, owners of wild animals, and any other individuals engaged in extremely hazardous activities have been held liable for damages caused by those activities, even when they were not at fault. Those who were interested in creating a more equitable system for injured consumers turned to strict liability doctrine as a good starting point.

Strict liability: Liability without regard to fault for particularly dangerous activities.

Product liability doctrine is a hybrid. It grew out of strict liability law, with a few contract law and tort law elements thrown in for good measure. The idea behind product liability doctrine was deceptively simple: Now manufacturers *could* be liable for injuries caused by defective products, even when the manufacturer could show that it was not at fault in the production, manufacture and distribution of the product. Injury alone was enough to establish liability.

Product liability: Imposing liability on a manufacturer for producing a defective product.

Of course, this was a radical departure from the existing law and a fundamental change in judicial philosophy. As a result, it was fought at nearly every level of the judicial system, from local lawsuits to rulings of the highest courts. The product liability doctrine received a significant boost in 1916 when the state of New York adopted it through a decision by its highest court. The decision still ranks as one of the most significant cases of the 20th century: *MacPherson v. Buick Motor Co.*[3]

> *Getting to the Essentials:*   Product liability is, in many ways, a hybrid between traditional tort actions and contract law.

The *MacPherson* case held that manufacturers who created products that could injure consumers must be responsible for the injuries that these products cause, even when the manufacturers could clearly demonstrate that they were not at fault. In the next few sections, we will examine the general parameters of a product liability suit.

Sidebar: Excerpt from *MacPherson*

"If the nature of a thing is such that it is reasonably certain to place life and limb in peril when negligently made, it is then a thing of danger. Its nature gives warning of the consequences to be expected. If to the element of danger there is added knowledge that the thing will be used by persons other than the purchaser, and used without new tests then, irrespective of contract, the manufacturer of this thing of danger is under a duty to make it carefully."[4]

> *Getting to the Essentials:*   The "MacPherson Doctrine" has grown from a simple case involving a defective automobile tire to form the basis of an entire branch of law, namely product liability suits.

A. Product Liability Does Not Involve a Finding of Fault

The basic premise behind product liability lawsuits is that a manufacturer can lose a lawsuit even when it can show that it did nothing wrong. It is not a defense to the suit that the manufacturer did not violate any laws in creating a product or that it did not deviate from accepted norms. It is no defense that the manufacturer created this product the same way that it has created hundreds or thousands of similar products that did not cause injury. Product liability is liability without fault, and therefore the manufacturer can be successfully sued even when it can prove that it did nothing wrong in creating the product.

B. What Can Be the Basis of a Product Liability Lawsuit?

Product liability lawsuits involve physical or financial injuries. However, a consumer is not permitted to bring a product liability lawsuit when he or she is simply dissatisfied with the performance of a product. The basic requirement of the suit is that there is an injury, either physical or financial. Dissatisfaction does not qualify as a kind of injury; at least as far as product liability lawsuits are concerned. When a product fails to live up to a consumer's expectations, this is usually considered to be a breach of warranty case.

---

3. 217 N.Y. 382, 111 N.E. 1050 (1916).
4. *MacPherson v. Buick Motor Co.*, 217 N.Y. 382, 111 N.E. 1050, 1055 (1916).

Consumers are allowed to sue under breach of warranty, but these cases are separate and distinct from product liability suits. For that reason, we will discuss warranties separately. (See Chapter 4)

Getting to the Essentials:	Product liability placed the burden of injury on manufacturers; it has unquestionably contributed to better and safer products, although there are many who claim that product liability has actually hampered innovation by placing too great a strain on companies to take risks and create new products.

C. Arguments For and Against Product Liability Cases

Product liability litigation is based on the premise that of the two parties involved—the individual consumer and the company that created the product—the company is in a better situation to remedy the danger than is the consumer. The theory underpinning these cases is that if a company is sued successfully for a dangerous product, the company will have a financial incentive to change the product to make it safer. Over time, this natural tendency toward creating better products will ultimately result in most products being made better, stronger and safer. One could certainly argue that with the extent of product liability lawsuits brought in the United States, this reasoning has shown to be correct. After all, the United States has one of the strongest economies while at the same time creating products that are generally far safer than products produced fifty or one hundred years ago. Although detractors would point out that product liability suits have damaged the U.S. economy, America is the world's remaining super power, with an enormously strong and vibrant economy, even in the face of product liability verdicts that far exceed amounts seen in most other countries. In the United States, products are continually refined and made safer and more effective for the consumer. Many argue that this is a direct result of product liability litigation placing the burden on the manufacturers to create safer products. Others might argue that safer products are the products of other forces and that the American economy perseveres despite huge jury awards. This issue is hotly debated.

Getting to the Essentials:	The theory underlying product liability suits is that of the two parties involved, the consumer and the manufacturer, society is better served by placing the burden of compensating injured consumers on the manufacturer.

D. Proving a Product Liability Case

All product liability lawsuits have some basic elements that the plaintiff must prove before he or she is entitled to an award of damages by the court. These elements include:

1. The plaintiff was injured by a product
2. That the injury was the result of a defective design
3. That the product was created or manufactured by the defendant

1. The Plaintiff Was Injured by a Product

The first requirement of a product liability lawsuit is that the plaintiff must prove that a product injured him or her. No matter how defective a product is, no matter how faulty the design, without proof of injury there can be no case. The plaintiff's injury could be physical, such as wounds or other trauma received from a defective product, but it can also be financial. If the plaintiff can show that his or her personal property was damaged by a defective product, the plaintiff can prove injury and establish the first element of a product liability lawsuit.

a. Proving a Defect

What qualifies as "defect" under product liability law? Most states recognize three different, accepted categories of defects. They include:

- Design defects
- Manufacturing defects
- Marketing defects

i. Design Defects

A design defect is a problem with a product that is a result of an innate, structural problem. There is something about the product that is faulty and can cause injury. The design defect could cause personal injury to a consumer or result in financial or property loss.

ii. Manufacturing Defects

A manufacturing defect is a defect that arises in the way that the product was produced. It might occur because of substandard ingredients or through an error in the production process.

iii. Marketing Defects

A marketing defect is based on the method that the company used to promote the product. Some products are not harmful when used in some contexts, while they are extremely dangerous when used in others. The typical toaster, for example, works extremely well, and quite safely, sitting on the kitchen counter, but will undoubtedly cause injury or electrocution when dropped into water. When a consumer alleges a marketing defect, he or she is saying that the way that the company promoted the product led directly to its misuse.

2. That the Injury Was the Result of a Defective Design

The second element in a product liability lawsuit is that the plaintiff must prove that the product that caused the injury was defectively designed or manufactured. Although this sounds like the most difficult element of a product liability lawsuit to prove, in everyday practice, satisfying element number two is usually straightforward. The plaintiff must present evidence, usually in the form of expert testimony, that the product that injured him or her had a defective design or some foreseeable use that could result in injury. Once the plaintiff has presented this evidence, the second element is proven.

3. That the Product Was Created or Manufactured by the Defendant

The third and final element of a product liability suit is proof that the defendant created or manufactured the defective product. This is also an easy element for the plaintiff to prove, especially given the fact that courts have been very liberal in determining the identity of manufacturers. In some instances, such as when a specific manufacturer cannot be identified, courts have imposed a "**market share theory**" to assess liability against all possible manufacturers of a product. Liability for a defective product was therefore spread across a number of potential defendants, with no single defendant bearing the entire financial brunt of a jury award.

> **Market share theory:** The premise that in any particular industry, 70% is owned by a small number of companies. When it is impossible to identify a specific manufacturer, courts will assess damages against the companies with the largest market share.

E. State Statutes on Product Liability

Although the critical product liability case was decided in New York in 1916, the doctrine was slow to catch on in other states. By the 1950s, all states had some form of product liability doctrine that allowed consumers to bring actions against manufacturers when they were injured by products, regardless of whether or not the manufacturer was at fault. Not all states that adopted product liability doctrine followed the New York example of basing liability exclusively on the theory that a manufacturer would be liable for any foreseeable injury from one of its products. Instead, they have followed diverse theories in recognizing product liability.

Product liability law has developed piecemeal across the country. In some situations courts have adopted product liability theory on their own initiative. They have essentially created a brand-new area of law by judicial decree. In other states, legislatures have enacted state statutes that clearly define the scope of product liability lawsuits. See Figure 3-4.

Figure 3-4. Product Liability Statute.

Inherently Unsafe Products

(a) In a products liability action, a manufacturer or seller shall not be liable if:

(1) the product is inherently unsafe and the product is known to be unsafe by the ordinary consumer who consumes the product with the ordinary knowledge common to the community; and

(2) the product is a common consumer product intended for personal consumption, such as sugar, castor oil, alcohol, tobacco, and butter, as identified in Comment i to Section 402A of the Restatement (Second) of Torts.

(b) For purposes of this section, the term "products liability action" does not include an action based on manufacturing defect or breach of an express warranty.[5]

---

5. (Texas) V.T.C.A., Civil Practice & Remedies Code § 82.004.

1. Different States/Different Theories of Product Liability

Because different states adopted different bases of recovery in product liability, we will simply summarize the most prominent of these reasons. In states that had a strong history of strict liability law, for example, product liability developed as a separate branch of that law. However, not all states recognized strict liability. In those states, product liability derives from contract law. Those states simply removed the privity of contract requirement and allowed consumers to sue manufacturers under breach of contract (or breach of warranty). Still other states opted for a modification of tort law principles to create product liability actions. It is important to understand how product liability was initially created in a particular state because it affects the way that the case proceeds. A product liability case that is based on contract theory will proceed very differently from one based on strict liability principles.

> *Getting to the Essentials:*　In different states, product liability lawsuits can be based on negligence theory, strict liability doctrine or some variation of consumer warranty theory.

F. Model Uniform Products Liability Act

Because of these different approaches to product liability, the Department of Commerce drafted a model act to serve as a guideline for the various states. The Model Uniform Products Liability Act was designed to act in much the same way as other proposed acts. The UPLA was presented as a complete Act, with proposed statutes, definitions and other elements that would enable states to simply adopt the measure. However, this model act has not reached the same level of acceptance as previous attempts, such as the Uniform Commercial Code or the Uniform Deceptive Trade Practices Act (Chapter 2). As a result, the state of the law on product liability varies from state to state.

G. Federal Legislation Related to Product Liability

The federal government has also created statutes governing various aspects of product liability. For instance, the U.S. Congress has created the Consumer Product Safety Commission. This commission has the responsibility for developing safety standards, enforcing these standards, forcing the recall of defective or dangerous products, researching products for their possible dangerousness and monitoring imported products.

The Consumer Product Safety Commission has sweeping powers when it comes to monitoring and recalling products. Usually it works through individual companies, orchestrating the recall of dangerous products by mutual agreement. However, the Commission does have the power to force recall of specific products. It also maintains an extremely informative Web site at www.cpsc.gov.

Figure 3-5. Consumer Product Safety Commission.

(a) Establishment; Chairman

An independent regulatory commission is hereby established, to be known as the Consumer Product Safety Commission, consisting of five Commissioners who shall be appointed by the President, by and with the advice and consent of the Senate. In making such appointments, the President shall consider individuals who, by reason of their background and expertise in areas related to consumer products and protection of the public from risks to safety, are qualified to serve as members of the Commission. The Chairman shall be appointed by the President, by and with the advice and consent of the Senate, from among the members of the Commission. An individual may be appointed as a member of the Commission and as Chairman at the same time. Any member of the Commission may be removed by the President for neglect of duty or malfeasance in office but for no other cause.[6]

These federal and state laws have imposed duties on manufacturers and producers. These duties include:

- The duty to test and inspect
- The duty to comply with health and safety regulations
- The duty to monitor "inherently dangerous objects"

1. The Duty to Test and Inspect

Various state and federal laws require a manufacturer to both test and inspect its products to ensure that they are not dangerous. This duty extends throughout the production process, from origination to final processing and distribution. When the product is complicated, the manufacturer must make more extensive provisions for testing and inspection than are required when the production is simple and straightforward. When production is multi-layered, such as that required to create an automobile, then the manufacturer must test at every stage of the production process.

Figure 3-6. Medical Examiners and Coroners Alert Project. Consumer Product and Safety Commission. October 2008 through September 2009.[7]

Asphyxiation/Suffocation

*A 9-month-old female was found unresponsive in her crib lying face down with her head in a corner of the crib. She was wrapped in a blanket with only her legs exposed. The blanket was 62" x 48" in size with a flexible heart shaped plastic decoration that illuminates in the corner of the blanket. The medical examiner suspects that this plastic decoration may have created a suffocation hazard. The cause of death was sudden unexplained infant death; prone sleep position, loose bedding. (Johnson County Medical Examiner Department, Iowa City, IA)**

*A 3-week-old male infant was found unresponsive after being placed to sleep on an infant support/nursing pillow. The infant was propped up in/on a pillow to sleep for the night. The mother had placed the baby on her queen size bed and they both fell asleep. Approximately six hours later the mother awoke and found the infant still in/on the pillow unresponsive. The cause of death was positional asphyxia. (Genessee County Medical Examiner's Office, Flint, MI) **

*A 3-month-old male victim was found deceased inside a portable crib. The infant was at a licensed day care provider. He was placed down for a nap on his stomach in a portable crib, which had an elevated sleeping platform. The victim was found unresponsive lying face down in a crease produced by the crib platform that was partly folded. He was pronounced deceased at the hospital. The cause of death was due to entrapment in collapsed crib sleeping platform. (Commonwealth of Virginia, Office of the Chief Medical Examiner, Northern Virginia District, Fairfax, VA)

*A 2-year-old male was standing on a couch by a window looking outside. When the father checked on his son, he noticed that the curtain cord (rope type) of the window shade was wrapped around his neck

---

6. 15 U.S.C.A. § 2053.

7. Medical Examiners and Coroners Alert Project (MECAP), Consumer Product Safety Commission, Oct. 2008 through Sep. 2009.

and he was unresponsive. The curtain cord was attached to an anchor which was attached to a window sill. The child was transported to a hospital where he later died. The cause of death was asphyxia due to ligature hanging. (Stearns County Medical Examiner's Office, St. Cloud, MN)**

*A 4-year-old girl and a 5 year-old-boy suffocated in a trunk while playing hide-and go-seek with their parents. They were celebrating the little girl's birthday. The mother found the children unresponsive and entrapped inside a wicker wooden trunk. The cause of death was Asphyxia. (District Twenty Medical Examiner's Office, Collier County, Naples, FL)

*Cases selected for CPSC follow-up investigation

**MECAP reports filed electronically.

2. The Duty to Comply with Health and Safety Regulations

Manufacturers also have the obligation to comply with health and safety regulations. They may be subject to inspection by both state and federal safety inspectors. What is interesting about this particular duty is that complying with it does not relieve the manufacturer of liability. The basic premise of product liability law is that a manufacturer can be liable even if it can show that it complied with all federal and state regulations. Product liability is liability without regard to fault, so a manufacturer cannot avoid responsibility for the damages done by a product by pointing to an unblemished safety record.

3. Inherently Dangerous Objects

What happens when a manufacturer is in the business of creating dangerous products? Handgun manufacturers deliberately create products that are designed to inflict injury or death. Does this mean that the manufacturer is responsible for every wound inflicted by the product? Obviously, that cannot be the case. When dealing with inherently dangerous objects, the law will make a manufacturer liable for injuries caused by the malfunctioning of the product, not for functioning the way it was designed. This means that a person who has been shot cannot sue a handgun manufacturer, but a person who is injured by a misfire can. Product liability allows suits in situations where the product does not work properly, not for injuries intentionally carried out by others.

H. Tort Reform and Product Liability

In recent years there has been a strong push towards reforming the tort laws in the United States. Reformers have taken special aim at product liability lawsuits, seeing them as essentially groundless actions that cripple research and development funds for manufacturers while awarding windfall profits to consumers. Tort reformers point to cases where consumers have reportedly received huge verdicts for relatively minor injuries. The theory offered by tort reformers sounds very much like the state of the law in the 1800s. In those times, judges argued that making manufacturers liable for all injuries caused by defective products would essentially cripple the companies and lead to the instability of the United States economy. In some ways we may be coming full circle on the issue of product liability.

Case Excerpt

When a pool pump causes severe brain damage.

Sta-Rite Industries, Inc. v. Levey[8]

SCHWARTZ, Chief Judge.

While visiting his mother at the Village Apartments, fourteen year old Lorenzo Peterson decided, along with a teenage friend, to swim in the complex's pool. During that innocent excursion he suffered severe brain injuries which occurred when, after removing an unsecured protective grate, he was caught in the powerful suction of the exposed drain. The efforts of numerous rescuers could not pull him out and, by the time the suction was released after it had become necessary to break down the locked door of a shack which housed the on and off switch, almost twelve minutes had passed. The boy had become catastrophically brain damaged and, at the time of the trial, was in a permanent vegetative state.

Footnote: We have been told that during the pendency of this appeal, indeed after oral argument, Lorenzo died.

His representatives brought claims against Roberta Segal, the owner of the Village Apartments, and All Florida Distributors, Inc., the company she hired to maintain and operate the pool. These potential defendants settled the cases against them for four million and three million dollars respectively. In this case, Sta-Rite Industries, Inc., the manufacturer of the pump, appeals from a judgment entered on a $104,409,053.20 jury verdict for the plaintiff, based on product liability theories that: (a) the pump was defectively designed; and (b) the failure properly to warn the owner and users of the pool of the dangers posed by permitting the drain to become exposed.

While we do not agree with Sta-Rite's primary contention on appeal that the evidence was insufficient to create a jury question as to its liability on either theory, we find reversible error in the trial court's treatment of the owner and maintenance company as Fabre defendants. We also conclude that the damage verdict cannot stand and that any new trial must involve the issues, not only of the respective responsibilities of Sta-Rite, the owner, and maintenance company, but of damages as well.

I.

We first conclude that the evidence supports the jury verdict as to Sta-Rite's liability on both the defective product and reasonable warning issues:

1. Defective design.

The plaintiff's most prominent theory was that Sta-Rite's pump was "defectively designed," because it did not contain a device which would automatically turn off the pump and its powerful suction effect within a few, harmless seconds after the drain had become clogged by a "foreign object" such as Lorenzo's body. In the light of the reasonable foreseeability, raised by many similar incidents, that the drain cover would become improperly secured and thereafter removed with the horrendous consequences which might follow, we conclude that this theory is well sustained by the

---

8. 2004 WL 2955038, 4 (Fla. App. 3 Dist., 2004).

evidence. Sta-Rite's primary contention to the contrary was that such a device was not reasonably available to a pump manufacturer when this one was sold to the apartment owner. This is simply not correct. The plaintiff introduced extensive evidence, both expert and lay, which showed that such a device was indeed feasible at that time.

Footnote in case: Quoting the plaintiff's brief:

Paul McKain, a fire-rescue paramedic, testified that in the 1990's he and his brother-in-law took this well-known technology and developed a successful vacuum kill-switch for swimming pool pumps in McKain's home and his sister's swimming pool as a stand-alone product—utilizing "floor sweepings," "very common pieces of electronic equipment" obtained from "Radio-Shack." This device has since been tested and found workable by other experts—including Sta-Rite's own expert at trial. Mr. McKain repeatedly testified that the device was based on technology and scientific knowledge that was widely-known "for decades" long before 1989 when the Sta-Rite pump herein was manufactured....

Sta-Rite surrebuts this evidence with a contention that the available technology did not include a perfected re-start mechanism which would automatically turn the pump back on—with the result that the system would be stopped for a period of time whenever, for example, a towel or leaves became caught in the drain. In our view, however, this makes no real difference. Applying the familiar risk-utility analysis, it was for the jury to say whether the mere inconvenience caused by a temporary shutdown while the obstruction was cleared was outweighed by the dangers of failing to have a switch-off at all. Of the cases which support this conclusion, we think that Martin Marietta is among the closest. There, the court upheld a products liability case based on the negligent failure properly to design an ejection system so as to preclude its operation while the plane was still on the ground and the consequent death of a test pilot, even though the danger would not have come into fruition without the intervening and quite unlikely disposal of a specific safety device during maintenance.

2. Failure to Warn.

There is little argument that a jury question was also presented as to the liability of Sta-Rite in failing reasonably to warn the purchaser and users of the pool about the extreme danger presented by a failure properly to maintain the grate, particularly in the light of similar severe accidents which occurred both before and after the sale of the pump in question. As accurately stated in the plaintiff's brief:

It is undisputed that no warning of any kind appeared on the Sta-Rite pump.... In 1997, some eight years after the pump in this case was manufactured, Sta-Rite placed a proper warning on its pumps manufactured from that point on:

Warning. Hazardous suction. Risk of drowning or disembowelment from hair or body entrapment against suction outlets.

Keep covers on suction outlets at all times. Covers must be screw-fastened to outlets and agency certified to be anti-entrapment and anti-hair-entanglement.

Do not use pool unless all suction outlets are covered with undamaged, correctly installed covers or grates that are screw-fastened and agency certified to be anti-entrapment and anti-hair entanglement.

Pool must have at least two suction outlets per pump, spaced at least three feet apart.

But Sta-Rite failed to send this warning to its distributors to see to it that prior purchasers of this pump (including the Village Apartments in this case) received it— although it could have easily done so.

As a result, no such warning got to the owner of the Village Apartments prior to Lorenzo's tragic entrapment in this case.

Sta-Rite's riposte to this evidence, however, is that inadequate warnings could not have been a legal cause of this accident because (a) Segal had in the past done no more than simply relay to All Florida any information about the pool, including the arguably insufficient warnings Sta-Rite had previously given her and, (b) All Florida already knew of the risks involved anyway. We do not agree with this line of argument.

As we have previously held in Munoz v. South Miami Hospital, Inc., 764 So.2d 854 (Fla. 3d DCA 2000), review denied, 789 So.2d 348 (Fla.2001), one who does not warn with the urgency and intensity deemed required under the circumstances cannot say that failure would have made no difference. This is the case even when, as in Munoz the person to be warned—there, a physician who should have been informed by hospital employees of his newborn patient's dangerous condition—specifically claims that such a warning would not have affected his conduct. It is all the more true because, in this case, Segal explicitly testified that if she had been given the stringent warnings the jury could have found were required she would have taken appropriate action, including informing All Florida.

While it is true that, as its employees acknowledged, All Florida was previously aware of a generalized requirement that the grate should be kept attached to the pool, the fact is that, despite that knowledge, the maintenance company did not in fact fix the grate in time to avoid the accident. Again, it must be assumed that a sufficiently emphatic warning would have made the difference. Indeed this is the very basis of the rule that warnings must be given with the urgency the circumstances, especially the potential dangers involved, require.

Case Questions

1. What happened to Lorenzo in this case?

2. According to the Court, was Sta-Rite's pump defectively designed?

3. Was there technology available at the time of Lorenzo's incident which would have prevented the tragedy?

4. Did Sta-Rite put any warning signs on its product?

5. Does the court maintain that a sufficiently urgent warning might have had some impact on this case?

Chapter Summary

Product liability law developed out of a need to provide injured consumers with a remedy through the court system. Prior to the development of product liability lawsuits, injured consumers had only two options: contract law and tort law. Bringing a product liability lawsuit under traditional contract law theories involved meeting the hurdle of privity. Privity is a requirement that a person who brings a contract lawsuit prove that there is a legally defined relationship between the parties. Because consumers and manufacturers have no legally defined, contractual relationship, most contract lawsuits resulted in verdicts for the manufacturers. Similar problems resulted when consumers attempted to use traditional tort law as a means to prove a product liability lawsuit. A negligent tort case has four elements: duty, breach, causation and damages, all of which must be proven before the plaintiff is permitted to recover anything from the defendant. Although proof of causation and damages normally presented no difficulties to an injured consumer, the first two elements, duty and breach, often presented insurmountable obstacles to a plaintiff. Because of the difficulties involved in suing under either contract law or tort law, states began adopting product liability doctrine as a means to allow injured consumers some way of receiving compensation from manufacturers who created defective products.

Under the theory of product liability, a manufacturer could be liable to an injured consumer even though the manufacturer was not at fault in creating the product. As long as the plaintiff could prove the basic elements of a product liability lawsuit: the plaintiff was injured by a product, that the injury was the result of a defective design and the product was created or manufactured by the defendant, the plaintiff could succeed on a product liability lawsuit.

Web Sites

- Consumer Product Safety Commission
  http://www.cpsc.gov/

Key Terms

Product liability	Damages
Privity	Strict liability
Negligence theory	Design defect
Tort law	Manufacturing defect
Duty	Marketing defect
Breach	Market share theory
Causation	Model Uniform Products Liability Act
Consumer Product Safety Commission	

Review Questions

1. Explain the basis of a product liability lawsuit.
2. Describe the development of product liability lawsuits in the United States.
3. Explain court philosophy regarding product liability lawsuits in the 1800s.
4. Before the creation of product liability doctrine, what were the two options for injured consumers?
5. What is privity?
6. What difficulties does a plaintiff have in pursuing a product liability suit under traditional contract law theories?
7. What are the elements of the traditional negligence action?
8. Which of the elements of a traditional negligence action presented the greatest problems for consumers injured by defective products?
9. What was the impetus for creating product liability doctrine in the early part of the 20th century?
10. What is strict liability and how does it compare to product liability?
11. What is the significance of the MacPherson case?
12. Give two arguments: one for and one against product liability.
13. What are the elements of a product liability lawsuit?
14. What is a design defect?
15. What is market share theory?
16. Locate a recent product recall and explain for what reason those products were recalled. What are the reasons for the recall, what result did the recall have and what potential lawsuits that could arise?

Chapter 4

Warranties

Chapter Objectives

- Explain the differences between implied and express warranties
- Describe important federal legislation that impacts the area of warranties
- Define the role of state law in the enforcement of warranties
- Explain "lemon laws" as they apply to transactions

I. What Are Warranties?

A warranty is a promise or an assurance that a seller makes about a product. Warranties come in a wide variety of formats. For instance, a manufacturer or seller might provide a written guarantee about the product's performance. On the other hand, the law might impose a warranty even in situations where the seller or a manufacturer does not provide one. In this chapter, we will examine the law regarding warranties, beginning with a discussion of the differences between express warranties and implied warranties and then proceeding on to important federal and state law governing warranties.

Warranty: A promise, assurance or guarantee that a particular fact or condition is true.

Before we can discuss the differences between various types of warranties, it is important to understand why the law of warranties is so important. In the modern era, consumers have the right to expect that a product will perform as advertised. This wasn't always the case. In fact, we can divide the law on warranties into three specific eras, each one a reflection of the society that created them.

A. A Short History of the Law of Warranties

Under the old common law, the manufacturer of a product was responsible for any harm that it caused. The idea was to put the burden of creating safe and useful products squarely on the people best suited to ensure those features in the finished product. Although not strictly classified as warranties, a manufacturer's responsibility arose more from a tort law basis than a contractual one. Under tort law, a person can be responsible for an action (or a failure to act) that causes harm to another. Tort law is alive and well when you consider the vast numbers of car wreck cases that are litigated every year, but the idea of tort as the basis for manufacturing warranties seems a little odd. However, if you consider that in the Middle Ages and later, a consumer was likely to be personally acquainted with a manufacturer, that they had both a business and a personal relationship, the idea of basing a cause of action for a dangerous device on tort law principles begins to make more sense.

However, the situation changed dramatically with the Industrial Revolution. With the swift changes in manufacturing processes, and the rise of huge, multi-national corporations, interchangeable parts and mass transportation, the relationship between manufacturer and consumer changed dramatically. The courts were also faced with the problem of making sure that the fledgling economy was allowed to grow without the possibility of litigation tearing it down before it had even taken root. Courts in the Industrial Revolution were notoriously pro-business and this approach was reflected in the law of warranties as much as any other area. Instead of making the manufacturer responsible for defects or injuries caused by harmful products, courts opted for a theory of caveat emptor. Under the theory of "let the buyer beware," consumers were responsible for ensuring that products would meet their needs and that they were safe for the purposes intended. *McFarland v. Newman*[1] is a case that is often cited as the point where the tide in the United States changed from protecting the consumer to imposing a strict standard of caveat emptor.

Caveat emptor: (Latin) "Let the buyer beware."

Sidebar: Excerpt from the McFarland v. Newman case:

"The relation of buyer and seller, unlike that of attorney and client, or guardian and ward, is not a confidential one; and if the buyer, instead of exacting an explicit warranty, chooses to rely on the bare opinion of one who knows no more about the matter than he does himself, he has himself to blame for it. If he will buy on the seller's responsibility, let him evince it by demanding the proper security; else let him be taken to have bought on his own. He who is so simple as to contract without a specification of the terms, is not a fit subject of judicial guardianship. Reposing no confidence in each other, and dealing at arms' length, no more should be required of parties to a sale, than to use no falsehood; and to require more of them, would put a stop to commerce itself in driving every one out of it by the terror of endless litigation."[2]

In the 20th century, the law of warranties underwent another change, one that proves that in law nothing is ever completely forgotten. The rule of caveat emptor often resulted in harsh rulings. As courts wrestled with these issues, the law of warranty became more important. Courts and legislatures began imposing legal requirements on manufacturers and sellers to provide some assurance that the products they were providing to the consumer actually performed according to the statements made. These legal requirements came in the form of express and implied warranties. Under modern analysis, warranties are not a function of the contractual relationship between the parties. Instead, they arise separately, almost like the obligations we see in tort law cases. In the modern era, manufacturers must contend with a wide range of warranties and consumers receive protections on many different levels, some of them based on contract law theories, some based on the law of warranties. Although it is tempting to approach the topic of warranties as if it is now perfectly settled, with contract law creating part of the basis and tort law providing the other, the situation is not so simple. The law of warranties remains complex

---

1. *McFarland V. Newman*, 99 Watts 55 (1839).
2. Id.

and varies from jurisdiction to jurisdiction. We will consider the general principles of warranty law, keeping in mind that the bases of these laws can be quite different from state to state and even from the state to the federal level.

> **Getting to the Essentials:** Prior to modern times, the rule of caveat emptor was the law of the land. It translates as, "let the buyer beware."

Example 4-1

Last week, Amy purchased a brand-new laptop computer. She discovered that the CD drive does not function. When she took the laptop back to store where she purchased it, the seller informed her that she must take up the malfunctioning CD drive with the manufacturer, which is located on the other side of the country. The store claims that it has no responsibility for the products that it sells. Is this a correct statement of the law? Under the old system of laws, the answer would be yes.

If the situation outlined in Example 4-1 seems unjust, that was the state of the law in the 18th, 19th and well into the 20th century.

B. Express Warranties

An express warranty is a promise, assurance or guarantee given by the manufacturer or seller about the product. In many ways, express warranties are the easiest type to analyze. They specifically rely on the statements made between the parties at the time of the sale. An express warranty can be made verbally or in writing. There is a wide range of express warranties that could be made about a particular product. An express warranty might assure a consumer that a product will perform under specific conditions, or that it has safety features, or that it has been evaluated for health risks. For an example of statutory limitations on express warranties, see Figure 4-1.

> **Express warranty:** A pledge, promise or assurance made orally or in writing that provides details about a product.

Figure 4-1. Express Warranties under the Uniform Commercial Code.

U.C.C. §2-313 Express Warranties by Affirmation, Promise, Description, Sample

(1) Express warranties by the seller are created as follows:

(a) Any affirmation of fact or promise made by the seller to the buyer which relates to the goods and becomes part of the basis of the bargain creates an express warranty that the goods shall conform to the affirmation or promise.

(b) Any description of the goods which is made part of the basis of the bargain creates an express warranty that the goods shall conform to the description.

(c) Any sample or model which is made part of the basis of the bargain creates an express warranty that the whole of the goods shall conform to the sample or model.

(2) It is not necessary to the creation of an express warranty that the seller use formal words such as "warrant" or "guarantee" or that he have a specific intention to make a warranty, but an affirmation merely of the value of the goods or a statement purporting to be merely the seller's opinion or commendation of the goods does not create a warranty.

When a consumer wishes to sue a manufacturer or seller under an express warranty, the suit resembles a simple contract dispute. The consumer must prove that the statement was made, the product failed to perform as promised, the consumer suffered damages because of the failure and that the consumer notified the manufacturer. Once that proof is presented, the burden shifts to the defendant to deny the elements.

Figure 4-2. Elements of A Suit Under an Express Warranty.

1. Whether an express warranty was given

2. The product failed to conform to the warranty

3. The plaintiff suffered damages because of this failure

4. The plaintiff notified the manufacturer of the breach

---

1. Evidentiary Issues in Express Warranty Cases

The trial of an express warranty case carries some unique evidentiary issues. Because the case relies heavily on testimony about conversations and other statements, the jury must determine which party is more accurate in his or her testimony. There are also some evidentiary rules that figure prominently in such cases. One of the most important is the parol evidence rule.

a. Parol Evidence Rule

The parol evidence rule is an evidentiary rule that prevents oral testimony to modify the terms of a written contract. The rule itself is based squarely in common sense, although it can have drastic consequences in express warranty cases. Under the rule, a witness is not permitted to testify that despite the fact that a written contract says one thing, the parties understood it to mean something else. The parol evidence rule makes written documents speak for themselves and does not allow oral testimony to alter their terms. A strict application of the parol evidence rule to express warranty cases would result in consumer losses in the vast majority of suits. After all, the entire case for the plaintiff is built on oral testimony about the representations made by the manufacturer/seller during the negotiations. The courts have gotten around this difficulty by using a relaxed approach to the parol evidence rule in express warranty cases. Essentially, the rule is honored more in the breach than in the observance. This is not true in other types of disputes. The parol evidence rule is alive and well in contract cases, but not in express warranty cases.

Parol evidence rule: A rule that prohibits oral testimony to interpret or alter the terms of a written contract.

Getting to the Essentials: The parol evidence rule prevents testimony about the provisions of a written document.

b. Conflicts Between Oral and Written Warranties

If the parol evidence rule is watered down in express warranty cases, what happens in a situation where a seller tells the buyer one thing, but the written warranty says something else? What happens when the oral warranty directly contradicts the written warranty? Courts do not follow a strict rule that always gives greater weight to the written warranty over the purported oral warranty. Instead, the courts must look to the facts of each case, including the surrounding circumstances, the sophistication of the parties and other factors that help determine the reliability of the oral warranty.

c. Disclaiming Express Warranties

The legal issues surrounding disclaimers are complex and will be addressed later in this chapter, but it is important to mention here the rule about disclaiming warranties in regard to express warranties. Courts take a dim view of disclaiming express warranties. After all, an express warranty is a direct promise or assurance made to a consumer. Allowing a manufacturer to make such a promise and then 'take it back' with a blanket statement such as "this product is sold without any express warranties" would be very much like giving with one hand and taking with the other. Although implied warranties can, and routinely are waived, express warranties generally are not. Courts take the view that when there are two conflicting provisions, one an express warranty and one disclaiming all warranties, they will interpret the transaction so that the express warranty controls.

C. Implied Warranties

In contrast to express warranties, an implied warranty is a promise or an assurance that is assumed under the law but never expressed by the manufacturer or seller. Over time, the area of implied warranty has grown in direct response to consumer complaints and unfair and deceptive trade practices by manufacturers and sellers.

1. Types of Implied Warranties

There are several types of implied warranties, including:

- Warranty of Merchantability
- Warranty of Fitness for Purpose
- Warranty of Good and Workmanlike Performance

Figure 4-3. U.C.C.; Implied Warranties.

U.C.C. 2-314. Implied Warranty: Merchantability; Usage of Trade

(1) Unless excluded or modified (Section 2-316), a warranty that the goods shall be merchantable is implied in a contract for their sale if the seller is a merchant with respect to goods of that kind. Under this section the serving for value of food or drink to be consumed either on the premises or elsewhere is a sale.

(2) Goods to be merchantable must be at least such as

(a) pass without objection in the trade under the contract description; and

(b) in the case of fungible goods, are of fair average quality within the description; and

(c) are fit for the ordinary purposes for which such goods are used; and

(d) run, within the variations permitted by the agreement, of even kind, quality and quantity within each unit and among all units involved; and

(e) are adequately contained, packaged, and labeled as the agreement may require; and

(f) conform to the promises or affirmations of fact made on the container or label if any.

(3) Unless excluded or modified (Section 2-316) other implied warranties may arise from course of dealing or usage of trade.

> **Getting to the Essentials:** Implied warranties arise under the law, not from the relationship or contractual negotiations between the parties.

a. Warranty of Merchantability

The implied warranty of merchantability is the implied promise that the product will perform and have the same quality as other similar products currently on the market. Although the warranty of merchantability has a long history, most states have adopted the Uniform Commercial Code approach to the warranty. (See Figure 4-4.)

b. Warranty of Fitness for Purpose

Like the implied warranty of merchantability, the implied warranty of fitness for particular purpose is an implied promise that the product will perform to certain specifications. This warranty is harder to prove than the warranty of merchantability, because it relies on statements and understandings between the parties at the time of the sale. Consider the facts in Example 4-2.

Example 4-2

Rachel Right has a cooking show on television. She requires kitchen appliances of the highest quality and always buys professional grade tools. She visits "The Cook's Resource" store and tells Sally Salesperson that she wants to buy a professional quality food processor. Sally takes her to the Process-a-matic 2000 and tells Rachel that this food processor is the right one for her needs. After taping two shows, the Process-a-matic breaks down. It turns out that the machine is very low quality and never designed for the amount of work that Rachel had in mind. Does Rachel have a suit for breach of implied warranty of fitness for purpose?

Answer: Yes. Because Rachel relied on the representations by Sally, who directed her to this particular machine, knowing that Rachel needed a high-quality, professional grade appliance, Rachel has a good chance of winning a suit under breach of warranty.

One of the problems in presenting a case for breach of implied warranty of fitness for purpose is that it is heavily dependent on the statements and knowledge on both parties. The situation in Example 4-2 might come out differently if Sally had no reason to know that Rachel was a cooking show host or that she needed professional grade appliances.

c. Warranty of Good and Workmanlike Performance

So far, our discussions about implied warranties have centered on products. The warranty of good and workmanlike performance is actually based on performing a service, not creating a product. Service contracts differ from the purchase of products in many important ways. The old common law rules apply to most service products for the simple reason that these contracts generally are negotiated between individuals who have the power to alter terms and construct their own provisions about how and when the service will be provided. As a result, the warranty of good and workmanlike performance is generally not seen in relation to products.

II. Federal Law Regarding Warranties

Because of the problems inherent in attempting to decipher the law of warranties, and the complaints of consumers across the country, the U.S. Congress passed the Magnuson-Moss Warranty Act to clarify many of the issues relating to express and implied warranties and also to disclaimers and the function of state law.

A. Magnuson-Moss Warranty Act

The Magnuson-Moss Warranty Act was created in 1975. It was a direct response to problems that consumers were having with the provisions in the Uniform Commercial Code that attempted to clarify the issues of warranties. Specifically, the UCC did not provide adequate means of addressing consumer problems in regard to the promises that manufacturers made about the performance and use of their products.

The Act essentially creates another level of safeguards for consumers, without superseding available state or federal law. The Act also provides a new and arguably more effective means for consumers to challenge deceptive warranty practices. Although the act does not require that a product must have a warranty, if a company decides to include a written warranty with a product, it must comply with the provisions of the Magnuson-Moss Warranty Act.

If the Act does not require every manufacturer to include warranties with their products, why would any company bother to provide warranties? The simple answer is that market pressures often force manufacturers to include a wide variety of warranties because their competitors do so. When a consumer has a choice between two virtually identical products, priced in the same range, consumers consistently purchase the product that offers the better warranties.

1. Jurisdiction of MMWA

One of the basic questions that must always be asked when dealing with the Magnuson-Moss act is whether or not a particular transaction falls within the act's jurisdiction. For instance, the Act does not address issues surrounding oral warranties or implied warranties that specifically fall within the jurisdiction of the Uniform Commercial Code. In order to fall under the jurisdiction of the MMWA, the product must be something that is normally used for "personal, family, or household purposes." See Figure 4-4. Under the Act, there are certain disclosures that must be made and that generally give consumers a reference system by either requiring the words "full" or "limited" in order to describe the various warranties. The Act also requires that any warranty made by a manufacturer must be displayed prominently. The Act also requires that any warranty must be made available prior to purchase. If a manufacturer chooses to display a warranty on products, the Act sets the minimum standards that the manufacturer must meet, including the nature of the remedies for breach of warranty. Finally, the Act specifically provides that it does not usurp or displace the law of implied warranties available under state law.

2. Definitions under MMWA

The Magnuson-Moss Warranty Act creates its own set of definitions for a wide variety of terms and phrases that figure prominently in consumer protection actions. Arguably the most important of these is the definition of "consumer."

a. Defining Consumers under MMWA

Under MMWA, a consumer is defined as:

- a buyer, other than for purposes of resale, of any consumer product, or
- any person to whom that product is transferred during the duration of the implied or written warranty of service
- any other person who is entitled by the terms of that warranty or service contract, or under applicable state law, to enforce against the warrantor or service contractor the obligations of the warranty.[3]

Figure 4-4. Defining "Consumer" under MMWA.

The term "consumer" means a buyer (other than for purposes of resale) of any consumer product, any person to whom such product is transferred during the duration of an implied or written warranty (or service contract) applicable to the product, and any other person who is entitled by the terms of such warranty (or service contract) or under applicable State law to enforce against the warrantor (or service contractor) the obligations of the warranty (or service contract).

Under the Magnuson-Moss act there is a clear distinction between consumers and commercial buyers, with consumers receiving a greater degree of protection. In order to clarify the distinction between consumers and manufacturers, sellers and suppliers, MMWA defines exactly what constitutes this non-consumer classification. Under the act, a "supplier" is any person or company that is engaged in the business of making consumer products. This definition applies to suppliers who create products that either directly or indirectly find their way into consumers' hands.

> **Getting to the Essentials:**   The Magnuson-Moss Warranty Act was a significant change in warranty law in the United States.

Figure 4-5. "Supplier" under MMWA.

The term "supplier" means any person engaged in the business of making a consumer product directly or indirectly available to consumers.[4]

---

b. Consumer Products under MMWA

The MMWA also defines consumer product in order to clarify exactly what types of products fall under its jurisdiction. Consumer products are defined as any item of personal property that are bought and sold and that are normally used for personal, family or household purposes. The definition of consumer product applies to all personal property, even when the property is occasionally used for commercial purposes. A typical example is an automobile. A car may be purchased for personal use, but may also be used

---

3. 15 U.S.C.A. § 2301 (3).
4. 15 U.S.C.A. § 2301(4).

for commercial reasons as well. The automobile falls under the Magnuson-Moss Warranty Act even if it is occasionally used for commercial purposes. However, when an automobile is specifically purchased for a commercial purpose, it does not fall under MMWA, even if it is sometimes used for personal reasons.

Example 4-3

Todd purchases a tractor-trailer rig for his business as a long-haul truck driver. One weekend, a friend asks him if he will help him move his belongings by loading them in Todd's trailer. Is the rig covered under MMWA?

Answer: No. The tractor-trailer was purchased for a commercial purpose and simply because it also happened to be used for a personal errand does not change its classification under MMWA.

Figure 4-6. Defining "Consumer Product" Under the Magnuson-Moss Warranty Act.

The term "consumer product" means any tangible personal property which is distributed in commerce and which is normally used for personal, family, or household purposes (including any such property intended to be attached to or installed in any real property without regard to whether it is so attached or installed).[5]

Example 4-4

Terry has purchased a prefabricated home to erect on an acre of land outside of town. She is curious to know if the MMWA applies in her situation. Does it?

Answer: No. Because the prefabricated home is not an item that is routinely sold in regular commerce and is also destined to become a part of real, not personal property, it does not fall under the jurisdiction of the MMWA. (It might, however, fall under the jurisdiction of the Uniform Commercial Code).[6]

3. Enforcement under the Act

The Magnuson-Moss Warranty Act gives the Federal Trade Commission the power to enforce its regulations. The Federal Trade Commission regulates businesses through an informal dispute resolution procedure. The FTC usually reaches consent agreements with businesses about what their written warranties should require. These enforcements are often closely tied to state-based regulations, such as automobile "lemon laws" and other consumer protection statutes. Although there have been some class actions brought under the Act, most litigation on warranties is carried out in state court systems. The question in many of these cases surrounds the issue of what, precisely, the written warranty must state.

4. Written Warranties under the Magnuson-Moss Warranty Act

Under the Magnuson-Moss Warranty Act, a written warranty refers to any written document containing a promise made in connection with the sale of a consumer product. This promise must relate to the nature of the product, the workmanship or its even-

---

5. 15 U.S.C.A. § 2301(4).
6. *Hughes v. Siegel Enterprises, Inc.*, 627 F. Supp. 1231 (W.D. Arkansas, 1986).

tual use. Warranties also include provisions about refunds for defective products, repairs of defective products and the situations in which the manufacturer will replace a defective product.[7]

Figure 4-7. Rules Governing Contents of Warranties under MMWA.

(a) Full and conspicuous disclosure of terms and conditions; additional requirements for contents

In order to improve the adequacy of information available to consumers, prevent deception, and improve competition in the marketing of consumer products, any warrantor warranting a consumer product to a consumer by means of a written warranty shall, to the extent required by rules of the Commission, fully and conspicuously disclose in simple and readily understood language the terms and conditions of such warranty. Such rules may require inclusion in the written warranty of any of the following items among others:

(1) The clear identification of the names and addresses of the warrantors.

(2) The identity of the party or parties to whom the warranty is extended.

(3) The products or parts covered.

(4) A statement of what the warrantor will do in the event of a defect, malfunction, or failure to conform with such written warranty—at whose expense—and for what period of time.

(5) A statement of what the consumer must do and expenses he must bear.

(6) Exceptions and exclusions from the terms of the warranty.

(7) The step-by-step procedure which the consumer should take in order to obtain performance of any obligation under the warranty, including the identification of any person or class of persons authorized to perform the obligations set forth in the warranty.

(8) Information respecting the availability of any informal dispute settlement procedure offered by the warrantor and a recital, where the warranty so provides, that the purchaser may be required to resort to such procedure before pursuing any legal remedies in the courts.

(9) A brief, general description of the legal remedies available to the consumer.

(10) The time at which the warrantor will perform any obligations under the warranty.

(11) The period of time within which, after notice of a defect, malfunction, or failure to conform with the warranty, the warrantor will perform any obligations under the warranty.

(12) The characteristics or properties of the products, or parts thereof, that are not covered by the warranty.

(13) The elements of the warranty in words or phrases which would not mislead a reasonable, average consumer as to the nature or scope of the warranty.[8]

---

a. Statements Not Covered under MMWA

The Magnuson-Moss Warranty Act does not apply to the opinions from salespersons, commonly referred to as "puffing." When a salesperson claims that a particular product is the finest that he or she has ever seen, or is the "best in the world," these statements are not considered to be warranties. There is a certain amount of exaggeration and hyperbole that all consumers must put up with. However, when a statement makes a factual claim, it can be construed as a warranty. Consider Example 4-5.

---

7. 15 U.S.C.A. § 2301 (1).
8. 15 U.S.C.A. § 2302.

Example 4-5

Which of the following statements would be considered a warranty under MMWA?

1. "This computer has a great business look."

2. "The seats are made from fine, Corinthian leather."

3. "You won't find a better washing machine in this country."

Answer: If you answered #2, then you would be right. The first and third statements are opinions, not facts, and therefore do not qualify as warranties. But the second statement is a fact. If the seats are not actually made from the specified type of leather, the consumer would have an action against the manufacturer.

5. Implied Warranties under the Magnuson-Moss Warranty Act

When it comes to the issue of implied warranties, the Magnuson-Moss Warranty Act relies on state law. In fact, MMWA specifically provides that state law rules about implied warranties apply. Examples of implied warranties under state law include the warranty of merchantability, discussed at the beginning of this chapter and the warranties available under the Uniform Commercial Code (listed in Figure 4-1). Because MMWA supplements, but does not replace, available state law, the Act provides consumers with added protections. The remedies available to consumers vary depending on the applicable state laws. Some states provide greater monetary damages for consumers than do others. The Magnuson-Moss Warranty Act also prohibits the disclaimer of implied warranties under state law.

6. The Magnuson-Moss Warranty Act and Other Federal Law

The Magnuson-Moss Warranty Act was specifically designed not to supersede the authority of the Federal Trade Commission or to take the place of any other existing federal statute. Essentially the act was created as a way of harnessing federal and state laws in such a way as to make them all work together, instead of working against one another. The Act does proscribe certain practices, such as claims by manufacturers that attempt to waive all warranties, but it does not supersede other warranty law. Because of this approach, individual state laws are important on the issue of damages that can be awarded by consumers who claim that they have been injured by a defective product. The Act does not provide a new cause of action in federal courts, relying on individual state court systems instead.

7. What Is Required under the Magnuson-Moss Warranty Act?

The provisions of the Magnuson-Moss Warranty Act clearly require that any manufacturer or seller of a product that places a warranty on that product must disclose, in complete terms and in conspicuous language, the terms and conditions of the warranty. The warranty must be presented in simple and easy to understand language and must abide by the rules of the Federal Trade Commission. The requirement of simple and easy to understand language has its roots in contract law. When courts are called upon to clarify ambiguities in a contract, the general rule is that unclear language is construed against the party who created it. Under that principle, the manufacturer who created a warranty that is difficult to understand would bear the brunt of the court's scrutiny and any provisions that failed to clearly establish a consumer's rights would be applied against the manufacturer and for the benefit of the consumer.

Figure 4-8. Code of Federal Regulations: CHAPTER I—FEDERAL TRADE COMMISSION; PART 701: DISCLOSURE OF WRITTEN CONSUMER PRODUCT WARRANTY TERMS AND CONDITIONS.

Sec. 701.3 Written warranty terms.

(a) Any warrantor warranting to a consumer by means of a written warranty a consumer product actually costing the consumer more than

$15.00 shall clearly and conspicuously disclose in a single document in simple and readily understood language, the following items of information:

(1) The identity of the party or parties to whom the written warranty is extended, if the enforceability of the written warranty is limited to the original consumer purchaser or is otherwise limited to persons other than every consumer owner during the term of the warranty;

(2) A clear description and identification of products, or parts, or characteristics, or components or properties covered by and where necessary for clarification, excluded from the warranty;

(3) A statement of what the warrantor will do in the event of a defect, malfunction or failure to conform with the written warranty, including the items or services the warrantor will pay for or provide, and, where necessary for clarification, those which the warrantor will not pay for or provide;

(4) The point in time or event on which the warranty term commences, if different from the purchase date, and the time period or other measurement of warranty duration;

(5) A step-by-step explanation of the procedure which the consumer should follow in order to obtain performance of any warranty obligation, including the persons or class of persons authorized to perform warranty obligations. This includes the name(s) of the warrantor(s), together with: The mailing address(es) of the warrantor(s), and/or the name or title and the address of any employee or department of the warrantor responsible for the performance of warranty obligations, and/or a telephone number which consumers may use without charge to obtain information on warranty performance;

(6) Information respecting the availability of any informal dispute settlement mechanism elected by the warrantor in compliance with part 703 of this subchapter;

(7) Any limitations on the duration of implied warranties, disclosed on the face of the warranty as provided in section 108 of the Act, accompanied by the following statement:

Some States do not allow limitations on how long an implied warranty lasts, so the above limitation may not apply to you.

(8) Any exclusions of or limitations on relief such as incidental or consequential damages, accompanied by the following statement, which may be combined with the statement required in paragraph (a)(7) of this section:

Some States do not allow the exclusion or limitation of incidental or consequential damages, so the above limitation or exclusion may not apply to you.

(9) A statement in the following language:

This warranty gives you specific legal rights, and you may also have other rights which vary from State to State.

---

a. Full Warranty vs. Limited Warranty

Under MMWA, a "full warranty" refers to a written warranty that meets all of the minimum federal standards. If a warranty fails to meet those minimum federal standards, it is referred to as a limited warranty. Under the Act, a seller or manufacturer can list both full and limited warranties on the same product. However, these warranties must be displayed prominently and if both are present, they must be differentiated to the point where it is clear where one begins and the other ends. Under the Act, the penalty for failing to designate a warranty as a limited warranty is for a court to consider it a full warranty. This rule even applies if the section is titled "warranty" and then makes clear that it is a limited warranty in the body of the warranty itself.

III. State-Based Warranty Actions

On a state level, consumers can bring actions based on various statutes and common law principles. Under the old common law, a consumer could bring an action for breach of warranty under contract law, or based on so-called "Lemon laws."

A. "Lemon Laws"

All states have enacted some version of what is popularly called a lemon law. These laws are designed to give consumers a legal action against manufacturers for the sale of defective merchandise. Most lemon laws are aimed at automobile manufacturers and are closely modeled on the statute found in Figure 4-9.

> **Lemon law:** A state statute that protects automobile consumers by providing them with legal actions against car manufacturers.

Figure 4-9. Sample Lemon Law Statute.

(a) The owner of a motor vehicle or the owner's designated agent may make a complaint concerning a defect in a motor vehicle that is covered by a manufacturer's, converter's, or distributor's warranty agreement applicable to the vehicle.

(b) The complaint must be made in writing to the applicable dealer, manufacturer, converter, or distributor and must specify each defect in the vehicle that is covered by the warranty.

(c) The owner may also invoke the board's jurisdiction by sending a copy of the complaint to the board.

(d) A hearing may be scheduled on any complaint made under this section that is not privately resolved between the owner and the dealer, manufacturer, converter, or distributor.[9]

---

9. TX § 2301.204. Complaint Concerning Vehicle Defect.

Case Excerpt

An example of a state-based automobile "lemon law" in action.

Culberson v. Mercedes-Benz USA, Ltd.[10]

BERNES, Judge.

Plaintiff Yolanda Culberson appeals from the Fulton County Superior Court's order granting partial summary judgment to defendant Mercedes-Benz USA, LLC ("MBUSA") in her action for alleged unrepaired electrical and paint defects in her 2002 Mercedes-Benz C240W. Culberson brought claims for breach of express warranty, breach of implied warranty, and revocation of acceptance under the Uniform Commercial Code-Sales (OCGA § 11-2-101 et seq.) and the Magnuson-Moss Warranty Act (15 USC § 2301 et seq.) (the "Federal Warranty Act"). On appeal, Culberson challenges the trial court's grant of summary judgment to MBUSA on her express warranty claim and on her claims brought pursuant to the Federal Warranty Act. Finding no error, we affirm.

"To prevail at summary judgment under OCGA § 9-11-56, the moving party must demonstrate that there is no genuine issue of material fact and that the undisputed facts, viewed in the light most favorable to the nonmoving party, warrant judgment as a matter of law." Lau's Corp. v. Haskins, 261 Ga. 491 (405 S.E.2d 474) (1991), abrogated in part on other grounds by Robinson v. Kroger Co., 268 Ga. 735 (493 S.E.2d 403) (1997). "On appeal from the grant of summary judgment this Court conducts a de novo review …" Youngblood v. Gwinnett Rockdale Newton Cmty. Serv. Bd., 273 Ga. 715, 717– 718(4) (545 S.E.2d 875) (2001).

So viewed, the record shows that on or about May 25, 2002, Culberson purchased the complained-of vehicle from Atlanta Classic Cars, Inc., an authorized MBUSA dealership, for $38,625.53. The Service and Warranty Information manual that came with the vehicle contained a manufacturer's limited warranty (hereinafter referred to as the "Warranty Provision") which provided: "(MBUSA) warrants to the original owner and each subsequent owner of a new Mercedes-Benz passenger car that any authorized Mercedes-Benz Center will make any repairs or replacements necessary to correct defects in material or workmanship." Significantly, the manual also contained a provision (hereinafter referred to as the "Enforcement Provision") which stated as follows:

Warranty Enforcement Laws (Lemon Laws)

Laws in many states and federal laws permit owners and/or lessees to obtain a replacement vehicle or a refund of the purchase or lease price under certain circumstances. The provisions of these laws vary from state to state and vary from the federal law. To the extent allowed or not prohibited by applicable law, Mercedes-Benz USA, LLC requires that you first provide us with written notification of any alleged unrepaired defect or malfunction, or any other dissatisfaction you have experienced with your vehicle so that we have the opportunity to cure the problem or dissatisfaction ourselves. Giving MBUSA itself this direct notice and opportunity to cure enables us to supplement prior efforts by our authorized dealers so any ongoing problem can be resolved or the dissatisfaction addressed....

---

10. *Culberson v. Mercedes-Benz, USA Ltd.*, 274 Ga. App. 89, 616 S.E.2d 865 (2005).

Only two months after buying the vehicle, Culberson first returned it to Atlanta Classic Cars' repair facility in order to have a side window problem corrected. Over the following five months, Culberson returned the vehicle for repairs nine additional times based on multiple alleged problems, including continuing side window malfunctions and defects in the gas gauge and windshield wipers.

On or about November 8, 2002, Culberson's attorney forwarded a letter to MBUSA which gave the corporation notice that Culberson's vehicle had electrical and paint defects and advised MBUSA of Culberson's intent to proceed against MBUSA pursuant to the Georgia Lemon Law and/or the Federal Warranty Act. Although the letter also stated that it was intended to give "Notice to Manufacturer of Final Opportunity to Repair pursuant to OCGA § 10-1-784(a)(1)," the letter went on to state that Culberson was revoking her acceptance of the vehicle and was demanding return of all funds paid towards the vehicle.

MBUSA responded by letter, dated November 21, 2002, seeking to clarify Culberson's contentions and requesting a final opportunity to inspect the vehicle and to cure. The letter stated:

In accordance with the express provisions of the written warranty and the Federal Warranty Act you also are required to provide MBUSA with an opportunity to cure, prior to filing suit. Accordingly, please contact the undersigned directly so that MBUSA may schedule an inspection and have the required opportunity to cure.

On December 2, 2002, Culberson's counsel forwarded a response letter to MBUSA indicating that the company could conduct a "final inspection" of the vehicle so long as it gave notice at least fifteen days in advance. Notably, the response letter did not state that MBUSA itself would be provided a final opportunity to cure or repair any alleged defects in addition to being provided an opportunity to inspect the vehicle.

MBUSA was attempting to schedule an inspection when Culberson filed her complaint on December 31, 2002. Subsequently, MBUSA moved for summary judgment, which the trial court granted in part. The trial court ruled that Culberson's express warranty claim failed as a matter of law because she had not given MBUSA itself a final opportunity to cure the defects in the vehicle prior to filing suit, as required by the express terms of the Enforcement Provision. Likewise, the trial court concluded that Culberson had no viable claims under the Federal Warranty Act because she had not provided MBUSA its own reasonable opportunity to cure the defects under 15 USC § 2310(e).

1. Culberson contends that the trial court erred in granting summary judgment to MBUSA on her express warranty claim. Culberson does not disagree that she failed to provide MBUSA itself a final opportunity to cure the alleged defects in the vehicle; rather, she contends that it was sufficient for her to give Atlanta Classic Cars, an authorized dealership repair facility, an opportunity to cure. We disagree.

When a warrantee brings a breach of express warranty claim, the terms of the written warranty control. Dryvit Sys., Inc. v. Stein, 256 Ga.App. 327, 329, 568 S.E.2d 569 (2002); DeLoach v. General Motors, 187 Ga.App. 159, 159–160, 369 S.E.2d 484 (1988). Thus, a warrantee can succeed on a breach of the warranty claim only if she has first satisfied the express conditions precedent for enforcement "as prescribed" by the warranty. Dryvit Sys., Inc., 256 Ga.App. at 329(1).

Here, the trial court correctly concluded that compliance with the Enforcement Provision was a condition precedent to Culberson's judicial enforcement of her right under the limited warranty to seek a replacement vehicle or her money back. The plain language of the Enforcement Provision required Culberson to provide MBUSA itself an opportunity to cure any perceived defects in the vehicle prior to the filing of a warranty suit, over and above any opportunities provided to individual dealerships to repair the vehicle or replace defective parts. Because Culberson failed to satisfy that condition precedent in this case, she cannot proceed with her express warranty claim against MBUSA. Accordingly, the trial court properly granted summary judgment to MBUSA on the express warranty claim.

While the parenthetical subtitle of the Enforcement Provision refers to "Lemons Laws," there is nothing in the text of the Enforcement Provision itself that restricts its application to causes of action specifically brought under state Lemon Laws. Rather, the Enforcement Provision, read as a whole, makes clear that the parenthetical phrase was intended to be illustrative of "laws in many states and federal law (that) permit owners and/or lessees to obtain a replacement vehicle or a refund of the purchase price or lease price under certain circumstances." The remedies that Culberson sought in this case were of this very type, and so there is no principled reason for allowing her to proceed with her express warranty claim without first satisfying the condition precedent contained in the Enforcement Provision.

Culberson similarly contends that the trial court erred in granting summary judgment to MBUSA on all of her Federal Warranty Act claims because she satisfied the requirements of 15 USC. §2310(e) by allowing an authorized dealership repair facility an opportunity to repair the vehicle defects. We cannot agree.

15 USC §2310(3) provides that "No action ... may be brought ... for failure to comply with any obligation under any written or implied warranty ... unless the person obligated under the warranty ... is afforded a reasonable opportunity to cure such failure to comply." Compliance with the "reasonable opportunity to cure" requirement imposed by 15 USC §2310(e) is a condition precedent to pursuing successful claims under the Federal Warranty Act. Cunningham v. Fleetwood Homes of Georgia, Inc., 253 F3d 611, 618 (11th Cir.2001).

Here, the Warranty Provision read in conjunction with the Enforcement Provision shows that "the person obligated under the warranty" was MBUSA itself, not the individual dealership repair facilities like Atlanta Classic Cars. See Lewis v. Mercedes-Benz USA, LLC, Order at 8. Based on the unique language of the Enforcement Provision, it is clear that MBUSA did not delegate its right to cure vehicle defects to the individual dealership repair facilities. Thus, Culberson was required to give MBUSA its own reasonable opportunity to cure the defects in the vehicle, separate and distinct from any interactions or communications Culberson had with individual dealerships such as Atlanta Classic Cars. It follows that, having failed to provide MBUSA itself any opportunity to cure the defects in the vehicle prior to filing suit, Culberson failed to comply with the "reasonable opportunity to cure" requirement imposed by 15 U.S.C. §2310(e) of the Federal Warranty Act. We therefore conclude that trial court did not err by granting summary judgment to MBUSA on Culberson's Federal Warranty Act claims.

For the foregoing reasons, we affirm the trial court's grant of summary judgment to MBUSA on Culberson's claims for breach of express warranty and violations of the Federal Warranty Act. Neither MBUSA nor Culberson challenge any of the remaining rulings made by the trial court in its summary judgment order, and so we likewise affirm those rulings.

Judgment affirmed.

Case Questions

1. What grounds did the plaintiff base her case upon?
2. What did the plaintiff's letter to MBUSA allege?
3. What does the court hold about the provisions of an express warranty versus a written warranty?
4. Why was it so important that MBUSA have an opportunity to "cure" the problem?
5. How does the opportunity to cure the problem factor into the plaintiff's claim of a violation of the Federal Warranty Act?

IV. Disclaimers

Both federal and state laws allow manufacturers to disclaim certain warranties. For instance, advertising a product for sale, "as is," signifies that the seller is making no warranties of any kind and when a consumer purchases the product, he or she would be barred from bringing action under a breach of warranty theory. However, as we have already seen, state and federal law prohibits sellers and manufacturers from disclaiming all warranties, especially on new products. We have already seen that courts frown on disclaimers of express warranties and the Magnuson-Moss Warranty Act specifically prohibits disclaimers of implied warranties for any product governed under its provisions.

Case Excerpt

Does Magnuson-Moss prohibit the enforcement of binding arbitration agreements?

Davis v. Southern Energy Homes, Inc.[11]

DUBINA, Circuit Judge:

The important question presented in this appeal is whether the Magnuson-Moss Warranty Act permits or prohibits the enforcement of pre-dispute binding arbitration clauses within written warranties. We hold that the Magnuson-Moss Warranty Act permits binding arbitration and that a written warranty claim arising under the Magnuson-Moss Warranty Act may be subject to a valid pre-dispute binding arbitration agreement.

---

11. *Davis v. Southern Energy Homes, Inc.*, 305 F.3d 1268 (C.A. 11 (Ala.) 2002).

I. BACKGROUND

In October 1999, Michael Shane Davis and Heather N. Davis ("the Davises") purchased a manufactured home constructed by Southern Energy Homes, Inc. ("Southern"). When the Davises purchased the home, they signed a binding arbitration agreement contained within the manufactured home's written warranty. The Davises later discovered multiple defects in the home and notified Southern of the problems. After Southern failed to correct the defects to the Davises' satisfaction, the Davises filed suit in the Circuit Court of Lowndes County, Alabama, asserting claims for breach of express and implied warranties, violations of the Magnuson-Moss Warranty-Trade Commission Act ("MMWA" or "the Act"), negligent and wanton repair, and fraud. Southern removed the case to federal court and, in lieu of an answer, filed a Motion to Dismiss or, in the Alternative, to Compel Arbitration. The district court, relying on its prior decision in Yeomans v. Homes of Legend, Inc., 2001 WL 237313, No. 00-D-824-N (M.D. Ala. March 5, 2001), which found that the MMWA prohibits binding arbitration, denied Southern's motion. Southern timely appealed the district court's order denying Southern's Motion to Compel Arbitration.

II. ISSUES

Whether the Magnuson-Moss Warranty Act permits or precludes enforcement of binding arbitration agreements with respect to written warranty claims.

The MMWA and Binding Arbitration of Written Warranty Claims

In this appeal, Southern argues that, based upon the strong federal policy of enforcing valid arbitration agreements under the Federal Arbitration Act ("FAA"), the Davises must submit their written warranty claims to binding arbitration rather than file suit for breach of warranty. To support this argument, Southern notes that the Supreme Court continually enforces binding arbitration agreements of statutory claims and argues that the MMWA is similar to these other statutes because nothing in the MMWA's text, legislative history, or underlying purposes evinces that Congress intended to preclude binding arbitration of written warranty claims. Southern also asserts that the Federal Trade Commission's ("FTC") regulations and interpretations, which prohibit binding arbitration of MMWA claims, are unreasonable, and thus, we should accord them no deference.

The Davises, conversely, assert that arbitration is an improper forum for MMWA claims and that the Act's language, legislative history, and underlying purposes compel a conclusion that dispute settlement procedures cannot be binding under the MMWA. The Davises argue that § 2310(a) of the MMWA, which states that consumers must resort to a warrantor's informal dispute settlement mechanism before commencing a civil action, necessarily implies that the decision of any informal settlement procedure may not be binding. They reason that Congress' use of different terminology to describe the settlement procedures of § 2310(a) throughout the MMWA's text and legislative history, combined with the absence of any statutory definition for the terms, establishes that Congress used the terms "dispute settlement procedures" and "dispute settlement mechanisms" only as generic terms, and thereby included binding arbitration as a type of alternative dispute resolution procedure. The Davises also argue that this court must defer to the FTC regulations, which reject binding arbitration of written warranty claims arising under the MMWA, because the FTC reasonably interpreted the MMWA in these regulations.

We recognize that state and federal courts are sharply divided on whether the MMWA permits pre-dispute binding arbitration of written warranty claims. The Fifth Circuit is the only circuit court to directly address this issue and, in a divided panel decision, it held that the MMWA permits binding arbitration. After a thorough review of the MMWA and its legislative history, the FAA and the Supreme Court's application of the FAA to other federal statutes, we conclude that the MMWA permits the enforcement of valid binding arbitration agreements within written warranties.

1. MMWA

Congress passed the MMWA in 1975 in response to an increasing number of consumer complaints regarding the inadequacy of warranties on consumer goods. The purpose of the MMWA is "to improve the adequacy of information available to consumers, prevent deception, and improve competition in the marketing of consumer products...." 15 U.S.C. §2302(a) (1994). In order to advance these goals, §2310(d) of the MMWA provides a statutory private right of action to consumers "damaged by the failure of a supplier, warrantor, or service contractor to comply with any obligation under this chapter, or under a written warranty, implied warranty, or service contract...." Id. §2310(d)(1). Consumers may sue for a MMWA violation in either state or federal court. Id.

In order to encourage settlements by means other than civil lawsuits, §2310(a) allows a warrantor to include a provision for an informal dispute settlement mechanism in a warranty. Id. §2310(a)(3); see also H.R.Rep. No. 93-1107 (1974), reprinted in 1974 U.S.C.C.A.N. 7702, 7722 ("Congress declares it to be its policy to encourage warrantors to establish procedures whereby consumer disputes are fairly and expeditiously settled through informal dispute settlement mechanisms."). Although the MMWA does not define "informal dispute settlement procedure," it does provide that if a warrantor incorporates a §2310(a) informal dispute settlement procedure into the warranty, the provision must comply with the minimum requirements that the FTC prescribes. 15 U.S.C. §2310(a)(2). If the informal dispute settlement procedure properly complies with the FTC's minimum requirements, and if the written warranty requires that the consumer "resort to such procedure before pursuing any legal remedy under this section respecting such warranty, the consumer may not commence a civil action ... under subsection (d) of this section unless he initially resorts to such procedure...." Id. §2310(a)(3).

2. FAA

Congress enacted the FAA in 1925 to reverse the longstanding judicial hostility towards arbitration and "to place arbitration agreements on the same footing as other contracts." Section 2 of the FAA provides:

A written provision in any ... contract evidencing a transaction involving commerce to settle by arbitration a controversy thereafter arising out of such contract or transaction, or the refusal to perform the whole or any part thereof, or an agreement in writing to submit to arbitration an existing controversy arising out of such a contract, ... shall be valid, irrevocable, and enforceable, save upon such grounds as exist at law or in equity for the revocation of any contract. 9 U.S.C. §2 (1994).

The Supreme Court has interpreted §2 of the FAA as "a congressional declaration of a liberal federal policy favoring arbitration agreements." Moses H. Cone Mem'l Hosp. v. Mercury Constr. Corp., 460 U.S. 1, 24, 103 S.Ct. 927, 941, 74 L.Ed.2d 765 (1983).

3. McMahon Test

Turning to whether Congress intended to preclude arbitration of a statutory claim, we follow the Supreme Court's McMahon test. McMahon, 482 U.S. at 226–27, 107

S.Ct. at 2337–38. In McMahon, the Supreme Court instructed us to consider three factors in deducing Congress' intent: (1) the text of the statute; (2) its legislative history; and (3) whether "an inherent conflict between arbitration and the underlying purposes (of the statute)" exists. Id. at 227, 107 S.Ct. at 2338. The party opposing the enforcement of the arbitration agreement has the burden of showing that Congress intended to preclude arbitration of the statutory claim. Id. In applying the McMahon test, "questions of arbitrability must be addressed with a healthy regard for the federal policy favoring arbitration. "Gilmer, 500 U.S. at 26, 111 S.Ct. at 1652 (quoting Moses H. Cone Mem'l Hosp., 460 U.S. at 24, 103 S.Ct. at 941). Thus, we analyze each factor in turn to determine whether Congress clearly expressed an intention to preclude binding arbitration of MMWA claims.

a. McMahon Factor One: MMWA's Text

The MMWA's text does not expressly prohibit arbitration and, in fact, fails to directly mention either binding arbitration or the FAA. Nevertheless, the Davises argue that the MMWA reserves strictly a judicial forum for consumers by providing a private right of action for consumers. The Supreme Court, however, has held that a statute's provision for a private right of action alone is inadequate to show that Congress intended to prohibit arbitration. Gilmer, 500 U.S. at 29, 111 S.Ct. at 1653–54 (rejecting the argument that binding arbitration is improper "because it deprives claimants of the judicial forum provided for by the ADEA"). As the Fifth Circuit recently recognized, "binding arbitration generally is understood to be a substitute for filing a lawsuit, not a prerequisite." Walton, 298 F.3d at 475 (citing Mitsubishi Motors Corp., 473 U.S. at 628, 105 S.Ct. at 3354) ("By agreeing to arbitrate a statutory claim, a party does not forgo the substantive rights afforded by the statute; it only submits to their resolution in an arbitral, rather than judicial, forum."). Furthermore, the fact that the MMWA grants a judicial forum with concurrent jurisdiction in state and federal courts for MMWA claims is insufficient evidence that Congress intended to preclude binding arbitration. See McMahon, 482 U.S. at 227, 107 S.Ct. at 2338 (rejecting the argument that compulsory arbitration under the Securities Exchange Act of 1934 is improper because the statute provides that "the district courts of the United States ... shall have exclusive jurisdiction of violations of this title...."); see also Gilmer, 500 U.S. at 29, 111 S.Ct. at 1654 (noting that Congress' grant of concurrent jurisdiction in state and federal courts for ADEA claims is consistent with binding arbitration because "arbitration agreements, 'like the provision for concurrent jurisdiction, serve to advance the objective of allowing (claimants) a broader right to select the forum for resolving disputes, whether it be judicial or otherwise' ") (quoting Rodriguez de Quijas, 490 U.S. at 483, 109 S.Ct. at 1921).

The Davises also argue that because § 2310(d) lists only two exceptions to the private right of action, the internal dispute settlement procedure referenced in § 2310(a) and the class action exception referenced in § 2310(e), Congress intended to preclude any other method of dispute resolution, including binding arbitration. See Transamerica Mortgage Advisors, Inc. v. Lewis, 444 U.S. 11, 19–20, 100 S.Ct. 242, 247, 62 L.Ed.2d 146 (1979) ("Where a statute expressly provides a particular remedy or remedies, a court must be chary of reading others into it. When a statute limits a thing to be done in a particular mode, it includes the negative of any other mode.") (internal quotations and citations omitted). The § 2310(a) exception to a consumer's private right of action states that, if a warrantor establishes an informal dispute settlement procedure, a consumer must resort to the procedure "before pursuing any legal remedy under this section respecting such warranty." 15 U.S.C. § 2310(a)(3)(c). Section 2310(a) also states that "the consumer may not commence a civil action … unless he initially resorts to such procedure" and that "in any civil action arising out of a warranty obligation and relating to a matter considered in such a procedure, any decision in such procedure shall be admissible in evidence." Id. Based on this language, the Davises assert that Congress intended to allow only non-binding alternative dispute resolution procedures. We disagree.

In Cunningham v. Fleetwood Homes of Ga., Inc., we noted that the district court erred "in concluding that, standing alone, the presence of the non-binding § 2310 mechanism in the statutory text requires the conclusion that Magnuson-Moss claims may not be the subject of binding arbitration agreements." 253 F.3d 611, 619 (11th Cir.2001). The fact that the MMWA regulates § 2310(a) informal dispute settlement procedures does not mean that the Act precludes a court from enforcing a valid binding arbitration agreement. See id. at 620 (noting that a statute's provision for one out-of-court settlement mechanism does not necessarily preclude the enforcement of all alternative mechanisms); see also Gilmer, 500 U.S. at 29, 111 S.Ct. at 1654 (holding that the ADEA's provision for "out-of-court dispute resolution" is not inconsistent with permitting arbitration under the FAA and that it even "suggests that out-of-court dispute resolution, such as arbitration, is consistent with the statutory scheme established by Congress"). Thus, we are unpersuaded that Congress intended to bar binding arbitration agreements in the language of the MMWA.

b. McMahon Factor Two: Legislative History

The second factor the Supreme Court instructs us to examine in determining Congress' intent to preclude the application of the FAA is the MMWA's legislative history. See McMahon, 482 U.S. at 226–27, 107 S.Ct. at 2338. Like the MMWA's text, its legislative history only addresses "internal dispute settlement procedures;" it never directly addresses the role of binding arbitration or the FAA. In trying to show that Congress intended to bar binding arbitration, the Davises rely on the MMWA's House Report, which notes that "an adverse decision in any informal dispute settlement proceeding would not be a bar to a civil action on the warranty involved in the proceeding." H.R.Rep. No. 93–1107 (1974), reprinted in 1974 U.S.C.C.A.N. 7702, 7723. The Davises argue that Congress considered all methods of dispute resolution, including arbitration, before allowing warrantors to pursue only informal, non-binding settlement procedures. After a thorough reading of the MMWA's legislative history, we disagree.

For many years warranties have confused and misled the American consumer. A warranty is a complicated legal document whose full essence lies buried in myriads of reported legal decisions and in complicated State codes of commercial law. The consumer's understanding of what a warranty on a particular product means to him frequently does not coincide with the legal meaning…. Typically, a consumer today cannot bargain with consumer product manufacturers or suppliers to obtain a warranty or to adjust the terms of a warranty voluntarily offered. Since almost all consumer products sold today are typically done so with a contract of adhesion, there is no bargaining over contractual terms.

The Davises have proved only that the MMWA's legislative history is ambiguous at most. When considering a preliminary draft of the MMWA, the Senate reflected that "it is Congress' intent that warrantors of consumer products cooperate with government and private agencies to establish informal dispute settlement mechanisms that take care of consumer grievances without the aid of litigation or formal arbitration." S.Rep. No. 91-876, at 22–23 (1970) (emphasis added). As the Fifth Circuit concluded, "there is still no evidence that Congress intended binding arbitration to be considered an informal dispute settlement procedure. Therefore the fact that any informal dispute settlement procedure must be non-binding, does not imply that Congress meant to preclude binding arbitration, which is of a different nature." Walton, 298 F.3d at 476. In McMahon, the Supreme Court upheld binding arbitration even though the Securities Exchange Act of 1934's legislative history implied that Congress intended to adopt the Wilko attitude that arbitration is an inadequate forum in which to enforce statutory claims. McMahon, 482 U.S. at 238, 107 S.Ct. at 2343. Any congressional intent to prohibit arbitration in the MMWA's legislative history is considerably less clear than the legislative history of the Securities Exchange Act of 1934, which the Supreme Court held did not prohibit binding arbitration in McMahon. In light of this ambiguity, the Davises fail to carry their burden of showing a clear congressional intent to prohibit binding arbitration of MMWA claims. Thus, given the absence of any meaningful legislative history barring binding arbitration, coupled with the unquestionable federal policy favoring arbitration, we conclude that Congress did not express a clear intent in the MMWA's legislative history to bar binding arbitration agreements in written warranties.

c. McMahon Factor Three: The MMWA's Underlying Purposes

The last McMahon factor requires us to examine the purposes of the MMWA to determine whether the MMWA and the FAA conflict. See McMahon, 482 U.S. at 226–27, 107 S.Ct. at 2337–38. The MMWA expressly states three purposes: "to improve the adequacy of information available to consumers, prevent deception, and improve competition in the marketing of consumer products." 15 U.S.C. § 2302(a). These purposes are not in conflict with the FAA. In fact, the Supreme Court has repeatedly enforced arbitration of statutory claims where the underlying purpose of the statutes is to protect and inform consumers. See, e.g., Basic Inc. v. Levinson, 485 U.S. 224, 234, 108 S.Ct. 978, 985, 99 L.Ed.2d 194 (1988) (stating that a fundamental purpose of the Securities Acts is the disclosure of information to potential investors); Rodriguez de Quijas, 490 U.S. at 485–86, 109 S.Ct. at 1922 (holding that parties may arbitrate Securities Act of 1933 claims); McMahon, 482 U.S. at 242, 107 S.Ct. at 2345 (holding that parties may arbitrate Securities Exchange Act of 1934 claims). "Even claims arising under a statute designed to further important social policies may be arbitrated because so long as the prospective litigant effectively may vindicate (his or her) statutory cause of action in the arbitral forum, the statute serves its function." Green Tree Fin. Corp.-Ala. v. Randolph, 531 U.S. 79, 90, 121 S.Ct. 513, 521, 148 L.Ed.2d 373 (2000) (holding that parties may arbitrate Truth in Lending Act claims). Consumers can adequately vindicate their rights arising under the MMWA and written warranties in an arbitral forum. Thus, we conclude that the MMWA's consumer protection goals do not conflict with the FAA.

V. CONCLUSION

After a thorough review of the MMWA and the FAA, combined with the strong federal policy favoring arbitration, we hold that written warranty claims arising under the Magnuson-Moss Warranty Act may be subject to valid binding arbitration agreements. Accordingly, we reverse the judgment of the district court and remand this case for further proceedings consistent with this opinion.

Case Questions

1. What is the central question in this case?

2. According to Southern, why must this written warranty case be submitted to arbitration?

3. Many circuits are divided on this question. How did the Fifth Circuit rule?

4. What is the "McMahon" test?

5. According to the Court, did Congress intend to allow only non-binding alternative dispute resolution procedures?

Chapter Summary

A warranty is a pledge, promise or assurance from a manufacturer or seller about a product. In the past, the law on warranties has swung from consumer-oriented to manufacturer-oriented and back again. Under modern law, there are two broad divisions of warranties: express and implied. An express warranty is a written or oral statement about a product. An implied warranty is one imposed on the parties by law. The Magnuson-Moss Warranty Act creates federal law for warranties. Under MMWA, a manufacturer or seller must comply with certain minimum requirements for all written warranties. MMWA also supplements available state law, giving consumers additional remedies. One of those remedies is the so-called "lemon law," which gives automobile purchasers specific rights to sue manufacturers and sellers for defective automobiles.

Web Sites

- Guide to Magnuson-Moss Warranty Act
  http://www.ftc.gov/bcp/conline/pubs/buspubs/warranty.htm

- FTC Guide to Warranties and Used Cars
  http://www.ftc.gov/bcp/guides/usedcar-comply.pdf

- Lemon Law Information (Texas)
  http://www.dot.state.tx.us/mvd/lemon/lemonlaw.htm

- New York's Lemon Law
  http://www.oag.state.ny.us/consumer/cars/newcarlemon.html

Key Terms

Warranty   Parol evidence rule

Caveat emptor   Lemon law

Express warranty

Review Questions

1. What is a warranty?

2. What is the difference between an express warranty and an implied warranty?

3. How has the law of warranties changed over time?

4. What is the significance of the McFarlan v. Newman case?

5. What is caveat emptor?

6. What is the modern basis for warranties on consumer products?

7. Is it necessary, under modern law, for there to be a contractual relationship between a manufacturer and the consumer before a warranty applies? Explain your answer.

8. What is the significance of the Magnuson-Moss Warranty Act?

9. What is the definition of consumer under Magnuson-Moss Warranty Act?

10. Provide examples of statements that would be considered warranties under Magnuson-Moss Warranty Act.

11. What is a "lemon law?"

12. What is the difference between a full warranty and a limited warranty?

13. What is the significance of the lemon law case excerpt?

14. What is a disclaimer?

15. What is the implied warranty of merchantability?

Chapter 5

Internet Scams, Forgery, Credit Card Fraud and Identity Theft

Chapter Objectives

- Identify the elements of forgery
- Explain the elements of credit card fraud
- Describe typical Internet scams
- Identify how criminals carry out identify theft
- Describe the governmental agencies responsible for investigating and prosecuting fraud

I. Introduction

In this chapter, we will examine the issues surrounding various types of fraud, including forgery, Internet scams, credit card theft and identity theft. These areas have come under increasing focus in recent years with the growing problem of identity theft and security breaches at credit card companies that have resulted in the theft of millions of individual credit card numbers. The ease with which criminals can obtain and use this information, and the devastation these actions can bring to an individual's credit history, have made it one of the hot button topics of the new millennium.

As long as there have been human beings, there have been thieves. If you approach theft from a cost-benefit analysis, it has always been easier to steal someone else's resources than to create them from scratch. That cost-benefit analysis has changed over the centuries, and these days, a potential thief must weigh the potential downside of imprisonment versus the possible profits. The Internet has again altered this analysis, and for the near future, thieves will continue to see little risk and high potential rewards for carrying out scams, cons and outright thefts using advanced technology. Some of the new scams are simply old cons repackaged for modern times. Consider the West African letter, provided in Example 5-1.

Example 5-1

This email has just arrived in your inbox.

"My name is Ferringo Beraze, and I am the finance minister for the country of West Africa. We need to transfer $142.3 million American dollars to an account in the United States to pay for humanitarian and medical supplies. In order to process these accounts, we need someone in the United States to provide us with a temporary holding account for the $142.3 million. If you are a trustworthy individual who is interested in helping a humanitarian cause, please respond to this email with your checking account routing numbers. We will deposit the $142.3 million into this account for a period of at least 30 days. In order to compensate you for the inconvenience, we will allow you to keep the interest accumulated on this sum during that one-month period."

Is this a legitimate email?

Answer: No. First of all, any country that would need medical and other humanitarian supplies and had in excess of $142 million dollars could approach a regular bank and make a deposit. Any bank would be only too helpful to assist this 'country.' (You might also note that "West Africa" is not an actual country, but simply a region of Africa). Hopefully, your suspicions were triggered by the request for a checking account routing number. Why would thieves want that information? With your checking account information, they could create bogus checks, launder money and carry out dozens, if not hundreds of actions, including draining the available funds. They could do it all without even going to the bank. (See Figure 5-1.)

Figure 5-1. Amount Lost by Fraud Type.*

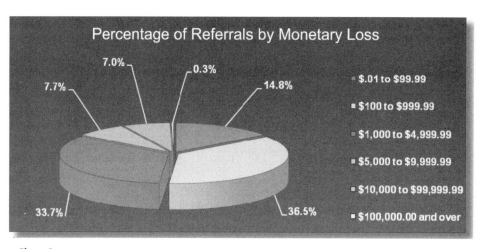

Chart 6

A key area of interest regarding Internet fraud is the average monetary loss incurred by complainants contacting IC3. Of the 72,940 fraudulent referrals processed by IC3 during 2008, 63,382 involved a victim who reported a monetary loss. The total dollar loss from all referred cases of fraud in 2008 was $264.6 million.

Amount Lost by Selected Fraud Type
for Individuals Reporting Monetary Loss

Complaint Type	% of Reported Total Loss	Of those who reported a loss the Average (median) $ Loss per Complaint
Check Fraud	7.8%	$3,000.00
Confidence Fraud	14.4%	$2,000.00
Nigerian Letter Fraud	5.2%	$1,650.00
Computer Fraud	3.8%	$1,000.00
Non-delivery (merchandise and payment)	28.6%	$800.00
Auction Fraud	16.3%	$610.00
Credit/Debit Card Fraud	4.7%	$223.00

Table1

The total dollar loss from all referred cases of fraud in 2008 was $264.6 million. That loss was greater than 2007 which reported a total loss of $239.1 million. The highest dollar loss per incident was reported by check fraud (median loss of $3,000). The lowest dollar loss was associated with credit/debit card fraud (median loss of $223.50).

* Internet Crime Complaint Center, Annual Report, 2008.

The interesting thing about this email is that it appeals to two basic human emotions: the desire to be helpful and the desire to make fast and easy money. If you calculate the daily interest on holding $140 million dollars, you would realize that at the end of the month, you could easily earn several hundred thousand dollars. Of course, that would never happen, but it does sound appealing. The other interesting thing about this email is that it has such strong historical roots.

The FBI and regional law enforcement agencies began setting up Nigerian White Collar Task Forces in the early 1990s, partly in response to letters by people pretending to be a foreign minister from the Nigerian government. These letters are almost identical to the email that is now circulating email boxes. But this is only one of the dozens of common scams currently being perpetrated on the Internet and World Wide Web.

A. Internet Scams

Internet scams are based on a single premise: a person contacts you needing personal information. With that information, he or she can create new accounts in your name, obtain credit cards, bill your existing cards, and add charges to your long distance telephone service, among many other activities. One of the most recent scams is phishing. (See Figure 5-2.)

Getting to the Essentials: Internet scams and frauds are increasing in frequency.

Figure 5-2. Internet Fraud Contact Methods.*

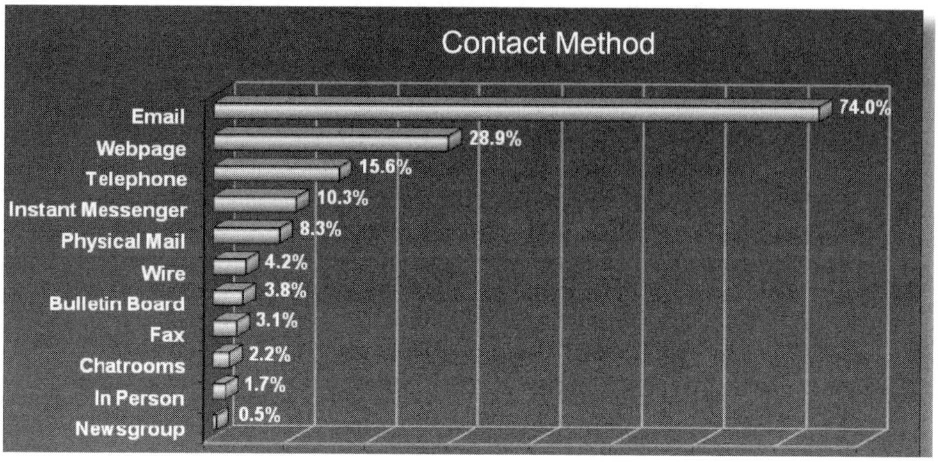

Chart 7

Although complainants in these cases may report multiple contact methods, few reported interacting face-to-face with the vast majority of perpetrators contact through e-mail (74.0%) or a webpage (28.9%). Others reportedly had phone contact (15.0%) with the perpetrator or corresponded through physical mail (8.3%). Interaction through chat rooms (2.2%) and in-person (1.7%) meetings were rarely reported.

  * Internet Crime Complaint Center, Annual Report, 2008.

1. Phishing

According to the Department of Justice, "phishing" is a scam where Internet savvy con artists use legitimate-looking emails and Web sites to request credit card numbers, Social Security numbers and other information that they use to defraud victims. Consider Example 5-2.

Example 5-2

Email

From: Bank of Corporate Credit, Security Department

Re: Your Account

Information has recently reached us that your account, listed above, has been penetrated by computer hackers and may be being used to conduct illegal activities. Please respond to this email immediately with your Social Security Number, Date of Birth and credit card numbers so that we may track recent activities and issue a new card if your accounts are, in fact, being used by criminals.

Of course this email is not legitimate, but because it appears to be from your bank, many people would be tempted to respond. Criminals have grown so sophisticated that they are now masquerading as bank security departments. Even if you examine the email address, you'd find that it appears to be legitimate. Truly computer-savvy criminals can create email accounts that closely mimic real sites. Another common scheme is cramming.

Phishing: The process of using email and Web sites that appear to be legitimate to gather sensitive information on consumers that can then be used for criminal activities.

Figure 5-3. Computer Security Incidents among Businesses.[1]

Table 3. Prevalence of computer security incidents among businesses, by type of incident, 2005

Type of incident	All businesses*	Businesses detecting incidents	
		Number	Percent
All incidents	7,636	5,081	67%
Cyber attack	7,626	4,398	58%
Computer virus	7,538	3,937	52
Denial of service	7,517	1,215	16
Vandalism or sabotage	7,500	350	5
Cyber theft	7,561	839	11%
Embezzlement	7,492	251	3
Fraud	7,488	364	5
Theft of intellectual property	7,492	227	3
Theft of personal or financial data	7,476	249	3
Other computer security incidents	7,492	1,792	24%

Note: Number of businesses and detail may sum to more than total because respondents could answer questions about more than one type of incident. See appendix table 3 for prevalence, by industry.

*Based on businesses that indicated whether they detected an incident.

---

2. Cramming

Cramming is the process of adding charges to a person's telephone bill. These days, a person can charge an amazing amount of services on a phone bill and con artists take advantage of this by adding charges for services individuals never requested.

Cramming: Adding unauthorized charges to a person's telephone bill.

B. Investigating Internet Fraud

The Internet Fraud Complaint Center is a joint venture of the FBI and National White Collar Crime Center. The link for the IFCC is provided at the end of this chapter. IFCC provides a comprehensive list of Internet-based fraud, and also provides a streamlined service so that victims can report crimes. The IFCC will then process the report and forward it to the appropriate state or federal agency. The IFCC acts as a clearinghouse for Internet fraud and addresses one of the biggest problems in Internet fraud: who is responsible for investigating the crime?

---

1. Cybercrime against Businesses, 2005. Bureau of Justice Statistics, Special Report, revised, 2008.

1. Jurisdictional Issues in Internet Fraud

Although television shows and other media present federal, state and local law enforcement as working closely together, the reality is often quite different. When a person has been scammed—such as by providing checking account information in response to the West African email in Example 5-1, who is responsible for investigating the crime? The victim would probably report the theft of his or her entire checking account funds to the local police, but they might not have the resources, or even the jurisdiction, to investigate the crime. For one thing, theft from federally insured banks and lending institutions brings the crime under federal jurisdiction. For another, where is the site of the crime? Would the defendant be prosecuted under your state's laws, or under the laws of the nation where he was when he sent the email and received your information? You can see that these crimes raise a host of complex legal issues. This sometimes turns fraud cases into a hot potato, bouncing from one jurisdiction to another until someone takes the case. However, the prevalence of Internet-based crime should not take away from some of the more traditional crimes, such as forgery and credit card fraud.

> *Getting to the Essentials:*   Jurisdiction is often a hotly contested issue in Internet-based scams and frauds, given the differences in location between victim and criminal. Some internet thieves are based in foreign countries.

Sidebar: A Web site that deals with jurisdictional issues related to Internet fraud is the National Fraud Information Center, http://www.fraud.org/. It has a fraud hotline and offers information about telemarketing fraud, Internet scams, counterfeit drugs and typical business scams.

Figure 5-4. Prevalence of computer security incidents.[2]

Table 1. Prevalence of computer security incidents, types of offenders, and reporting to law enforcement, 2005

Characteristic	Percent of businesses by type of incident			
	All incidents	Cyber attack	Cyber theft	Other
All businesses responding	67%	58%	11%	24%
Number of employees				
2-24	50%	44%	8%	15%
25-99	59	51	7	17
100-999	70	60	9	24
1,000 or more	82	72	20	36
Industries with the highest prevalence of cybercrime[a]				
Telecommunications	82%	74%	17%	32%
Computer system design	79	72	15	25
Manufacturing, durable goods	75	68	15	32

2. Cybercrime against Businesses, 2005. Bureau of Justice Statistics, Special Report, revised, 2008.

Suspected offender was an—[b]				
Insider	40%	27%	74%	30%
Outsider	71	74	32	72
Incidents were reported—[c]				
Within the business	80%	81%	46%	69%
To another organization	15	14	9	7
To law enforcement authorities	15	6	56	12

Note: A total of 7,818 businesses responded to the National Computer Security Survey. Detail may sum to more than 100% because businesses could detect multiple types of incidents.

[a]See appendix table 3 for all industries.

[b]Percentages are based on businesses that detected an incident and provided information on suspected offenders.

[c]Percentages are based on businesses that detected an incident and provided information on reporting incidents to authorities.

II. Forgery

Although Internet-based crimes are important, the more traditional crimes are still the most common. Among these tried-and-true criminal enterprises is forgery. Under the old common law, forgery consisted of writing someone else's signature on a document and passing it off as authentic. Modern forgery statutes have these same elements, but also include other techniques. For instance, it is forgery to:

- Write someone else's signature without permission
- Transfer a genuine signature to a bogus document
- Use a scanner or other technology to print another person's name on a document

Figure 5-5. Forgery in the First Degree.

(a) A person commits the offense of forgery in the first degree when, with intent to defraud, he knowingly makes, alters, or possesses any writing in a fictitious name or in such manner that the writing as made or altered purports to have been made by another person, at another time, with different provisions, or by authority of one who did not give such authority and utters or delivers such writing.

(b) A person convicted of the offense of forgery in the first degree shall be punished by imprisonment for not fewer than one nor more than ten years. O.C.G.A. § 16-9-1.

A. The Basic Elements of Forgery

The basic elements of forgery include:

- That the defendant did knowingly, and with the intent to defraud
- Make, alter or possess any writing
- Without authority and
- Utter or deliver such writing

In order to be convicted of forgery, the prosecution must prove each of the elements set out above. The first element requires that the prosecution must show that the defendant acted with full knowledge of what he or she was doing and that these actions were based on the intent to defraud another. How does the prosecution prove that the defendant intended to defraud someone else? Consider Example 5-3.

Example 5-3

Mary receives her husband's paycheck in the mail while he is out of town. She wants to deposit the check into their joint account, and writes his name on the back to indorse it. When she deposits the check, has she committed forgery?

Answer: No. This is not a forgery case for at least two reasons. The first has to do with authority. Mary's husband may have given her authority to sign his name. Some states even go so far as to say that spouses automatically have authority to sign each other's names, but even if the issue of authority is open to question, what about the intent to defraud? Did Mary present the check with intent to defraud someone else out of money or property? No. She merely deposited funds into her own account. Without some indication of intention to defraud, this is not a forgery case.

1. Make, Alter or Possess a Writing

The law of forgery applies to written documents. It is not forgery to print counterfeit money or to create fraudulent artwork. Those crimes are classified differently than forgery. In order to have forgery, there must be a writing. "Writing" is generally defined as any handwritten, typewritten, computer-generated, printed, or engraved document. Possession of a forged document will qualify as forgery in the second degree, discussed below.

2. Without Authority

Another element that the prosecution must prove on a forgery case is that the person who created the fraudulent document did so without permission. It is perfectly acceptable for one person to give another person permission to sign his or her name to a document. However, when a person signs the other person's name without authority, it is forgery.

3. Uttering and Delivering

One of the most important elements of forgery is **uttering** or delivering. In fact, uttering a document separates it from a lesser offense commonly referred to as forgery in the second degree. When a person utters a forged document, he or she passes it off to someone else as a valid and genuine document. Simply possessing a document does not satisfy the element of uttering. Before a person can be successfully prosecuted for forgery in the first degree, the prosecution must prove that the defendant presented the document to someone else and the document was a valid, legitimate document. If the prosecution cannot prove this element, the most a defendant can be charged with is forgery in the second degree. The difference between these two offenses is important when it comes to sentencing. Although the length of sentence varies from state to state, in most jurisdictions, forgery in the first degree can be punished by as long as 10 years in prison, while forgery in the second degree can result in a maximum sentence of only five years. Forgery in the first degree is always punished more severely than forgery in the second degree. This is why uttering and delivering the writing is such an important element in a forgery case.

Uttering: To present to another

> ***Getting to the Essentials:***   To "utter" a forged document is to present it to another as real and valid.

Case Excerpt

What constitutes "uttering?"

Grimes v. State 245 Ga.App. 277, 537 S.E.2d 720 (2000)

PHIPPS, Judge.

Kenneth Leon Grimes was found guilty of 13 counts of forgery in the first degree. In this appeal, Grimes asserts that the trial court erred in its recharge of the jury and also disputes the sufficiency of the evidence as well as the effectiveness of his trial counsel. After reviewing each of these issues, we affirm.

When viewed in the light most favorable to the verdict, the evidence established that Grimes, along with co-conspirator Denise Dixon, purchased about $200 worth of merchandise from Pep Boys using counterfeit bills. Store clerk Crystal Goodwin noticed that as Grimes and Dixon shopped they both appeared extremely nervous. Goodwin observed that Dixon's hands were heavily wrapped in bandaging. At the check-out register, Goodwin became more suspicious when Dixon produced a large sum of cash that appeared to have been washed. While at the check-out, Grimes instructed Dixon to be sure to get a receipt. Goodwin set aside the bills in a slot next to the customer service desk. At the end of her shift, Goodwin and her supervisor examined the bills closely and decided they were counterfeit. Pep Boys then contacted the United States Secret Service which began an investigation.

Secret Service Agent Scott Trew determined that the bills at issue were, in fact, counterfeit. He and Secret Service Agent Todd Kennedy interviewed Grimes. Initially, Grimes denied knowing anything about the counterfeit bills. But in a subsequent interview, Grimes admitted having picked up the counterfeit bills for Dixon, his then live-in girlfriend, from a man who had received them in a drug deal. Grimes knew when he obtained the bills that they were counterfeit. In a written statement, Grimes admitted accompanying Dixon to Pep Boys, then later proceeding to a different Pep Boys' location to procure a cash refund for the merchandise purchased with the counterfeit bills. Agent Kennedy explained that the process Grimes followed is a typical method by which counterfeit bills are placed into circulation and exchanged for genuine currency.

1. Grimes contends that the trial court erred in its recharge to the jury. He claims that the court impermissibly injected its opinion by providing the jury with numerous examples about the distinction between actual and constructive possession.

The jury had asked for a reexplanation of constructive possession. To comply with that request, using the pattern charge, the court gave the legal definitions of actual and constructive possession. The court then provided a few simple examples from everyday life to illustrate the two terms.

When a trial court correctly instructs the jury on the law but an exception is made to a hypothetical illustration offered by way of explanation, unless a showing is made that the illustration confused or misled the jury, this court will not narrowly scrutinize that illustration. Here, no such showing has been made. In any event, since the determinative issue was whether Grimes was a party to the crime, the illustrations on possession could hardly have misled or confused the jury. Contrary to Grimes's claims, the jury charge as a whole, including the recharge, was correct and not misleading. Nor did the recharge express or intimate any opinion by the trial court concerning any matter.

2. Grimes contends that the evidence was insufficient to support a finding that he participated in the crime of forgery as opposed to merely being present at Pep Boys. He further asserts that the State failed to prove that the counterfeit bills he picked up were the ones used at Pep Boys and that the counterfeit bills turned over to federal agents were those used by Dixon.

Grimes's argument overlooks two points: that a party to a crime may be held fully culpable for committing it and that a conviction for forgery can hinge on circumstantial evidence. A party to a crime may be prosecuted and convicted for the commission of the offense regardless of whether anyone else was prosecuted. Forgery in the first degree requires uttering or delivering such writing. Proof of uttering is met by evidence that the defendant offered to pass a forged writing to another person, declaring or asserting, directly or indirectly, by words or actions, that it was good. Thus, an intent to defraud, coupled with the possession of an altered writing and delivery thereof, is sufficient to prove forgery in the first degree.

Here, the evidence showed at a minimum that Grimes was a party to the crime of forgery. Grimes admitted that before the Pep Boys venture, he had met a friend of Dixon's at a prearranged location to obtain the counterfeit bills. While at Pep Boys, Grimes reminded Dixon to get a receipt. Later, using that receipt, Grimes went to another store operated by Pep Boys where he exchanged the merchandise for a cash refund. Construed in a light most favorable to the verdict, this evidence was sufficient to authorize a jury to find Grimes guilty beyond a reasonable doubt of committing forgery.

3. On appeal, Grimes contends, for the first time, that his trial counsel rendered ineffective assistance of counsel.

An ineffectiveness claim must be asserted at the earliest practicable moment and before appeal when the opportunity to raise such claim is available. The failure to do so results in a waiver of that issue. Here, new counsel was appointed in time to file a timely notice of appeal but did so without first filing a motion for new trial or otherwise seeking an evidentiary hearing on any claim of ineffective assistance of trial counsel. As a consequence, this claim is procedurally foreclosed.

Case Questions

1.   What crime are Grimes and Dixon accused of committing?
2.   What procedure do counterfeiters commonly use to exchange fake bills for real ones?

3. What are the two problems with Grimes' second argument?

4. How did the government prove that Grimes had "uttered" the counterfeit bills?

III. Credit Card Theft and Fraud

Credit card use is so prevalent in United States that virtually anything can be purchased with one. That convenience comes at a price. Credit card theft and fraud is one of the fastest-growing crimes in the United States. All states now have statutes penalizing the theft and unauthorized use of another person's credit cards.

Figure 5-6. California Statute on Credit Card Theft.

Fraudulent use of access cards or account information

Every person who, with the intent to defraud, (a) uses, for the purpose of obtaining money, goods, services, or anything else of value, an access card or access card account information that has been altered, obtained, or retained in violation of Section 484e or 484f, or an access card which he or she knows is forged, expired, or revoked, or (b) obtains money, goods, services, or anything else of value by representing without the consent of the cardholder that he or she is the holder of an access card and the card has not in fact been issued, is guilty of theft. If the value of all money, goods, services, and other things of value obtained in violation of this section exceeds four hundred. CA PENAL § 484d

On the federal level, the Secret Service has jurisdiction to investigate and prosecute credit card theft and fraud when such activities cross state lines or involve interstate commerce. Although it might seem odd that the Secret Service has this authority, its jurisdiction stems from its authority to review cases involving counterfeit money. In recent years, the United States Secret Service has formed special task forces with local law enforcement in order to combat this increasingly difficult and prevalent crime.

Credit card thieves can obtain credit card numbers and other information from a wide variety of sources. One of the easiest ways of obtaining misinformation is to get it from the individual by e-mail or telephone contact. Thieves may contact an individual consumer and request clarification on a recent "order," or ask seemingly innocuous questions in order to get the person to open up to them and provide information that they need about their accounts. This process is referred to as "social engineering," and was first used by hackers to obtain information from companies so that they could then access company accounts. The average credit card fraud results in a loss of $2000. Although the consumer may not be obligated to pay that entire amount, the fact that a merchant absorbs the cost simply means that society as a whole ends up paying the tab for credit card fraud.

Getting to the Essentials: Credit card theft includes actually stealing the physical card as well as using the credit card number to make unauthorized purchases.

A. Skimming

Another common method of obtaining credit card information is a process called "**skimming**." This involves the use of a small machine that can easily be concealed on the thief's body. Waiters and other service workers can simply swipe the customer's card through this small machine, called a "skimmer." This machine records the card information in electronic format. Skimmers can store hundreds of credit card numbers, which can later be downloaded onto computer systems and sold to other individuals.

Skimming: Using a handheld device to illegally copy credit card information.

IV. Identity Theft

The crime of identity theft is a relatively recent development in the criminal world. The term itself is so new that credit card companies, lending institutions and law enforcement cannot agree on what exactly constitutes identity theft. The most commonly accepted definition of identity theft occurs when someone uses personal information belonging to another to pass himself or herself off as that person to obtain financial gain. A criminal might obtain loans, new credit cards and even buy a home using someone else's credit history and personal information. Later, all of these assets will be liquidated, leaving the original person liable for all of the debts. What makes an identity theft so difficult to prosecute is that the criminal often uses the victim's name for all transactions, completely cutting himself out of the loop and making it that much harder to identify the real defendant. Victims often find it very difficult to convince credit card companies and other lenders that someone else obtained all of this financing. The effects on the victim's credit history can be devastating. It frequently takes years and a large financial investment for victims to clear their names.

Figure 5-7. Households Experiencing Identity Theft.[3]

Table 2. Age, race, Hispanic origin, region and location of residence of head of households experiencing identity theft

Head of household characteristic	Number of victimized households	Percent of all households in each category
Total	6,426,200	5.5%
Age		
18-24	545,100	7.0%
25-34	1,225,900	6.1
35-49	2,240,400	6.1
50-64	1,725,800	5.9
65 or older	689,100	3.0
Race		
White	5,410,100	5.6%
Black	693,700	4.8
Other race	255,800	4.9
More than one race	66,600	7.5
Hispanic origin		
Hispanic	551,900	4.4%
Non-Hispanic	5,850,200	5.6

---

3. Identity Theft, 2005. Bureau of Justice Statistics, Special Report, November 2007.

Region		
Northeast	997,600	4.7%
Midwest	1,394,600	5.0
South	2,157,000	5.0
West	1,877,000	7.4
Location of residence		
Urban	2,010,800	5.8%
Suburban	3,548,500	5.9
Rural	866,900	3.9

A person can commit identity theft with relatively little information. With the victim's full name, date of birth and Social Security number, a wide variety of lending institutions will extend credit, issue credit cards, and allow a criminal almost limitless access to financial opportunities. Both federal and state initiatives have attempted to make access to Social Security number information more difficult to obtain, but even these days acquiring some else's Social Security number is much easier than it should be. Here are some of the common methods that criminals use to obtain this information:

- Social engineering—asking the victim for the information while posing as a legitimate business.
- Trash—people often dispose of items containing important reference information, including their Social Security numbers, bank account statements, credit card numbers and a wide variety of other information that criminals can put to ready use.
- Purchase—criminals may pose as legitimate companies requesting background information or credit histories on individuals.
- Theft—criminals may simply steal the information from legitimate companies.

> **Getting to the Essentials:**   Identity theft consists of using someone else's private information for financial gain.

Case Excerpt

When is a private company liable for identity theft?

King Motor Co. of Fort Lauderdale v. Jones, 901 So.2d 1017 (Fla. App. 4 Dist., 2005)

TAYLOR, J.

Appellee, Judith Jones, became a victim of identity theft when she purchased a car at a dealership. She sued King Motor Company of Fort Lauderdale, Inc. (King Motor), alleging that a King Motor's salesman used the information contained on her credit application to steal her identity and make fraudulent purchases and bank account withdrawals. Her complaint included claims for negligence, gross negligence, unfair and deceptive trade practices, and a violation of the Credit Services Organization Act. In this appeal, King Motor challenges the trial court's order denying its motion to stay and compel arbitration. Because we agree with the trial court's ruling that appellee's claims are not subject to arbitration, we affirm.

We first note that the validity of the written arbitration agreement is not in dispute. Second, though the parties below advanced arguments concerning waiver of the right to arbitration, the record does not reflect a ruling on this issue. Third, appellant's point on appeal, that the arbitrator, rather than the judge, should have decided the issue of arbitrability, was not properly raised below. Therefore, the sole issue for our review is whether an arbitrable issue exists.

The language in the arbitration clause is as follows:

Buyer/lessee acknowledges and agrees that the vehicle the buyer/lessee is purchasing or leasing from the dealer has traveled in interstate commerce. Buyer/lessee thus acknowledges that the vehicle and other aspects of the sale, lease or financing transaction are involved in, affect, or have a direct impact upon interstate commerce.

Buyer/lessee and dealer agree that all claims, demands, disputes or controversies of every kind or nature between them arising from, concerning or relating to any of the negotiations involved in the sale/lease or financing of the vehicle, the terms and provision of the sale, lease, or financing arrangements, the arrangements for financing, the purchase of insurance, extended warranties, service contracts or other products purchased as an incident to the sale, lease or financing of the vehicle, the performance or condition of the vehicle, or any other aspects of the vehicle and its sale, lease or financing, shall be settled by binding arbitration, conducted pursuant to the provisions of the Federal Arbitration Act, 9. U.S.C. Section 1 et seq. and according to the commercial arbitration rules of the American Arbitration Association. Without limiting the generality of the foregoing, it is the intention of the buyer/lessee and the dealer to resolve by binding arbitration all disputes between them concerning the vehicle, its sale, lease or financing, and its condition, including disputes concerning the terms and conditions of the sale, lease, or financing, the condition of the vehicle, any damage to the vehicle, the terms and meaning of any of the documents signed or given in connection with the sale, lease or financing of the vehicle, or negotiations for the sale, lease or financing of the vehicle, or any terms conditions, representations or omissions made in connection with the financing, credit, life insurance, disability insurance, vehicle extended warranty or service contract or other products or services acquired as an incident to the sale, lease or financing of the vehicle.

Either party may demand arbitration, by filing.... Buyer/lessee and dealer further agree that any questions regarding whether a particular controversy is subject to arbitration shall be decided by the Arbitrator.

BUYER/LESSEE AND DEALER UNDERSTAND THAT THEY ARE AGREEING TO RESOLVE THE DISPUTES BETWEEN THEM DESCRIBED ABOVE BY BINDING ARBITRATION RATHER THAN BY LITIGATING IN COURT.

King Motor looks to the broad italicized language above to support its position that appellee's causes of action arise out of, or relate to, the sales contract and, particularly, the financing associated with the vehicle sale. Appellee counters that her causes of action do not arise from or concern the sales transaction, notwithstanding King Motor's contention that "but for" the sale, there would not have been a theft of her identity.

Seifert is instructive when considering whether a trial court should exclude certain tort and statutory claims from arbitration despite broad arbitration language. Deciding whether a particular claim is covered by a broad arbitration provision requires a determination of whether a significant relationship exists between the claim and the agreement containing the arbitration clause, regardless of the legal label attached to the dispute. *Seifert*, 750 So.2d at 637–38.

In *Seifert*, the plaintiff brought a wrongful death action against her house builder. She and her husband had contracted with the builder to construct a new house. After the Sieferts moved into the house, the husband left his car running in the garage. The air conditioning system, which was located in the garage, picked up the carbon monoxide emissions from the car and distributed them through the house, killing the husband. The wife, as personal representative of her husband's estate, sued the builder for negligence. The builder moved to submit the wrongful death action to arbitration, based on an arbitration clause in the purchase and sale contract providing for arbitration of "any controversy or claim arising under or related to this agreement or to the property." 750 So.2d at 635. The issue in Seifert was whether these arbitration terms in the purchase and sale contract required the wrongful death claim to be arbitrated.

The Fifth District Court of Appeal held that the issue was arbitrable because the claims arose under or related to the contract for construction of the home. U.S. Home Corp. v. Seifert, 699 So.2d 787 (Fla. 5th DCA 1997). However, the Florida Supreme Court quashed the decision, noting that "even in contracts containing broad arbitration provisions, the determination of whether a particular claim must be submitted to arbitration necessarily depends on the existence of some nexus between the dispute and the contract containing the arbitration clause." Seifert, 750 So.2d at 638. The supreme court disagreed that an agreement to arbitrate in a purchase and sale agreement necessarily requires "arbitration of a subsequent and independent tort action based upon common-law duties." Id. at 635. It further noted that "the mere fact that the dispute would not have arisen but for the existence of the contract and consequent relationship between the parties is insufficient by itself to transform a dispute into one 'arising out of or relating to' the agreement." Id. at 638.

After reviewing case law from Florida and other jurisdictions and comparing how various courts interpret arbitration clauses that include all claims or controversies "arising out of" the subject contract, the supreme court ultimately adopted the reasoning employed in our holding in Terminix International Co., L.P. v. Michaels, 668 So.2d 1013 (Fla. 4th DCA 1996). There, we relied upon and adopted the Arizona Court of Appeal's holding in Dusold v. Porta-John Corp., 167 Ariz. 358, 807 P.2d 526 (Ct.App.1990). The supreme court in Seifert quoted Dusold:

If the contract places the parties in a unique relationship that creates new duties not otherwise imposed by law, then a dispute regarding a breach of a contractually-imposed duty is one that arises from the contract. Analogously, such a claim would be one arising from the contract terms and therefore subject to arbitration where the contract required it. If, on the other hand, the duty alleged to be breached is one imposed by law in recognition of public policy and is generally owed to others besides the contracting parties, then a dispute regarding such a breach is not one arising from the contract, but sounds in tort. Therefore, a contractually-imposed arbitration requirement ... would not apply to such a claim. Seifert, at 639 (quoting Dusold, 807 P.2d at 529–31).

As mentioned above, this case involves tort claims based on King Motor's alleged breach of duty to keep customers' confidential and financial information safe. These claims do not implicate contractual duties created or governed by the contract but concern duties generally owed to the public, i.e., to others besides appellee Jones. None of the allegations in the complaint require reference to or construction of any portion of the purchase and sale or financing agreement between the parties. Because this action is predicated upon a theory of negligence unrelated to the rights and obligations of the contract, it does not have a sufficient relationship to the agreement as to fall within the arbitration provision. Accordingly, we affirm the trial court's denial of the stay and motion to compel arbitration.

AFFIRMED.

Case Questions

1. Do the parties in this case argue that the arbitration agreement was improper? Why or why not?

2. King Motor argues that this case should have been submitted to an arbitrator. Explain King Motor's argument.

3. Explain the court's reasoning why the arbitration clause had no relevance to this case.

4. Was King Motor under an obligation to protect consumer information to avoid identity theft? Explain.

Chapter Summary

There is a wide variety of Internet scams currently being practiced on the World Wide Web and through e-mail services. The scams range from requests for funds to legitimate-appearing e-mails that request personal information. Once a criminal obtains a person's credit card number or other personal information, the criminal can then charge items to that account or even establish a separate identity in what is commonly known as identity theft. Internet crimes involve difficult jurisdictional questions. For instance, when a victim is located in one state and a defendant in another, which state has jurisdiction over the crime? Traditional crimes, such as forgery, have long since settled these questions of jurisdiction. Forgery in the first degree is the crime of possessing or altering a document without permission and uttering or delivering the document to another. The topic of identity theft raises a host of issues including the individual's responsibility for keeping his or her information private as well as the responsibility of private companies to safely store information from thieves who wish to obtain it.

Web Sites

- Internet Fraud—U.S. Department of Justice
  http://www.internetfraud.usdoj.gov/

- Internet Fraud Complaint Center
  http://www1.ifccfbi.gov/index.asp
- U.S. Securities and Exchange Commission
  http://www.sec.gov/investor/pubs/cyberfraud.htm
- Fair Debt Collection Practices
  http://www.ftc.gov/bcp/conline/pubs/credit/fdc.htm
- U.S. Secret Service — Financial Crimes Division
  http://www.ustreas.gov/usss/financial_crimes.shtml
- Internet Fraud (FBI)
  http://www.fbi.gov/majcases/fraud/internetschemes.htm

Key Terms

Phishing   Uttering

Cramming   Skimming

Review Questions

1. How do Internet scams differ from traditional scams?
2. What is phishing?
3. What is the most common method to contact a potential victim in an Internet scam?
4. What is "cramming?"
5. Who is responsible for investigating Internet — based crimes?
6. Why are jurisdictional questions a prominent feature of Internet — based crimes?
7. What are the elements of first-degree forgery?
8. What is the difference between first-degree forgery and second-degree forgery?
9. What is "uttering?"
10. How do thieves acquire credit card information from their victims?
11. What is "skimming?"
12. What is identity theft?
13. What are some of the methods used to commit identity theft?
14. Why is identity theft such a growing problem in the United States?
15. Explain the significance of the *King Motor Company* case.

Chapter 6

Truth in Lending

Chapter Objectives

- Explain the basic features of the Federal Truth in Lending Act (TILA)
- Describe the function of Regulation Z
- List the types of disclosures that a creditor must make under TILA
- Analyze a TILA disclosure form
- Describe how enforcement actions are brought under TILA

I. The Federal Truth in Lending Act

The Federal Truth in Lending Act (TILA) was passed in 1968 in direct response to consumer complaints about mortgage lenders and other loan practices that disguise fees and other charges. According to the terms of the act, a lender must disclose specific types of information prior to the loan agreement. In fact, the Truth in Lending Act has a standard form that must be presented to a borrower that presents information in a clear and concise way. The basic idea behind the Truth in Lending Act was to provide consumers with a way of comparing lenders to one another. When consumers understand the various fees and the interest rates that can be assessed on their loans, they can more accurately assess competing lenders and sign up for terms that they find more agreeable.

The Federal Truth in Lending Act (TILA), 15 U.S.C. § 1601 requires lenders and other creditors to make specific disclosures to borrowers both prior to and during a credit transaction. The Federal Truth in Lending Act does not apply to business transactions. The Federal Truth in Lending Act only applies to transactions where there will be installment payments over time. It governs all fees associated with obtaining a loan, including periodic payments, finance charges, and any other charge associated with obtaining or maintaining the loan.

> *Getting to the Essentials:*   The Truth in Lending Act requires specific disclosures to help inform consumers.

Under the terms of TILA, all disclosures must be made before any documents finalize the loan agreement. These disclosures must be made in writing and the consumer is permitted to keep a copy of all disclosures. The terms must also specifically provide the nature and type of finance charges in language that the average adult would be able to understand. The Act also has specific requirements for terms such as "required finance charge." That term, and others, must be conspicuously set out in the Federal Truth in Lending Act disclosure. Disclosures must also provide the annual percentage rate. Finally, the Act requires that both the creditor and the borrower must be specifically and clearly identified.

A. Regulation Z

Regulation Z is the legislation used by the Board of Governors of the Federal Reserve System to implement the rules found in the Federal Truth in Lending Act. The purpose of Regulation Z is to promote the informed use of credit by consumers through the use of required disclosures on the part of lenders. Regulation Z also gives consumers the right to cancel certain credit transactions that involve liens or security interests on their residences and also regulates credit card transactions. Regulation Z requires disclosures about maximum interest rates and variable rate charges that apply to credit cards and other types of loans. The regulation covers all individual business transactions where credit is offered and any of the four conditions are met:

- Credit is offered or extended to consumers
- The offer of credit or extension of credit is done regularly
- Credit is subject to a finance charge or is payable in four or more regular installments
- The credit is primarily for personal, family or household use

Getting to the Essentials:	Regulation Z implements the statutory provisions of TILA.

Regulation Z: Legislation that imposes the provisions of TILA on creditors.

Regulation Z provides specific guidance about transactions that are not covered under the Federal Truth in Lending Act. These include business, commercial, agricultural or organizational credit. Under this definition, the extension of credit or loans to businesses or other commercial enterprises does not fall under the Federal Truth in Lending Act. The primary purpose of the act is to give consumers better information about the terms and charges that would be assessed against them when they are acquiring a loan or obtaining credit. The reason that TILA does not apply to commercial enterprises is a presumption that business owners and other commercial ventures would be more sophisticated than the average consumer, would have better information and also be able to negotiate their own terms with lenders—none of the factors available to a normal consumer. The Federal Truth in Lending Act also does not apply to extension of credit to corporations or governmental agencies. It also does not cover credit situations where the amount of the loan is greater than $25,000 and the principal dwelling is not used as collateral. Finally, other transactions that are exempt under regulations include public utility credits, securities or commodities accounts, home fuel budget plans and student loans.

B. Time of Disclosures

The creditor must make these disclosures before the first transactions are made under the plan. In addition to requiring disclosures, Regulation Z also requires periodic statements from the creditor, corresponding to each billing cycle for any account that has a debtor-credit balance of more than one dollar. If the creditor fails to meet these requirements, the creditor cannot collect any finance or other charges. The disclosures in open-ended credit arrangements must reflect all of the legal obligations assumed between the parties. In essence, Regulation Z operates to require the lender (or creditor) to divulge as much pertinent information to the consumer before the consumer assumes the legal obligation to repay. Recent changes in TILA now require notice to consumers within three business days of the application for credit. Consumers cannot be charged any fees prior to the TILA notice, except for credit report fees. In addition, changes that took effect in 2009 mandate that a closing cannot occur until seven business days have elapsed since the initial delivery of a TILA notice. Other changes in TILA also affect the consumer indirectly, including the application of unfair and deceptive trade practices legislation to the mortgage industry and limitations on the influence of appraisers in the mortgage process.

C. Finance Charges under the Federal Truth in Lending Act

Regulation Z specifically defines finance charge as "the cost of consumer credit" per dollar amount. It includes any charge payable directly or indirectly by the consumer and imposed directly or indirectly by the creditor as an incident to or a condition of the extension of credit." Under this broad definition, almost any charge associated with obtaining credit, from paying "points" in obtaining a mortgage loan to other assessments would be defined as finance charges. However, there are some charges associated with obtaining a loan that are specifically not covered by the Federal Truth in Lending Act. These include:

- Application fees
- Charges for late payments
- Charges for exceeding a credit limit
- Real estate related fees, including title examination, abstract title and title insurance policy premiums and
  - Preparing and recording deeds and mortgages
  - Notary and credit report fees
  - Property appraisal fees
  - Fees associated with escrow or trustee accounts

D. Initial Disclosure Statements

Before the creation of TILA and Regulation Z, consumers often had difficulty in determining credit rates, terms and fees associated with obtaining loans, credit cards and other credit. Among the items that must be disclosed include the finance charge, including when the finance charge will be charged and an explanation of how it will be determined. The disclosure must also include an explanation of the periodic rate that may be used to compute the finance charge and the annual percentage rate. Additional disclosures include an explanation of the method used to determine the balance and an explanation of how the finance charge amount will be determined.

E. Continuous Obligation of Creditors

Under Federal Truth in Lending, lenders have a continuing obligation to correct any information as the changes and must notify borrowers about inaccuracies in the finance or other charges.

II. Open-ended Credit

Open-ended credit arrangements fall under subpart B of Regulation Z. Under section 226.5, creditors must make clear and conspicuous disclosures, in writing, to prospective borrowers. These include "finance charge" and "annual percentage rate" disclosures. These disclosures must be provided conspicuously and in a table format as shown in Figure 6-1.

> *Getting to the Essentials:*   In open-ended credit arrangements, there is no fixed term or fixed amount financed.

Open-ended credit: Under the provisions of sub-part B of Regulation Z, a credit arrangement without a fixed term or a fixed amount borrowed.

Figure 6-1. Early Disclosure Model Form (Home-equity Plans).[1]

G-14(A) Early Disclosure Model Form (Home-equity Plans)

[Loan Applicant's Name]   [Date]
[Loan Applicant's Address]   [Name of Creditor]
                                                         [Loan Originator's Unique Identifier]

[Statement that the consumer has applied for a home-equity line of credit]

Borrowing Guidelines	
Credit Limit	[Disclosure of credit limit]
First Transaction	[Description of any minimum draw requirements at account opening]
Minimum Transaction	[Description of any minimum draw requirements after account opening]
Minimum Balance	[Description of any minimum outstanding balance requirement]
Limits on Number of Credit Transactions	[Description of any limitations on the number of extensions of credit]
Limits on Amount of Credit Borrowed	[Description of any limitations on the amount of credit that may be obtained during any time period]

Annual Percentage Rate	
Annual Percentage Rate (APR)	[APR(s) applicable to the payment plans disclosed in the table, including introductory APR information] [For variable APRs, the following (1) description that the APR varies, (2) how the APR is determined, (3) the frequency of changes in the APR, (4) description of any limitations on changes in the APR (except for minimum and maximum APRs) or a statement that no annual limitation exists, as applicable, and (5) description of any rules relating to changes in the index value and the APR, including preferred rate provisions and rate carryover provisions, if any]

---

1. Board of the Governors of the Federal Reserve System, Model Form G-14(A).

Maximum APR	[Maximum APR(s) applicable to the payment plans disclosed in the table]
Minimum APR	[Minimum APR(s) applicable to the payment plans disclosed in the table]
Historical Changes to Prime Rate	[Description of the lowest and highest value of the index in the past 15 years]

Fees	
Refundability of Fees	[Description of a consumer's rights to refund of fees]
Total Account Opening Fees	[Description of total one-time account opening fees] [Description of itemized one-time account opening fees]
[Annual Fee/Monthly Fees]	[Description of fees imposed by the creditor for availability of the plan]
Early Termination Fee	[Description of fees imposed by the creditor for early termination of the plan by the consumer]
Required [insert name of required insurance, or debt cancellation or suspension coverage]	[Description of cost of insurance, or debt cancellation or suspension plan] [Cross reference to additional information]
Other Fees	[Statements about other fees]

Borrowing and Repayment Terms	
Length of Credit Plan	[Disclosures of length of plan, length of draw period, and length of any repayment period] [If there is no repayment period on the plan, a statement that after the draw period ends, the consumer must repay the remaining balance in full] [A statement that the consumer can borrow money during the draw period] [If a repayment period is provided, a statement that the consumer cannot borrow money during the repayment period] [A statement indicating whether minimum payments are due in the draw period and any repayment period]
Balloon Payment	[Statement that paying only the minimum periodic payments may not repay any of the principal or may repay less than the outstanding balance by the end of the plan] [Statement that a balloon payment may result or will result, as applicable]

Payment Plans
[Statement indicating that the table shows how the creditor determines minimum required payments for two plans offered by the creditor]
[Statement that other payment plans are available]
[Statement that consumer should ask the creditor for additional details about these other payment plans]

Plan A	[Explanation of how the minimum periodic payment will be determined and the timing of the payments for this plan] [Statement about balloon payment for this plan] [Statement about payment limitations] [Statement about negative amortization]
Plan B	[Explanation of how the minimum periodic payment will be determined and the timing of the payments for this plan] [Statement about balloon payment for this plan] [Statement about payment limitations] [Statement about negative amortization]

Plan Comparison: Sample Payments on an $(credit limit) Balance
[Statement that the sample payments show the first periodic payments if the consumer borrows the maximum credit available when the account is opened and does not borrow any more money]
[Statement that the sample payments are not the consumer's actual payments]
[Statement that the actual payments each period will depend on the amount that the consumer has borrowed and the interest rate that period]

Sample Payments under Plan A			
APR	Borrowing Period (Years __ to __) First Payment	[Balance at Start of Repayment Period]	[Repayment Period (Years __ to __) First Payment]
____% (current)	$____	[$____]	[$____]
____% (max.)	$____	[$____]	[$____]

Sample Payments under Plan B			
APR	Borrowing Period (Years __ to __) First Payment	[Balance at Start of Repayment Period]	[Repayment Period (Years __ to __) First Payment]
____% (current)	$____	[$____]	[$____]
____% (max.)	$____	[$____]	[$____]

Plan A vs. Plan B
[Identification of which plan results in the least amount of interest, and which plan results in the most amount of interest]
[Statements about balloon payments]

[Fixed Interest Rate Option]
[Statements about fixed-rate and -term payment plans] [Statement that consumer should ask creditor for details about fixed-rate and -term payment plans]

Risks	
You Could Lose Your Home	[Statements about security interest in the consumer's dwelling and risk to home]
You May Not Be Able to Borrow From Your Line of Credit	[Statements about possible actions by creditor on HELOC plan]
The Interest You Pay May Not Be Tax-Deductible	[Statements about tax implications]

→ [Statement that the consumer has no obligation to accept the terms disclosed in the table] [Identification of any disclosed term that is subject to change prior to opening the plan, or a statement that all terms disclosed could change before the plan is opened, as applicable]

→ [Statement that the consumer may be entitled to a refund of all fees paid if the consumer decides not to open the plan] [Cross reference to the "Fees" section in the table]

→ [Statement about asking questions]

→ [Statement about Board's website]

[If the creditor has a provision for the consumer's signature, a statement that a signature by the consumer only confirms receipt of the disclosure statement]

[_____

Borrower's Signature   Date]

Figure 6-2. Regulation Z, Sub-Part B

(a) Required disclosures by creditor

Before opening any account under an open end consumer credit plan, the creditor shall disclose to the person to whom credit is to be extended each of the following items, to the extent applicable:

(1) The conditions under which a finance charge may be imposed, including the time period (if any) within which any credit extended may be repaid without incurring a finance charge, except that the creditor may, at his election and without disclosure, impose no such finance charge if payment is received after the termination of such time period. If no such time period is provided, the creditor shall disclose such fact.

(2) The method of determining the balance upon which a finance charge will be imposed.

(3) The method of determining the amount of the finance charge, including any minimum or fixed amount imposed as a finance charge.

(4) Where one or more periodic rates may be used to compute the finance charge, each such rate, the range of balances to which it is applicable, and the corresponding nominal annual percentage rate determined by multiplying the periodic rate by the number of periods in a year.

(5) Identification of other charges which may be imposed as part of the plan, and their method of computation, in accordance with regulations of the Board.

(6) In cases where the credit is or will be secured, a statement that a security interest has been or will be taken in (A) the property purchased as part of the credit transaction, or (B) property not purchased as part of the credit transaction identified by item or type.

(7) A statement, in a form prescribed by regulations of the Board of the protection provided by sections 1666 and 1666i of this title to an obligor and the creditor's responsibilities under

sections 1666a and 1666i of this title. With respect to one billing cycle per calendar year, at intervals of not less than six months or more than eighteen months, the creditor shall transmit such statement to each obligor to whom the creditor is required to transmit a statement pursuant to subsection (b) of this section for such billing cycle.

A. Credit Cards

Credit cards fall into the category of open-ended credit agreements. That means there is no fixed term or fixed amount that is borrowed. Instead, the charge revolves from month to month. Under TILA, the creditor must provide the borrower with periodic statements updating the account status for credit cards. Most credit card creditors provide monthly statements to their borrowers. The statements list all transactions for the month, including purchases, cash advances and interest payments. They must also show how any payments received have been assessed against interest and principal.

> *Getting to the Essentials:* Credit cards are the most common example of open-ended credit transactions under TILA.

1. Credit Card Applications and Solicitations

Whenever a credit card company solicits new business, it must make specific disclosures in the solicitation. Regulation Z even goes so far as to define what a solicitation is. Under the regulation, a "solicitation" refers to an offer by the credit card issuer to open a creditor charge card account and it does not require the consumer to complete an application.

2. Credit Card Disclosures

In situations involving credit cards and other open-ended credit arrangements, the Federal Truth in Lending Act requires conspicuous disclosures in tabular format of all the following information:

- Annual percentage rate
- Fees for issuance or availability
- Minimum finance charge
- Transaction charges
- Grace period
- Balance computation method
- Statement on charge card payments
- Cash advance fees
- Late payment fees
- Over the limit fees
- Balance transfer fee

a. Annual Percentage Rate

The **annual percentage rate** is defined under Regulation Z as each periodic rate that is applied to compute the finance charge, outstanding balance, cash advances, and balance transfers for a credit card account. The annual percentage rate is actually a measure of the cost of credit, expressed as a yearly rate. Under Regulation Z, the annual percentage rate must be disclosed in at least 18-point type. If the rate varies, the credit card issuer must disclose that fact as well. The annual percentage rate is calculated under several different methods, all of which must be disclosed to the consumer. For instance, the creditor might simply calculate the annual percentage rate by multiplying the periodic rate of the billing rate by the number of periods in the year. Another method is to divide the total finance charge for the billing cycle by the sum of the balances to which it applies and multiplying by the number of billing cycles in the year. Whatever method is used by the creditor, it must be disclosed in the Federal Truth in Lending Act disclosure forms made available to the consumer prior to completing the transaction.

> **Annual percentage rate:** The amount that credit costs a consumer on a yearly basis.

b. Fees for Issuance or Availability

Regulation Z requires that the creditor must disclose any annual or periodic fees that can be imposed as a result of either issuing the card or making it available. These fees include activity or inactivity assessments for situations where consumers either use their card more than is anticipated or fail to use the card at all during a specific period.

c. Minimum Finance Charge

Creditors must disclose any minimum or fixed finance charges that can be imposed during the billing cycle.

d. Transaction Charges

Creditors must also disclose any fees associated with using the card to make purchases. Transaction charges are those fees assessed either against the consumer or the merchant for processing the payment. Transaction fees for merchants can vary widely and sometimes explain why some businesses do not accept certain credit cards. It also applies to consumers who may or may not be charged periodic transaction fees simply for using the card in the first place.

e. Grace Period

In addition to making all of the disclosures we have set out so far, the Federal Truth in Lending Act also requires that the creditor must provide a specific grace period within which any credit extended for purchases may be repaid without incurring a finance charge. If the creditor does not allow any grace periods, the creditor must disclose that. If the grace period varies, the creditor must also disclose how it varies by giving a range of days, including a minimum number of days in which the consumer can repay credit extended without incurring finance charge.

f. Balance Computation Method

The creditor must disclose how it computes balances. Regulation Z provides several enumerated **balance computation methods** that a creditor can either refer to by name or explain its own method of computing the balance. This is one of the disclosures that can appear outside the table format required under Regulation Z. The regulation allows certain types of balance competition methods to be named in the disclosures. These include:

- Average Daily Balance (including new purchases)
- Average Daily Balance (excluding new purchases)
- Two Cycle Average Daily Balance (including new purchases)
- Two Cycle Average Daily Balance (excluding new purchases)
- Adjusted Balance
- Previous Balance

Balance computation method: The method used to calculate interest fees and balances on open-ended credit transactions.

i. Average Daily Balance (Including New Purchases)

Under this method, the balance on a credit card is calculated by adding the outstanding balance and any new purchases, while also deducting payments and credits for each day in the billing cycle, then dividing by the number of days in the billing cycle.

ii. Average Daily Balance (Excluding New Purchases)

The average daily balance method, excluding new purchases, is calculated by adding the outstanding balance without factoring in new purchases, deducting any payments and credits for each day in the billing cycle, and then dividing by the total number of days in that cycle.

iii. Two Cycle Average Daily Balance (Including New Purchases)

Under the two cycle average daily balance, including new purchases method, the balance on the account is calculated as the sum of the average daily balances for two billing cycles. The first balance is the current billing cycle balance and is made by adding the outstanding balance, including new purchases and deducting payments and credits for each day of the billing cycle, and then dividing by the number of days in the billing cycle. The second balance is for the preceding billing cycle in is made in the same way as the first balance.

iv. Two Cycle Average Daily Balance (Excluding New Purchases)

The calculations for the two cycle average daily balance, excluding new purchases, is done exactly the same way as the previous paragraph, except that new purchases are not added to the calculations.

v. Adjusted Balance

Under the adjusted balance method of computation, the balance is calculated by deducting payments and credits made during the billing cycle from the outstanding balance that existed at the beginning of the billing cycle.

vi. Previous Balance

The previous balance computation method is perhaps the simplest of the computing methods. It is simply the amount of the outstanding balance from the beginning of the billing cycle.

g. Statement on Charge Card Payments

TILA also requires that the creditor issue a statement listing the use of the credit card and that payments are due for the period in question.

h. Cash Advance Fees

If the creditor imposes any fees for cash advances on credit cards, these must also be disclosed.

i. Late Payment Fees

When a creditor imposes additional fees for overdue payments, this fact must also be disclosed in the credit agreement and the TILA disclosures.

j. Over-the-limit Fees

Most credit card companies impose some kind of fee when the consumer exceeds the available credit limit. If they do, they must disclose this fact.

k. Balance Transfer Fee

In recent years, credit card companies have promoted the option of switching balances held on one credit card to a different card. The new card offers better terms, but if the new credit card company charges a fee for this transfer, this must also be disclosed.

3. Billing Errors on Credit Card Transactions

Creditors are not allowed to close the consumer's account simply because the consumer has exercised his or her rights under the Federal Truth in Lending Act by challenging fees, assessments or other charges. Under Regulation Z, a consumer has the right to challenge particular assessments in writing as billing errors, as long as the notice is not received later than 60 days after the periodic statement showing the error. In order to be valid, the consumer's written notice must identify the consumer's name and account number and the nature of the consumer's belief that there has been a billing error. When this notice has been received, the creditor has 30 days to take appropriate action to resolve the issue.

III. Closed-end Credit Agreements

In a **closed-end credit agreement**, such as a mortgage, there is both a fixed term and a fixed amount borrowed. In that situation, the lender must not only provide a Federal Truth in Lending disclosure form, but also a schedule showing how payment amounts will be distributed between interest payments and principal repayment. Recent changes in TILA and Regulation Z include a new category of loans, called "higher-priced mortgage" loans. Under the new rules, TILA and Regulation Z apply to home refinance loans, home equity loans, construction loans and any extension of credit based on the consumer's dwelling. The changes also require earlier disclosures of TILA and Regulation Z requirements.

Closed-end credit arrangement: A credit transaction where the terms, including interest rate and amount borrowed, are known before the agreement is consummated.

A. Required Disclosures in Closed-end Credit Transactions

Closed-end credit transactions refer to situations where the amount borrowed and the term of repayment are both fixed. The classic example of a closed-end transaction is a mortgage. In a closed-end credit transaction, the creditor must make specific types of disclosures, similar to ones that must be made in open-ended credit transactions. The consumer has the right to keep a copy of these disclosures and they must be made in a particular format, in clear and conspicuous terms. The disclosures required include:

- Identification of creditor
- The amount financed
- Itemization of amount financed
- Finance charge
- Annual percentage rate
- Variable rate
- Payment schedule
- Total of payments
- Demand feature
- Total sale price
- Prepayment provisions
- Late payment
- Security interest
- Insurance and debt cancellation provisions
- Security interest charges
- Contract reference

- Assumption policy
- Required deposit

> ***Getting to the Essentials:***   Closed-end credit transactions involve known terms and a specific amount borrowed.

1. Identification of Creditor

The first requirement of a closed-end credit transaction is that the creditor must fully and completely identify who is extending credit.

2. The Amount Financed

The disclosures must actually provide the phrase "the amount financed" and a brief description of the credit extended to the consumer. This disclosure will also provide background on how the amount financed is actually calculated.

3. Itemization of Amount Financed

Creditors must also disclose, in a separate written itemization, the total amount financed including a good-faith estimate of the settlement costs provided for real estate transactions. This is a requirement under the Real Estate Settlement Procedures Act. Under that act, whenever financing involves mortgages, the lender must provide a booklet summarizing the entire credit transaction and providing a good-faith estimate concerning all credit charges and other fees associated with closing residential real estate loans.

4. Finance Charge

The finance charge disclosure tells the consumer the total amount that the credit arrangement will eventually cost. This disclosure must be given after the sentence "the dollar amount credit will cost you."

5. Annual Percentage Rate

Like open-ended credit transactions, closed-end credit arrangements must also provide information about the annual percentage rate. This figure is calculated in much the same way as was discussed under open-ended credit transactions. This amount must be given in the following sentence, "the cost of your credit as a yearly rate."

6. Variable Rate

There are many circumstances in which a borrower might apply for a variable rate loans, including variable rate mortgages. When a creditor offers a variable rate on the loan, the creditor must provide information about how and under what circumstances the rate will increase, any limitations on the rate increase and an example of how the payment terms would change based on that variable rate.

7. *Payment Schedule*

For closed-end credit transactions, the creditor must provide a **payment schedule** that includes the number, amounts and timing of payments that will repay the loan. This payment schedule will list each of the payments according to the periodic payment schedule, usually monthly and will list the amount of each payment, from first to last, including the largest and smallest payment. The provision for the smallest payment is usually the last payment where only a small amount is left on the balance of the loan.

> **Payment schedule:** A provision of a closed-end credit agreement which shows all payments required under the loan.

8. *Total of Payments*

The total of payments disclosure requires that the creditor provide a descriptive explanation of the total amount of the creditor will pay, usually at the conclusion of the sentence that begins, "the amount you will have paid when you have made all schedule payments." For many consumers, this figure can come as quite a surprise. Over the full term of the loan, a consumer may pay two or three times the amount of the original purchase price.

9. *Demand Feature*

A demand feature is a provision in the loan arrangement that allows the creditor to demand full payment of the existing balance without any prior notice. In residential mortgages, these are very rare.

10. *Total Sale Price*

The total sale price is the sum of the initial cash price, plus any finance charges and credit charges associated with obtaining the loan. This must be disclosed to the consumer in the following terms, "the total price of your purchase on credit, including your down payment of $_____."

11. *Prepayment Provisions*

If the creditor imposes any fee for early payments, this fact must be disclosed to the consumer in the Truth in Lending disclosure statement.

12. *Late Payments*

Just as we saw in open-ended credit arrangements, if the creditor imposes a late payment fee, this fact must be disclosed to the consumer, along with details about how the fee is determined.

13. *Security Interest*

The Federal Truth in Lending Act also requires that when a creditor obtains a **security interest** in property owned by the borrower, that the creditor disclose how and when it has the power to seize that property for nonpayment of the loan. A security interest refers to any item of property at the borrower pledges as collateral for the loan. If the borrower defaults on the loan, the creditor has a right to seize the property in satisfaction of the outstanding debt. Consider Example 6-1.

Example 6-1

Maria recently negotiated the purchase of an automobile. Part of the Federal Truth in Lending Act disclosure forms revealed that title to the automobile would be held by ABC lenders as collateral for the loan. When Maria makes the final payment on the loan, ABC lenders is obligated to transfer title to her. However, in the event that Maria defaults on the car loan, ABC lenders would have the right to repossess the automobile and resell it. Maria knows this because Federal Truth in Lending Act disclosure forms require ABC lenders to reveal this factor in prior to completing the loan transaction.

Security Interest: The pledge of real or personal property as collateral for a loan.

Another common example of a security interest occurs in mortgage lending. Few people have the cash on hand to purchase a home outright. Instead, they must arrange mortgage financing offering the house as collateral for the loan. It is tempting to think that car loans and home loans work in essentially the same way, but that would be incorrect. Pledging real property as security for a loan is different than pledging personal property. Because the car is personal property, the lender is authorized to repossess the car in the event of a loan default. However, the situation changes radically when real property is pledged as collateral for a loan. In that situation, the lender must institute foreclosure proceedings, often involving a court order, before the real property can be auctioned off for the outstanding debt. Unlike car loans, a mortgage lender does not hold title to the real estate. The borrower holds title and the lender has the right to bring a foreclosure action in the event of a default.

14. Insurance and Debt Cancellation Provisions

Creditors are permitted to exclude charges for premiums on credit insurance, life insurance, accident or health insurance from the calculation of finance charges, as long as the creditor does not require these types of insurance to secure the loan.

15. Security Interest Charges

As long as the creditor itemizes and discloses taxes and fees that are required to be paid to public officials for perfecting, releasing and satisfying a security interest, these taxes and fees are not calculated as part of the finance charge.

16. Contract Reference

The disclosure forms should also include a reference to the fact that the contract entered into between the consumer and creditor is the appropriate document for all information concerning the credit arrangement and is a legally binding document that sets the terms and conditions of the credit arrangement. In other words, the written contract replaces any and all verbal agreements between the parties. Under this clause, a consumer would be unable to challenge a contract by stating that his or her understanding was different than the written contract because of the way that it was described. This clause negates any other verbal discussions and makes the written contract the sum total of the agreement between the creditor and the consumer.

17. Assumption Policy

An assumption policy disclosure reveals the fact that a residential mortgage may be sold or transferred to some other creditor during the life of the loan. This disclosure allows the creditor to make that transaction. This clause is quite common in mortgage loans and the resale of mortgages to others happens with great frequency. In fact, some commentators have said that the cause of the recent financial crisis was, in part, precipitated by the sale of mortgage backed securities that were split apart and sold as investments. The distance between the person paying the loan and the person reaping the benefit of the payments became so attenuated that it was nearly impossible for creditors to renegotiate loans with defaulting debtors, thus leading to more and more foreclosures.

18. Required Deposit

When a creditor requires the consumer to maintain a specific amount on deposit as a condition for receiving the loan, this fact must be disclosed in the Truth in Lending disclosure forms. The disclosure must also include a statement that the deposit is not affected by the annual percentage rate. This clause may also include provisions allowing the release of the deposited funds after the consumer has consistently met regular payments for a set period of time, often one year.

B. Right of Rescission

Whenever any credit arrangement involves a lien or foreclosure right in the consumer's principal residence, the consumer has the right to rescind the credit arrangement. The **right of rescission** extends for three business days following the offer of credit, delivery of the notice required under the Federal Truth in Lending Act, or delivery of material disclosures required under Regulation Z, whichever event occurs last. Under the Act, if the creditor fails to deliver material disclosures as required, the consumer has three years to rescind the contract.

> **Right of rescission:** The consumer's right to cancel the credit arrangement within three business days of consummation.

1. Notice of Rescission

The creditor is responsible for delivering the notice of the right to rescdind to the borrower. The notice must include the following information, noted in conspicuous and clear type:

- The creditor's acquisition of a security interest in the consumer's principal dwelling or residence
- The consumer's right to rescind
- How the consumer can exercise his right to rescind, including the address that the notice must be sent to

- The effect of rescission
- The date when the right to rescind expires

IV. Enforcement of Federal Truth in Lending Act

What happens when a creditor violates the Federal Truth in Lending Act by omitting certain facts in disclosure statements or failing to provide other information? What agency is responsible for enforcing TILA? The provisions of the Consumer Credit Protection Act provide the answers to these questions. The Federal Trade Commission has the general responsibility for enforcing the provisions of the act, but there are also provisions that allow individual consumers to sue under Truth in Lending and Regulation Z.

A. Federal Trade Commission

15 U.S.C.A. § 1607 gives the Federal Trade Commission the right to promulgate rules and enforce the general provisions of the Federal Truth in Lending Act. Regulation Z is a direct result of that authority. The act also authorizes various other agencies to intercede when the credit arrangement involves national lending institutions, state lending institutions or the Federal Deposit Insurance Corporation.

Figure 6-3. Enforcement of Truth in Lending Act.

Federal Trade Commission as overall enforcing agency

Except to the extent that enforcement of the requirements imposed under this subchapter is specifically committed to some other Government agency under subsection (a) of this section, the Federal Trade Commission shall enforce such requirements.[2]

B. Consumer Actions under TILA

One of the most important provisions of the Truth in Lending Act is the power it gives to consumers to bring independent civil actions against lenders who fail to comply with the disclosure requirements of the act. Consumers are entitled to damages that are twice the finance charge imposed on the credit transaction. Consumers are entitled to a minimum of $100 for each such transgression or maximum of $1000 without regard to how many transactions occurred. When a case is brought in state court, the litigants must follow the rules of that court, and not federal rules. TILA does not provide its own internal procedural rules. As a result, a state-based TILA action varies depending on the jurisdiction where it is brought. Creditors are responsible for any violation in their disclosure requirements, even if there is no harm to the consumer. However, if the creditor can show that it corrected the error within 60 days of learning of it, prior to any civil suit to enforce the provisions of TILA, then none of the civil sanctions under TILA will apply.

---

2. 15 U.S.C.A. § 1607.

Figure 6-4. Civil Liability under TILA.

(a) Individual or class action for damages; amount of award; factors determining amount of award

Except as otherwise provided in this section, any creditor who fails to comply with any requirement imposed under this part, including any requirement under section 1635 of this title, or part D or E of this subchapter with respect to any person is liable to such person in an amount equal to the sum of—

(1) any actual damage sustained by such person as a result of the failure;

(2)(A) (i) in the case of an individual action, twice the amount of any finance charge in connection with the transaction, (ii) in the case of an individual action relating to a consumer lease under part E of this subchapter, 25 per centum of the total amount of monthly payments under the lease, except that the liability under this subparagraph shall not be less than $100 nor greater than $1,000, or (iii) in the case of an individual action relating to a credit transaction not under an open end credit plan that is secured by real property or a dwelling, not less than $200 or greater than $2,000; or

(B) in the case of a class action, such amount as the court may allow, except that as to each member of the class no minimum recovery shall be applicable, and the total recovery under this subparagraph in any class action or series of class actions arising out of the same failure to comply by the same creditor shall not be more than the lesser of $500,000 or 1 per centum of the net worth of the creditor;

(3) in the case of any successful action to enforce the foregoing liability or in any action in which a person is determined to have a right of rescission under section 1635 of this title, the costs of the action, together with a reasonable attorney's fee as determined by the court; and

(4) in the case of a failure to comply with any requirement under section 1639 of this title, an amount equal to the sum of all finance charges and fees paid by the consumer, unless the creditor demonstrates that the failure to comply is not material.[3]

1. Criminal Liability under TILA

In addition to civil actions, TILA also authorizes criminal prosecution when a creditor willfully and knowingly violates the terms of regulation Z. See Figure 6-5.

Figure 6-5. Criminal Liability for Willful and Knowing Violation of TILA.

Whoever willfully and knowingly

(1) gives false or inaccurate information or fails to provide information which he is required to disclose under the provisions of this subchapter or any regulation issued thereunder,

(2) uses any chart or table authorized by the Board under section 1606 of this title in such a manner as to consistently understate the annual percentage rate determined under section 1606(a)(1)(A) of this title, or

(3) otherwise fails to comply with any requirement imposed under this subchapter, shall be fined not more than $5,000 or imprisoned not more than one year, or both.[4]

2. Preemption of State Law

Generally, actions brought under TILA preempt state law application. Preemption of state law is a common feature of federal statutes. Under the United States Constitution

---

3. 15 U.S.C.A. § 1640.
4. 15 U.S.C.A. § 1611.

supremacy clause, whenever there is a conflict between federal statutes and state statutes, federal statutes take precedence. However, if there is no conflict between a state-based consumer protection action and the provisions of TILA, then both may apply. A consumer can bring an action in United States District Court or any state court for a violation of the provisions of TILA.

Case Excerpt

How do courts calculate annual percentage rate (APR)?

Rucker v. Sheehy Alexandria, Inc. 228 F.Supp.2d 711 (E.D.Va.,2002)

MEMORANDUM OPINION

ELLIS, District Judge.

This action arises from the sale and spot delivery[1] of an automobile. The consumer drove away in the automobile after signing a first sales agreement conditioned on certain financing. When that financing fell through, the consumer returned to the dealership some ten days later and signed a second sales agreement, which was backdated ten days and based on different financing.

FN1. In a spot delivery transaction, the buyer takes possession of the vehicle pursuant to financing terms which have been agreed upon by the parties, but not yet accepted by a third party lender. In the event the lender rejects the financing terms, the agreement between the buyer and the seller is null and void. A spot delivery sale is used to allow the buyer to take possession of the car before the financing is approved.

The novel question presented is whether the disclosures in the second agreement violate the Truth in Lending Act (TILA), 15 U.S.C. § 1601 et seq., by calculating the annual percentage rate of interest (APR) on the basis of the date on the backdated agreement rather than the date the transaction was consummated.

I.

The record reflects the following undisputed material facts: Plaintiff Emily Rucker is a Virginia citizen who purchased a car in April 2001 from the defendant Sheehy Alexandria, Inc., a automobile dealer doing business under the name of Sheehy Honda. On April 3, 2001, Rucker contracted to purchase a 1998 Honda Civic from Sheehy. She executed a buyer's order, a retail installment sales contract (RISC), and a bailment agreement. Under the terms of the April 3 RISC, Rucker provided a $1,000 down payment and financed $13,576.68 at 22.95% APR over 5 years. The total finance charge was $9,582.72, resulting in total payments on the car, including down payment, of

---

1. In a spot delivery transaction, the buyer takes possession of the vehicle pursuant to financing terms which have been agreed upon by the parties, but not yet accepted by a third party lender. In the event the lender rejects the financing terms, the agreement between the buyer and the seller is null and void. A spot delivery sale is used to allow the buyer to take possession of the car before the financing is approved.

$24,159.40. The first monthly payment of $386.99 was due on May 18, 2001, 45 days after the consummation of the transaction. The buyer's order and bailment agreement made clear that this was a spot delivery, because the sale was conditioned upon financing being obtained from a third party lender according to the terms of the RISC within five days from the date of the agreements. Rucker drove the car home on April 3. Sheehy was unable to obtain financing on the terms offered in the first RISC. In a series of six facsimile transmissions, all dated April 3, the financing companies contacted by Sheehy declined to make the loan on the proposed terms. By its terms, the April 3 agreement became null and void when Sheehy was unable to obtain financing within five days. Nonetheless, Sheehy made no effort to contact Rucker at that time and ask her to return the car.

On April 13, 2001, Sheehy received a counteroffer from Mercury Finance, approving a loan of up to $11,000 at an APR of 24.95%. After receiving this counteroffer Sheehy asked Rucker, who was still in possession of the car, to return to the dealership. Although the parties dispute what reason the dealership gave Rucker for returning, it is clear that Sheehy did not tell her that the original financing offer had fallen through. Upon Rucker's return on or after April 13, 2001, a second agreement was reached, according to which Rucker provided an additional $1,000 down payment, while the dealer eliminated a $943.77 extended service warranty from the contract, and lowered the price of the car by $614.65. These changes lowered the amount financed to meet the lender's limit. Under the terms of the second RISC, Rucker financed $10,998.77 at 24.95% over 4 years. The finance charge came to $6,672.91, resulting in total payments under the second deal of $19,671.68. The first monthly payment, now $368.16, was still due on May 18, 2001.

The terms of the two agreements are summarized in the table below:

	April 3	April 13
Sale Price	$12,998.00	$12,383.35
Total Cash Price (including taxes and fees)	$13,632.91	$12,998.77
Extended service warranty	$ 943.77	not provided
Down Payment	$ 1,000	$ 2,000
Amount Financed	$13,576.68	$10,998.77
Annual Percentage Rate	22.95%	24.95%
(APR)		(beginning on April 3)
Finance Charge	$9,582.72	$6,672.91
Total Payments (including down payment)	$24,159.40	$19,671.58
Term of Loan	5 years	4 years
Monthly Payment	$386.99	$368.16
First Payment Due	May 18, 2001	May 18, 2001

A comparison of these agreements reveals that, even though the monthly payment and the total payment over the life of the loan were lower in the April 13 agreement, the terms of the April 13 agreement were less favorable to Rucker than the April 3 terms had been. Under the April 13 agreement, Rucker was required to pay more money down, and to pay off the loan over a shorter period of time. Also, she was charged a higher APR to finance a smaller sum. Additionally, she received less value under the April 13 deal, since the extended warranty, a near $1,000 value, was not included in that transaction as it had been in the April 3 agreement. The only concrete benefit of the second deal was the dealership's reduction in price of $614.65.

Although the second agreement was reached on or about April 13, the April 13 buyer's order and RISC were backdated to April 3, the date of the original and now void agreement between the parties and the date Rucker took possession of the car. The April 13 RISC, therefore, provides no clue on its face that it actually represents a second offer which was entered into well after Rucker took possession of the car. Most significantly for this case, the backdating of the April 13 RISC also resulted in Rucker being charged interest beginning on April 3, even though the agreement pursuant to which that interest was calculated and charged was not reached until ten days later. According to Sheehy, it is industry practice for car dealers to use the date of delivery of the vehicle on subsequent agreements reached in spot delivery transactions, and banks will only accept buyer's orders containing the date of delivery of the vehicle.

On these facts, Rucker filed a complaint asserting the following claims:

Count I: violation of the Fair Credit Reporting Act, 15 U.S.C. § 1681 et seq.

Count II: violations of TILA, 15 U.S.C. § 1601 et seq.

Count III: violation of the Magnuson-Moss Warranty Act, 15 U.S.C. § 2301 et seq.

Count IV: violations of the Virginia Consumer Protection Act, Va.Code § 59.1-196 et seq.

Count V: Breach of Contract

Count VI: Fraud

Rucker filed a motion for partial summary judgment with respect to Count II and Sheehy filed a cross motion for summary judgment on all counts. On September 10, 2002, after oral argument on the motions, Sheehy's motion for summary judgment was granted with respect to Counts I, III and V, and denied with respect to Counts IV and VI. The cross motions for summary judgment on Count II were taken under advisement. For the reasons stated in court and presented below, Rucker was granted summary judgment on the Count II TILA claim by Order dated October 9, 2002.

II.

No controlling circuit authority addresses the question whether the backdating of the April 13 RISC constitutes a violation of TILA, 15 U.S.C. § 1601 et seq. Accordingly, analysis of the question presented properly begins with an examination of the stated purposes of the statute and the relevant statutory and regulatory language.

The goal of TILA is to "assure a meaningful disclosure of credit terms" to promote the "informed use of credit" and to "protect the consumer against inaccurate and unfair credit billing … practices." TILA, 15 U.S.C. § 1601(a). To this end, TILA requires lenders to make certain prominent disclosures when extending credit, including the amount financed, all finance charges, and the APR. Id. at § 1638(a). The disclosed APR must be accurate to within one-eighth of one per cent of the properly calculated actual APR. See 15 U.S.C. § 1606(c). And, Regulation Z, promulgated by the Federal Reserve pursuant to TILA, provides detailed and complex instructions for accurate APR calculation. See 12 C.F.R. § 226 app. J(b)(2).

Consistent with TILA's goals, the timing of these required disclosures is critical. The required information must be disclosed "before credit is extended," 15 U.S.C. at § 1638(b)(1), or, according to Regulation Z, "before consumption of the transaction," 12 C.F.R. § 226.17. Consummation, in turn, is defined by Regulation Z as "the time that a consumer becomes contractually obligated on a credit transaction." 12 C.F.R. § 226.2(a)(13); see Cades v. H & R Block, Inc., 43 F.3d 869, 876 (4th Cir.1994); Harper v. Lindsay Chevrolet, 212 F.Supp.2d 582, 587 (E.D.Va.2002). In this respect, the Fourth Circuit recently held that the then-existing industry practice of providing the disclosures only after the consumer had signed the agreement was a clear violation of TILA and Regulation Z. See Polk v. Crown Auto, Inc., 221 F.3d 691, 692 (4th Cir.2000).

The April 13 RISC agreement presents two questions concerning TILA compliance. First, were the required disclosures timely, even though the agreement retroactively charged interest dating to April 3, ten days before the disclosures occurred? Second, was the APR properly calculated based on the nominal date of the agreement rather than the actual date of its signing? The answer to these questions hinges on the determination of the proper "consummation date" for the purposes of TILA.

Rucker contends that April 13 is the proper consummation date. Although Sheehy's arguments have been somewhat inconsistent, the most recent filing asserts that the deal "must have been consummated on April 3, 2001," although the terms of the April 3 RISC were superseded by the April 13 RISC. Yet, both parties agree that the April 3 agreement was rendered null and void by its terms when financing on the originally agreed upon terms was not obtained within five days. The April 3 date of the first agreement is therefore not relevant in considering the parties' current contractual obligations. The fact that Rucker took possession of the car on April 3 is likewise irrelevant. According to Regulation Z, consummation occurs not when the consumer takes possession of the product, but at the "time that a consumer becomes contractually obligated on a credit transaction," 12 C.F.R. § 226.2(a)(13); see Cades v. H & R Block, Inc., 43 F.3d at 876. Not until the April 13 agreement was signed by the parties did they become "obligated on a credit transaction." This second agreement is the surviving agreement by which the parties remain bound, and according to which Rucker has continued to make her payments due on the loan. In sum, because Rucker did not become obligated on the credit transaction until April 13, that is the date the transaction was consummated under TILA.

Two conclusions flow inexorably from the conclusion that April 13 is the proper date for the consummation of the transaction. First, the required TILA disclosures were timely. It is undisputed in the record that the April 13 RISC was filled out with all the required terms when it was presented for Rucker's signature. That is sufficient to meet the TILA temporal requirements set forth in § 1638(b)(1) and Regulation Z. See Harper, 212 F.Supp.2d at 587; 15 U.S.C. § 1638(b)(1); 12 C.F.R. § 226.17. The backdating of the second RISC agreement does not alter the fact that the required information was disclosed to Rucker before she became contractually obligated.

The second conclusion that follows from the April 13 consummation date is that the APR figure disclosed on the April 13 RISC is inaccurate. The APR must be calculated according to the Regulation Z instructions. See 12 C.F.R. 226 app. J(b). According to the current version of Regulation Z, "the term of the transaction begins on the date of its consummation, except that if the finance charge or any portion of it is earned beginning on a later date, the term begins on a later date." See id. (emphasis added). Thus, the Regulation Z does not permit calculation of the APR based on an interest accrual date which is earlier than the consummation date. By contrast, the previous version of Regulation Z was more flexible, directing only that the "term of the transaction commences on the date of its consummation, except that if the finance charge begins to accrue on any other date, the term of the transaction shall be the date the finance charge begins to accrue." See 12 C.F.R. § 226.40(b)(1) (pre-October 1, 1982 version) (emphasis added). Under the current Regulation Z, however, "accrual dates prior to the date of consummation are apparently prohibited."

In this case, the APR should have been calculated based on a term starting April 13, the consummation date, not April 3, the nominal date of the April 13 agreement. Based on the amount financed, the finance charges and the monthly payment schedule presented in the April 13 RISC, the properly calculated APR, using an accrual date of April 13, was 25.35%. See Pl. Supp. Br. Ex. C. Using the improper accrual date of April 3 led to the disclosed APR of 24.95%. See Pl. Supp. Br. Ex. D. This .4% difference is outside the one-eighth of one percent, or .125% tolerance allowed by the statute, resulting in a violation of TILA. See 15 U.S.C. § 1606(c). Thus, Rucker is entitled to statutory damages for the improper disclosure of the APR on the April 13 RISC.

To be sure, this seems to be no more than a minor technical error. Yet, it is clear that such errors may not be ignored. TILA is a technical statute, and should be strictly enforced. See Mars v. Spartanburg Chrysler Plymouth, Inc., 713 F.2d 65, 67 (4th Cir.1983) (holding that TILA should be "absolutely complied with and strictly enforced," and finding a violation for improper type size and minor variations in required language). Moreover, this technical TILA regulation supports the statute's substantive goals by fostering "meaningful disclosure of credit terms" and "protecting the consumer against inaccurate and unfair credit billing … practices." 15 U.S.C. § 1601(a). Allowing the imposition of interest accrual dates prior to the consummation date undermines the clarity and usefulness of the disclosed information, particularly the APR. Altering the length of the first payment period can have a significant effect on the APR; in this case the interest accrual date ten days prior to the consummation date lowered the disclosed APR by .4%, or almost one half of one percent. The potential for APR manipulation clearly undermines the comparability of APR figures. And, few consumers are aware of the effect that the interest accrual date has on the APR. Moreover, TILA does not require that the interest accrual date be displayed prominently along with other key disclosures, such as the APR itself or the finance charge. See 12 C.F.R. §§ 226.17, 226.18. In this case, the retroactive interest accrual date used by the dealer was arguably signaled by the backdating of the agreement. Yet, the nominal contract date appears only after Rucker's signature at the bottom of the second page, far removed from the prominent TILA disclosures at the top of the first page. Its significance is hardly self-evident. Even if consumers were aware of the sensitivity of the APR to changes in interest accrual dates, they would need to perform complex calculations to gauge the difference between the APR calculated on the nominal date of a backdated agreement versus the actual date of consummation. There is no reason for consumers to bear this burden. The implementing regulations simplify matters by prohibiting earlier accrual dates which would result in understated APRs. This renders the disclosures more comparable and helps to "assure a meaningful disclosure" of the APR. 15 U.S.C. § 1601(a).

The prohibition against the use of interest accrual dates that antedate the consummation of transactions not only provides consumers greater opportunity to shop for better terms, but also furthers the fairness of credit contracts. This ban on retroactive interest obligations ensures that the terms of the transaction are set in stone before the consumer becomes obligated, so that a lender cannot surprise a consumer with higher than expected or suddenly changing rates. This furthers TILA's goal of "protecting the consumer against inaccurate and unfair credit billing ... practices." 15 U.S.C. § 1601(a).

The combination of spot delivery contracts and the industry practice of backdating documents to the original delivery date creates a real potential for abuse. Detractors of spot delivery transactions point out that such transactions allow the following fraudulent "yo-yo" sales strategy: A dealer lures a prospective buyer with a financing deal which is unlikely to win approval. The buyer is then allowed to drive away in the car and consider herself the owner for a period of time, only to be called back in when the financing terms are rejected. Back at the dealership, the buyer is persuaded to sign a second deal, backdated to the original date of delivery, with less favorable financing terms. At this point, the buyer is quite likely to sign the deal, even if she may have balked at the terms as an original matter. Psychologically, the buyer has been given a week to become attached to the car, and is less likely to shop around. The buyer is likely unaware of her right to return the car she thinks she has already bought. Indeed, she may not have been told that the original financing fell through, and she may be misled into thinking that the second deal is a better deal. In these circumstances, a buyer will not wish to return the car and face the embarrassment of having to explain to family and friends that she lost the car because she was not creditworthy. Once the backdated contract is signed, there is no evidence on the face of the controlling legal documents that the terms of the deal which the consumer signed actually changed after she took possession of the car. Some of the elements of a yo-yo sales scheme appear in the present case, except that there is no record evidence here that the dealer set out to mislead the consumer through a yo-yo strategy. In any event, the potential for abuse is obvious in transactions involving a spot delivery and backdating of a RISC.

It is noteworthy, however, that neither TILA nor Regulation Z prohibits spot delivery transactions; absent some independent showing of fraud or misrepresentation spot delivery transactions are not illegal. Nor does the spot delivery in this case run afoul of TILA. Instead, the TILA transgression here results from the backdating of the second RISC and the corresponding use of the earlier date to calculate the APR improperly in violation of TILA's Regulation Z. Sheehy should have properly dated the second RISC, and charged interest beginning on the consummation date. If Sheehy wants to recover payment from the consumer for the use of the car prior to the second agreement, it should explicitly provide for some rent to be paid for this time period in the original conditional contract.

The only question remaining on Rucker's TILA claim is what damages are due to her as a result of the violation. The civil liability provisions of TILA allow plaintiffs to sue for "any actual damage sustained" as a result of defendant's failure to comply with the statute. See 15 U.S.C. § 1640(a)(1). Rucker claims actual damages of $76.22, the amount of extra interest charged during the first payment period because of the additional ten days of interest accrued due to the backdating. Yet, Rucker is not entitled to recover actual damages in this case. This is so because the record indicates that she read none of the documents presented to her in either the April 3 or the April 13 agreement. Therefore, she cannot show that she relied on the disclosures in those documents in any way. There is no evidence that she would have negotiated further or shopped around for better credit terms had the APR been properly presented; thus Rucker cannot show that the APR violation proximately caused her any injury. See Hodges, 180 F.Supp.2d at 792 n. 6 ("To recover actual damages, the plaintiff must show a real loss or injury proximately caused by the defendant's TILA violation. In order to show causation, the plaintiff must show that (1) he read the TILA disclosure statement; (2) he understood the charges being disclosed; (3) had the disclosure statement been accurate, he would have sought a lower price, and (4) he would have obtained a lower price.").

TILA also provides statutory damages for the violation of selected requirements, including the required disclosure of the APR. See 15 U.S.C. § 1640(a)(4) (indicating that statutory damages are available for violations of § 1638(a)(4) (the APR disclosure requirement)). Statutory damages are set at "twice the amount of any finance charge in connection with the transaction," bounded by a statutory minimum of $100 and a statutory maximum of $1,000. Rucker has shown that Sheehy improperly calculated and disclosed the APR, in violation of § 1638(a)(4) and the implementing regulations, and therefore is entitled to statutory damages. The amount financed in the April 13 RISC was $6,672.91. Therefore, Rucker is entitled to the statutory maximum of $1,000.

An appropriate Order has issued.

Case Questions

1. What is the basic transaction involved in this case?
2. What is the unique question presented in this case about calculating APR?
3. How did the terms of the second financing deal differ from the first?
4. According to the court, what is the purpose of TILA?
5. When does "consummation" of a deal occur, according to Regulation Z?

Chapter Summary

The Federal Truth in Lending Act was passed in 1968 in response to widespread abuses and misinformation from creditors. Under TILA, creditors must make specific disclosures to borrowers, including annual percentage rate (APR) and other terms. Regulation Z, which implements TILA, also requires that these disclosures must be made in a specific format and in clear and easy to understand language. TILA makes a distinction between open-ended credit transactions, such as credit cards and closed-end transactions, such as mortgage loans. Under TILA, different disclosures are required depending on which category a transaction falls into. The Federal Trade Commission has the responsibility for enforcing the provisions of TILA.

Web Sites

- U.S. Treasury Department (Overview of TILA)
  http://www.occ.treas.gov/handbook/til.pdf

- Clarke County, Nevada—Explanation of TILA and State Law
  http://clarkcountylegal.com/tila.htm
- Federal Deposit Insurance Corporation—Text of Regulation Z
  http://www.fdic.gov/regulations/laws/rules/6500-1400.html

Key Terms

Regulation Z   Closed-end credit agreement

Open-ended credit   Payment schedule

Annual percentage rate   Security Interest

Balance computation method   Right of rescission

Review Questions

1. When was the Federal Truth in Lending Act created?

2. What is the purpose of TILA?

3. What is the relationship between TILA and Regulation Z?

4. What governmental agency is responsible for enforcing TILA?

5. What four basic conditions must be met before TILA applies to a credit transaction?

6. When must disclosures under TILA be made?

7. What is an open-ended credit transaction?

8. What limitations does Regulation Z attach to credit offers and solicitations?

9. What is an annual percentage rate (APR)?

10. What is a grace period under an open-ended credit arrangement?

11. What is the "balance of computation" method?

12. What remedies does a consumer have for billing errors on credit card statements?

13. What is a closed-end credit transaction?

14. What is a payment schedule under a closed-end credit arrangement?

15. What is a security interest under a closed-end credit transaction?

16. What is the right of rescission? How long does a consumer have to rescind a credit arrangement?

17. What does this chapter's case excerpt say about calculating APR and other time deadlines under TILA?

18. What role does the FTC play in TILA and Regulation Z?

Chapter 7

Predatory Lending & Other Questionable Lending Practices

Chapter Objectives

- Explain predatory lending
- Describe predatory lending practices and methods
- List and describe the effects of questionable lending practices on consumers
- Explain the impact of questionable lending practices on an individual consumer's credit history
- Describe the disadvantages of payday loans, tax refund loans and other short-term lending practices

I. Questionable Lending Practices

In this chapter, we will examine the issues surrounding predatory lending and other questionable lending practices. Throughout history, there have been individuals only too willing to help separate others from their money. We have dealt with fraud in a previous chapter, now it is time to focus on the practices that may not necessarily be illegal, but at least are questionable. They involve not only predatory lending, but also other practices such as payday loans, rent-to-own contracts and tax refund loans. We will examine each of these practices, noting their common features, the problems that they cause for consumers and the overall damage that they do to the American economy.

A. The Housing Market

Many questionable lending schemes are closely tied to the purchase or refinance of real estate. Home purchases have steadily increased in the last 30 years even taking into account the corresponding rise in population. According to the 2000 Census, 66.2% of the housing units in the United States were owned by the residents. That is a vast market for lenders who are in the business of providing residential mortgages and second mortgages. Unfortunately, it is also a powerful temptation for unscrupulous lenders to take advantage of segments of that market for their own gain. We will not discuss the vast majority of the mortgage market lenders who do their best to provide appropriate financing for consumers. Instead, this chapter will focus on the small, but growing percentage of unscrupulous lenders who provide loans to low and middle-income individuals, without regard for their ability to repay the loan, with no regard for the equity that these individuals have built up in their homes and provide fees and services that the consumer neither wants or needs.

II. Predatory Lending

Predatory lending practices cover a wide range of activities, from charging excessive fees on loans to more complex schemes designed to drain away a borrower's equity, while charging exorbitant fees for routine transactions. According to the Department of Housing and Urban Development (HUD), predatory lending practices include any of the following:

- Encouraging borrowers to exaggerate or outright lie about their income, debts, expenses and cash on hand
- Lending more money to borrowers than they actually need, knowing that the borrower lacks the ability to repay it
- Charging higher than average interest rates for factors other than credit history
- Charging fees for unnecessary services or protections
- Charging fees for non-existent services
- High pre-payment penalties
- Stripping equity from homeowners
- Use of high pressure sales tactics to get borrowers to accept loans that will not benefit them

Predatory lending: Using tactics and practices that are not industry standards and that trick or intimidate customers into accepting terms, fees and services that do not benefit them.

> *Getting to the Essentials:*   Predatory lending uses questionable, immoral or illegal methods to get consumers to obtain loans.

A. Encouraging Borrowers to Lie About Their Income and Debts

One common tactic that predatory lenders use is to encourage their customers to lie, or exaggerate, their income. The higher the income, the more money the individual will be able to borrow. This benefits the predatory lender in very specific ways. Because the lender's fees are tied directly to the amount financed, the more debt that the borrower takes on, the higher the fees. Consider Example 7-1.

Example 7-1

Purely Vicious Lenders, Inc. has encouraged David to exaggerate his income from $32,000 to $42,000 per year. Because of this, David is able to borrow more money than he originally sought. Like all of us, David would like to have more money, and when the broker at Purely Vicious Lenders insists that by declaring his income at a higher rate, he'll end up with more money at the conclusion of the transaction, David agrees. However, because the bank charges fees totaling 6% of the loan balance, when David borrows $50,000 instead of $40,000, how much more money does PVL recover?

If David had borrowed $40,000 with fees of 6%, he would have to pay $2400 in fees. However, when he borrows $50,000, his fees equal $3000. The net result is that David walks away from the transaction with $47,000, but he has paid higher fees in order to obtain it.

1. Financing Fees

Another attractive and seemingly painless feature that lenders provide is the financing of the fees along with the principal of the loan. Suppose that David did not pay the $3000 in fees upfront, but, instead, chose to finance them as part of his loan package? In that case, David would be borrowing $53,000 and would pay interest on the fees that were already unnaturally high in the first place.

> *Getting to the Essentials:*   Charging excessive fees is a common tactic among predatory lenders.

B. Charging High Interest Rates

Another common tactic used by predatory lenders is to charge interest rates that are higher than the rates available to traditional lenders. Predatory lenders can justify these higher than average fees because the people who come to them for loans often have spotty credit histories. A credit report showing a history of late payments, bad debt and other negative entries can cause traditional banks and lending institutions to consider the consumer to be too high a risk for their lending programs. However, predatory lenders realize that many of these consumers are desperate and are willing to pay higher interest rates in order to obtain the financing that they require. Of course, higher interest payments result in higher profits for the lender.

Consumers with bad credit are often referred to as "**sub-prime**" borrowers. The term refers to the interest rate that the borrower will be assessed. The more checkered the consumer's credit history, the more likely he or she will be charged an interest rate that is several percentage points higher than the one that a person with excellent credit would receive.

Sub-prime borrower: A borrower with poor credit who only qualifies for higher than average interest loans.

C. Charging High Fees

Another common feature of predatory lending practices is for the lender to charge the borrower high fees to obtain the loan. Many lenders assess points for a loan. Points are specific interest rates that are assessed against a loan as a fee. A point is 1 percent of the total loan. See Example 7-2.

Example 7-2

Maria has applied for a $72,000 loan with two points assessed as a fee. How much is the fee?

Answer: Because points are interest rates, two points equals two percent. Maria's fees would equal 2% of $72,000 or $1440.

When dealing with sub-prime borrowers, it is very common for the lender to assess points against the loan. For borrowers with good credit, points may be negotiable. A borrower with a good credit history might negotiate away the points in order to obtain the loan. Other borrowers might shop around, questioning local lenders about which ones assess points as fees for the loan, and which ones do not. However, with sub-prime borrowers, there is usually little or no room for negotiation. The loan is offered on a "take it or leave it" basis, with the points assessed as originally stated.

Sidebar: In many European companies, points are not used.

There are times when borrowers with excellent credit might prefer a loan with points to a loan without one. A loan with points assessed up front might result in a lower interest rate for the borrower. In the long term, this lower interest rate will mean that more of the monthly payment goes towards paying down principal, instead of interest fees. However, predatory lenders often charge excessive points on their loans, equal to 4, 5 or even 6% of the loan.

Predatory lenders often target low to middle income individuals. Although the fees that they charge must be disclosed, they are easy to bury in the paperwork and disclosures that are now a routine part of any loan transaction. As a result, many individuals do not realize that they are agreeing to these fees, or even that the fees are negotiable. Legitimate lenders often limit their fees and service charges to less than 1% of the loan amount. Predatory lenders, on the other hand, routinely charge up to 5% of the loan amount.

D. Pre-payment Penalties

A pre-payment penalty is a fee assessed against a borrower who pays off a loan before its maturity, or when a borrower pays above the regular monthly amount. You might think that lenders would be happy to receive these extra payments, but they are not. Paying off a loan early cuts down on the interest that the lender will earn over the life of the loan. As a result, many sub-prime lenders impose pre-payment penalties on borrowers. Some lenders justify these pre-payment penalties because of the higher chance that the borrower will refinance the loan at some point. A pre-payment penalty that imposes a 5% fee based on the remaining balance of the loan often keeps borrowers from refinancing. Consider Example 7-3.

Example 7-3

Maria borrowed $85,000 at 12% interest to purchase her home a few years ago. Her loan has a 5% pre-payment penalty. She keeps hearing that the interest rates have declined and wants to refinance the loan. The current balance on her mortgage is $73,400. How much would she have to pay as a pre-payment penalty?

Answer: Multiplying $73,400 by the 5% pre-payment penalty, Maria would pay a fee of $3640 in order to refinance. This fee would be in addition to any other fees that she would pay for the new loan. This fee would probably discourage her from going through with the refinance.

> *Getting to the Essentials:*   Pre-payment penalties discourage borrowers from refinancing loans by imposing a fee on paying off the balance too early.

Among legitimate lenders, only about 2% of home loans carry prepayment penalty clauses. Among predatory lenders, prepayment penalties are the rule rather than the exception. National secondary mortgage purchasers, such as Fannie Mae and Freddie Mac, will no longer purchase loans that contain prepayment penalties where the prepayment penalty remains with the loan for longer than three years. Those institutions changed their policies after realizing that predatory lenders were using prepayment penalties as a way to prevent sub-prime borrowers from negotiating a better loan after a few years.

Pre-payment penalties do play a role in legitimate lending, but only in limited circumstances. Borrowers with excellent credit usually never hear about pre-payment penalties. However, if the borrower negotiates a loan with pre-payment penalties (thus increasing the possibility that the loan will be held longer) the borrower's interest rate charge on the loan could be lower.

E. Stripping Equity

Another side effect of unscrupulous sales tactics is the gradual stripping away of a consumer's accumulated value in his or her home. Equity refers to the difference between the market value of an item and the amount that the borrower owes on it.

Example 7-4

Derrick purchased his home seven years ago. The sale price was $102,000. He was been making regular payments since he bought the home. He now owes $88,000 on his mortgage. A recent appraisal placed the value of Derrick's home at $124,000. How much equity does he have?

Answer: Assuming that Derrick could sell his home for the appraised value of $124,000, then his equity would be the difference between the home's value and what Derrick owes on it.

$124,000
− $88,000
─────────
$36,000

Derrick has $36,000 in equity in his home. He can go to a local lender and borrow against that equity by obtaining a second mortgage on his home.

> *Getting to the Essentials:*   Equity is the difference between what a person owes on property and what it is actually worth.

However, as borrowers pledge their equity as collateral for their loans, they risk stripping away any value in the home. If Derrick borrows against the equity in his home in the example provided above, then Derrick has no equity left. Of course, he won't get the full $36,000 as a loan. The lender will assess fees.

Example 7-5

Suppose that Derrick wishes to borrow against his equity? The secondary mortgage lender he seeks out charges fees that amount to 6% of the loan amount. How much will Derrick have left over, once he completes the transaction?

Answer: Multiply $36,000 by 6%. The answer is $2160. Derrick will get $33,840. That might not seem like a bad bargain, but the actual fees will actually come closer to the example provided in Figure 7-1. Added to the fact that Derrick will pay all of these fees, he will also face foreclosure on his home if he fails to make payments on the new loan. He will also be paying a higher interest rate than the one he pays on his first mortgage.

Example 7-6

Sheila is considering taking out a second mortgage on her home for $15,000. Cut Rate Lenders is only too happy to assist her. CRL will charge an interest rate of 15.68% for a 10-year loan. If she makes every payment, how much will she actually pay out of cost?

Answer: She will pay $29,306, in addition to the fees assessed against her to obtain the loan in the first place.

F. High Pressure Sales Tactics

Another common feature of predatory lenders is the tactics that they use to get borrowers to sign on the bottom line. For instance, lenders might engage in questionable practices, such as mass mailings, touting the good life and how easy it would be to attain by simply obtaining a second mortgage or a loan. They might offer information that is false, such as claims that the Federal Housing Administration (FHA) will prevent a loan from going into foreclosure. The Federal Housing Administration does not issue insurance policies to protect borrowers against loan or title defects. Other tactics include:

- Requesting the borrower to sign blank loan documents, as part of "escrow"
- Loan terms and fee amounts that differ substantially from those provided on the Good Faith Estimate
- Telling borrowers that refinancing can help their credit history

G. Other Predatory Lending Practices

As we have already seen, there are many lending practices that predatory lenders have been using for decades. However, there are some methods that are relatively new and that consumers should be aware of. They include:

- Yield Spread Premiums
- Unreasonable arbitration clauses

Figure 7-1. Indicators of Predatory Lending.

- Excessive fees and surcharges on a loan
- Broker kickbacks
- Prepayment penalties
- Loan churning or loan flipping
- Unnecessary and unneeded loan products
- Unreasonable arbitration clauses

---

1. Yield Spread Premiums

These days, it is common for a borrower to seek the assistance of a mortgage broker to locate the best possible deal on a loan. Brokers not only provide information, but also help with preparing the paperwork, providing services such as appraisals and evaluations of credit reports, among others. Traditionally, a mortgage broker would be compensated for these services by receiving a fee equivalent to 1% of the total loan amount. Brokers might also charge additional fees for some of their services. However, **yield spread premiums** allow the broker to collect even more money, but this time the remuneration is paid by the lender, not the borrower. When the borrower obtains a loan at a higher than average rate, the difference between the average, or par, lending rate and the new rate (the "sub-par") rate is paid to the broker as a fee for using a particular lender. These fees can range into several thousand dollars per transaction.

> **Yield spread premium:** A fee paid to a mortgage broker who arranges for a loan that provides an interest rate above the going rate.

The idea behind yield spread premiums was originally to give the borrower the choice between higher up-front fees and a lower rate, or lower up-front fees and a higher rate. However, the practical application has amounted to a kickback to brokers for negotiating the loan. The practice is questionable, because it creates an appearance of impropriety for a broker who is supposed to be arranging the best possible credit terms for his or her client to receive compensation from a lending institution when the broker recommends a loan with a higher interest rate.

H. Unreasonable Arbitration Clauses

The courts have generally upheld arbitration clauses, as long as they are fully disclosed. Under a mandatory arbitration clause, the borrower agrees not to sue the lender should any dispute arise about the loan. Instead, the borrower agrees to submit to mandatory arbitration, which is an informal hearing to determine the rights and responsibilities of both parties. Some mandatory arbitration clauses also insist the arbitration must occur in the lender's home state, not the state where the loan was given.

> *Getting to the Essentials:*   Arbitration clauses consist of hearings held out of court for disputes between the lender and borrower.

I. Consequences of Predatory Lending

When predatory lenders target poor and minority neighborhoods they can have a devastating impact on the economy. When consumers lose money to fees and surcharges on loans they have less money that they can use for other items. Predatory lenders target areas that are on the fringe of society. Traditionally, obtaining favorable loan treatment in these areas has been difficult because so few lending institutions serve these communities. This leaves the area open to predatory lenders.

In addition to causing more economic hardship, predatory lending practices also contribute to the loss of equity in homes and increase the overall foreclosure rate. This tends to put an area into a downward spiral of urban or suburban blight. While there are drastic effects on the community, there are also important consequences for individual consumers.

Consumers who stay on the debt treadmill eventually find that they cannot meet their debt load and their credit histories begin to suffer. More and more late payments appear on their records, resulting in higher interest rates when they can even qualify for a loan. The higher interest rates and fees contribute to a vicious cycle of debt load that eventually leads to outright default and foreclosure or to bankruptcy.

The most common target for predatory and other unscrupulous lenders are those individuals with poor credit histories. When a consumer refinances an existing loan, predatory lenders include excessive fees and charges that offer no practical benefit to the borrower and only seek to enrich the lender. The problem with predatory lending practices is that until very recently, they were all perfectly legal. There has been a push in recent years on both the state and federal level to outlaw some of these predatory lending practices, but unscrupulous lenders come up with ways of getting around the legislation.

II. Other Questionable Lending Practices

As we will see later in this chapter, many predatory lending practices have been ruled illegal by the passage of both state and federal laws. However, there are some questionable lending practices that remain perfectly legal, but that can still cause hardship for consumers. Unscrupulous lenders often target low-income individuals, the elderly, recent immigrants and others with high interest loans and unnecessary fees. Among the questionable lending practices we will examine in this section are:

- Overdraft loan programs
- Credit Repair Agencies
- Loan churning or loan "flipping"
- Credit Insurance
- Payday loans
- Tax refund loans
- Car title loans
- Rent-to-own
- Balloon payments

A. Overdraft Loan Programs

In the past, banks have always had the option of paying or declining checks when a deposit holder exceeded the balance on the account. However, there is a new approach to overdraft that has caused some controversy. Instead of simply paying or declining the check, banks have created overdraft loan programs. These programs differ from traditional overdraft protection that simply draws funds from another account to pay a check that exceeds the available funds. Under that traditional approach, when a customer repeatedly exceeded the account limits the most common method would be to close the account or advise the customer that overdrafts would no longer be honored. However, some lending institutions have now come up with a third option: charging fees for overdraft protection. When a customer writes a check for more than the available funds, the bank issues a short-term credit to the customer. The credit pays the check, but then acts as a separate loan, with an extremely high interest rate. Many of these programs are designed to generate additional income for the lending institution by increasing the number of overdraft fees by changing the definition of what constitutes overdraft.

Some studies estimate that borrowers are paying more than $10 billion per year in fees for overdraft protection on loans. Many of these overdraft protection accounts are not covered under the Federal Truth in Lending Act. Borrowers can also be enrolled in these accounts without giving informed consent. According to the Federal Deposit Insurance Corporation (FDIC), financial institutions received $38 billion in service charges on overdraft accounts in 2003. That amount of money will continue to attract new and unscrupulous lenders to an already burgeoning market. Some experts in the field estimate that 20% percent of the checking accounts in the United States generate 80% of the overdraft fees.[1]

Despite consumer concerns, overdraft protection accounts continue to grow. The average fees on overdraft loans increased over 30% between 1998 and 2003, according to the Federal Reserve.[2] When a consumer is required to pay high overdraft fees on checking accounts, the end result is a lower monthly balance for the consumer. More and more of the consumer's money ends up in the hands of the lender in the form of assessed fees, leading to correspondingly less money for the consumer. Some institutions include overdraft loans as an automatic feature for checking accounts that are specifically targeted at low and middle-income individuals.

B. Credit Repair

Some companies offer programs to help consumers "fix" bad credit. They offer foolproof methods for making bad entries on a credit history disappear. Of course, they do this service for a price. Credit repair companies sometimes advocate illegal tactics, such as trying to create a new credit history by using a variation of the consumer's Social Security number, or by using guerrilla tactics to remove perfectly true entries on a person's credit history. (One such technique is to repeatedly challenge an entry until the original creditor gives up contesting it). These companies also suggest that consumers take out small loans and pay them back on time, creating positive entries on credit histories. Nat-

---

1. High Cost and Hidden from View: the $10 Billion Overdraft Loan Market, p. 5.
2. Federal Reserve Bulletin, Retail Fees of Depository Institutions, 1997–2001.

urally enough, the companies also offer small term loans at high interest rates that can easily serve that purpose. However, most of these techniques are questionable, if not completely illegal. As we will see in the next chapter, there are methods that a consumer can use to challenge incorrect information on a credit report, but there is no way for a company to "fix" bad credit.

> *Getting to the Essentials:*   There are very few legal methods to "repair" a person's credit history.

C. Loan Churning or "Loan Flipping"

When a lender churns or flips a loan, the lender is replacing one loan with another. The second loan offers no benefit to the consumer, but gives the lender new opportunities to charge fees and surcharges. The fees that are incurred every time a new loan is initiated can quickly eat up the borrower's equity. Lenders may use high-pressure tactics or even misleading information to encourage borrowers to refinance an existing loan before it reaches maturity in order to collect new fees and raise the interest rate.

D. Insurance Schemes

In addition to fees and surcharges, many lenders also offer other products, including insurance programs. These insurance programs promise to compensate the consumer, or to pay the loan balances in the event of an accident, illness, death or firing of a borrower, but many of them have been under scrutiny. Single premium insurance is an excellent example of a questionable credit insurance program. When a borrower applies for a loan, lenders would often suggest purchasing credit insurance as a way of protecting the borrower's credit history. Credit insurance would pay the bills in the event that the borrower is unable to do so. However, after many consumer complaints, mortgage backers such as Freddie Mac, Fannie Mae and Ginnie Mae have all backed away from single premium credit insurance. Their concerns are that there are so many conditions placed on the actual payment of benefits under the program that many consumers never seem to qualify. As a result, Freddie Mac and others have announced policies refusing to deal with lenders that require single premium credit insurance for their loans.

Single premium credit insurance is an insurance policy that is supposed to pay the consumer's scheduled loan payments in the event that the policyholder is injured, ill or otherwise unable to work. There is only a single payment, paid up front and often financed as part of the loan. This effectively makes the premium part of the overall financing and can result in additional interest charges for the lender. (After all, if the interest charges are based on the amount financed, and the premium is added to that amount, then the lender receives more money in fees).

Figure 7-2. Avoiding Loan Fraud.

- Check on information about home prices in the neighborhood. (Some consumers fail to investigate the housing market and end up paying too much for their home.)
- Hire a licensed home inspector.
- Compare lenders, costs and fees assessed. If one lender is offering a lower interest rate, is that lender making up for it by charging "points?"

- Consumers should never borrow more money than they actually need.
- They should not sign blank documents

E. Payday Loans

Payday lending is also referred to as cash advance. In its simplest form, payday lending is the process of allowing a consumer to write a postdated check for the amount of the loan plus fees in exchange for receiving immediate cash. The entire balance of the loan is due on the date indicated on the postdated check. In order to qualify for payday lending, the consumer needs some form of personal identification, a checking account and some form of income. The income does not necessarily have to come from a job. Government benefits, such as workers compensation and Social Security benefits can also qualify.

The downside of payday loans is that they fall between the cracks of the credit regulations in the United States. Payday lenders are permitted to charge triple digit interest rates on short-term loans, with fees as high as 400% APR.

When the customer is unable to repay the loan within two weeks, the lender requires a "rollover" loan that has additional fees and costs. This new loan has additional fees and the consumer eventually finds himself or herself on a never-ending treadmill of debt. The entire loan must be repaid in full at the end of two weeks. There are no installment payments.

Payday lenders make most of their money with repeat business, making loans to the same customers over and over again. Some consumers "rob Peter to pay Paul" by borrowing from one payday lender to repay another. Lenders also encourage consumers to borrow the maximum amount possible, without regard to the consumer's credit history or ability to repay the loan. When the customer is unable to pay the postdated check, he or she faces additional fees and the possibility of criminal charges for writing a bad check. Some estimates put the cost of payday lending at $3.4 billion every year. This is the cost to consumers for the privilege of borrowing against their own paychecks.

F. Tax Refund Loans

Tax refund loans, also known as tax refund anticipation loans, are similar to payday loans. Tax refund loans are usually offered by tax preparers, used-car dealerships and others as a way of extending short-term credit using the taxpayer's anticipated tax refund as collateral for the loan. What seems attractive, the opportunity of borrowing against a refund, often turns into an ugly picture with lenders charging interest rates anywhere from 40% to 400%. According to one study, $1.5 billion that should have gone to taxpayers was diverted to lenders to pay fees on tax refund loans.

G. Car Title Loans

When a consumer has the title to his or her car, it can be used as collateral for a short-term loan. These loans, like payday loans and tax refund loans, fall outside the normal rules and regulations governing lending and usury. Lenders can charge triple digit interest rates for the money that they lend consumers who provide their car titles as collateral. If the consumer defaults on the loan, the lender seizes the automobile.

H. Rent-to-own Contracts

Another common questionable lending practice involves rent-to-own contracts. Under the typical rent-to-own arrangement, an appliance dealer offers to finance the purchase of an appliance, such as a television, refrigerator or piece of furniture. The payments for these items could be as low as $15 per month. That amount of money is very attractive to low and middle-income people who could not afford to pay for the item out right. Consider Example 7-7.

Example 7-7

Mohammed would like to purchase a $250 television set, but doesn't have the money. He goes to a local rent-to-own establishment where the payments to receive a television immediately are $13 per week for 80 weeks. Mohammed signs the rental agreement and takes the television home that same day. How much will he end up paying for the television?

Answer: $13 for 80 weeks is $824. Because the price of the television set is only $250, Mohammed ends up paying more than twice the actual value of the television.

Rent-to-own agreements are often portrayed as leases. They are touted as having several advantages over outright purchasing. For one thing, rent-to-own companies allow a customer to upgrade the appliance to a newer model after a six-month period. However, this arrangement isn't as advantageous as it sounds. After six months, the consumer has paid more than the value of the original item and must surrender possession of it to acquire the newer model. Now the consumer faces new fees and assessments, and will again pay more than the purchase price over the term of the "lease."

As a result of rent-to-own agreements, many consumers find themselves in a downward spiral of debt. They continue to pay exorbitant rates for everyday appliances. Given the situation, one would wonder why any consumer would engage in a rent-to-own agreement. The simple answer is that these consumers are unable to pay for the item outright and are only able to come up with minimal amounts per week to pay for their appliances.

I. Balloon Payments

Another tactic used by questionable lenders is to disguise monthly payments by including a provision for a balloon payment in the lending agreement. A balloon payment is a final payment that can be as large as half of the entire balance, due at some point in the future. When lenders offer terms to consumers, most concentrate on the monthly payments, reasoning that if they can afford the monthly payment, they should be all right in obtaining the loan. However, some fail to notice the balloon payment provision, requiring payment of the entire balance in as little as 24 months. When the consumer cannot make the payment, then the lender defaults the loan and forecloses on the property.

Figure 7-3. Freddie Mac's Policies Against Predatory Lending.

- No longer purchasing sub-prime loans
- Refusing to work with any predatory lenders

- Requiring complete disclosures about fees and terms
- Avoiding single premium credit insurance mortgages

Case Excerpt

An example of predatory lending?

Monetary Funding Group, Inc. v. Pluchino[3]

STEVENS, J.

STATEMENT OF THE CASE

This is an action instituted by the plaintiff, Monetary Funding Group, Inc., against the defendant, John Pluchino, seeking to foreclose on a mortgage held by the plaintiff on defendant's property located at 621 Washington Avenue, Bridgeport, Connecticut. In response to the complaint, the defendant filed eleven special defenses alleging unconscionability, unclean hands, violation of the implied covenant of good faith and fair dealing, and violation of the Connecticut Unfair Trade Practices Act (CUTPA), General Statutes § 42-110a et seq. The one-count counterclaim also alleges a violation of CUTPA. A bench trial was held before the court on March 25, 2003. The parties filed post-trial memoranda and the court makes the following findings.

In the spring of 2000, the defendant needed financing to purchase a convenience store and a laundromat business. Prior to this time, the defendant had owned and operated a gas station and radiator business for more than thirty years, and he had recently converted this business into a restaurant. The defendant testified that when he sought a loan from a commercial bank to purchase the store and laundromat, he was turned down because the bank was not satisfied with the stability of his income from the recently started restaurant business.

The defendant then contacted the plaintiff regarding a loan. The defendant talked with Paul Dwyer, the president of Monetary Funding, and informed Dwyer that he needed $20,000 to purchase the business. On April 13, 2000, the defendant executed a promissory note payable to the plaintiff for $25,000. The note had an interest rate of 15 percent per annum. The terms of the note required that three months of interest be paid in advance. The note fully matured after ninety days, and was secured by a mortgage on the property located at 621 Washington Avenue, Bridgeport, Connecticut.

A disclosure statement prepared by the plaintiff and given to the defendant indicated that from the loan proceeds, the defendant would pay the plaintiff a $3,000 origination fee, a $400 processing fee and $937.50 for three months, prepaid interest. On cross-examination, Dwyer testified that the standard origination fee was between 2 and 6 percent. Dwyer further testified that the $3,000 origination fee, which represented a 15 percent fee, was an "arbitrary" figure chosen for the defendant's loan. The disclosure statement also indicated that the "annual percentage rate" was

---

3. 2003 WL 22133826, (Conn. Super., 2003), 867 A.2d 841.

28 percent. The evidence established that the actual annual percentage rate for this transaction was higher than 28 percent.

As evidenced by the term of the promissory note, the $25,000 loan was extended to the defendant for ninety days, and the parties contemplated that at the end of this period, the loan would be restructured through a refinancing. The evidence conflicts on exactly why the transaction was structured this way. The defendant testified that he was in no rush to receive the loan as he was under no pressure to purchase the business and he only needed to borrow $20,000 for this purchase. At the end of the ninety-day period, his understanding was that the note would be restructured into an installment loan. He also testified that the parties discussed his possible interest in purchasing the building housing the business, but that he would pursue this issue only after purchasing the business and evaluating its progress. Dwyer testified that the parties initially discussed the purchase of the business, as well as the building where it was located, and that a loan of $80,000 was necessary for this purpose. According to Dwyer, only after this initial discussion did the defendant decide to borrow the $20,000.

In any event, the court finds from the evidence that the defendant only sought to borrow $20,000 and that Dwyer indicated to him that the up-front costs for this loan would be between $4,000 and $5,000. At the end of ninety days, the defendant expected that the loan would be restructured into an installment loan, most likely with another lender. The terms, conditions, or costs of this restructured financing were not discussed with or explained to the defendant when the $25,000 note and mortgage were executed.

Dwyer testified that he had no expectation that the defendant would have the financial ability to pay the $25,000 note when it came due on July 18, 2000, the end of the ninety-day term. He expected that the only way the plaintiff would be able to pay the loan at maturity would be through the refinancing.

In or about January 2001, the plaintiff located a lender willing to refinance the loan. When the defendant attended the closing and reviewed the documents for this refinancing, he became aware for the first time that this refinancing involved an $80,000 loan from InterBay. The closing statement provided to the defendant for this loan indicated the following:

Amount of Loan	$80,000.00
Less:	
Monetary Funding group Payoff	$28,678.31
Monetary Funding Group Broker's Fee	4,800.00
Bridgeport Tax Collector	2,776.27
InterBay Loan Origination Fee	1,600.00
InterBay Closing Costs	1,168.17
InterBay Closing Fee	850.00
Title Insurance	310.00
Title Search	267.00
UCC Search	16.00
Eugene D. Micci, Esq.	800.00
Recording Fees	13.00
	$38,721.25

Thus, this closing statement indicated that not only was the plaintiff's loan being paid off, but that the plaintiff was also to receive a broker's fee of $4,800. InterBay was to receive a loan origination fee of $1,600, a closing fee of $850, and unidentified "closing costs" of $1,168.17. Consequently, what was ultimately offered by the plaintiff to the defendant was an $80,000 loan transaction in which the defendant would receive an initial net advance of $20,000, followed by an additional net advance of $38,721.25. In summary, the defendant would receive in hand $58,721.25, and incur a total of $21,278.75 in up-front interest, fees, costs and expenses—$5,000 for the first transaction and $16,278.75 for the second transaction.

The defendant refused to proceed with this refinancing, indicating that he wanted to have an attorney review the papers, but by this time, he was already in default under the terms of the $25,000 note, as this note had fully matured on July 18, 2000. The defendant never executed the documents to refinance the debt through Inter-Bay and did not repay the loan. As a result of the defendant's default on the note, the plaintiff instituted this foreclosure action.

There is no dispute that the plaintiff is in default under the terms of the note and mortgage. The evidence established that $36,380 is due on the note as calculated through March 25, 2003, plus a $1,250 late fee, costs and attorney fees. The gravamen of the parties' dispute over the complaint is whether the defendant has proven any of his special defenses to preclude the enforcement of the mortgage.

DISCUSSION

I

Unclean Hands

Under Connecticut law, the plaintiff's action to foreclose a mortgage is an equitable proceeding. "It is a fundamental principle of equity jurisprudence that for a complainant to show that he is entitled to the benefit of equity he must establish that he comes into court with clean hands ... The clean hands doctrine is applied not for the protection of the parties but for the protection of the court ... It is applied not by way of punishment but on considerations that make for the advancement of right and justice ... The doctrine of unclean bands expresses the principle that where a plaintiff seeks equitable relief, he must show that his conduct has been fair, equitable and honest as to the particular controversy in issue ... Unless the plaintiff's conduct is of such a character as to be condemned and pronounced wrongful by honest and fair-minded people, the doctrine of unclean hands does not apply. The party seeking to invoke the clean hands doctrine to bar equitable relief must show that his opponent engaged in wilful misconduct with regard to the matter in litigation."

The plaintiff relies on lower court cases such as Mechanics & Farmers Savings Bank, FSB v. Delco Development Co., Inc., 43 Conn. Sup. 408, 420, 656 A.2d 1075 (1993), to argue that the doctrine of unclean hands is inapplicable in foreclosure cases. This view has been expressly rejected by appellate court precedent, holding that the unclean hands doctrine may be asserted as a special defense in a foreclosure action.

The defendant's special defenses are set out in an overlapping and redundant manner. In summary, the first, second, third, and fourth special defenses allege that the plaintiff has unclean hands because of the high annual percentage rate, the note's "balloon payment," and the plaintiff's knowledge that the defendant was unable to pay the loan. He further claims that the loan is an example of "predatory lending."

In the ninth special defense, the defendant claims that the plaintiff has unclean hands because it was an "oppressive bargainer." Except for those facts articulated above on which the court bases its conclusion that plaintiff has unclean hands, the court finds that the defendant has failed to prove that the plaintiff was an "oppressive bargainer."

Relying on Patricia E. Obara, "Predatory Lending," 118 Banking L.J. 541 (2001), the plaintiff defines "predatory lending" as: making unaffordable loans based on the assets of the borrower rather than on the borrower's ability to repay an obligation; inducing a borrower to refinance the loan repeatedly in order to charge high points and fees each time the loan is refinanced or flipped; or engaging in fraud or deception to conceal the true nature of the loan obligation or ancillary products from an unsuspecting or unsophisticated borrower. (Defendant's Trial Memorandum, p. 10.)

Based on the following findings, the court agrees with the defendant that the plaintiff has "unclean hands." Although this was a commercial transaction, the defendant was an unsophisticated borrower and unrepresented by counsel. The plaintiff charged an arbitrarily high origination fee and misrepresented the annual percentage rate for the loan. The plaintiff conducted no bona fide evaluation of the defendant's ability to repay the loan and concedes knowing that the defendant did not have the financial ability to comply with the payment terms of the note.

Although the plaintiff knew that a refinancing was necessary in order for the defendant to repay the loan according to its terms, the plaintiff had no discussion with the defendant to evaluate or determine the amount, terms or conditions of this refinancing. In short, there was no basis to evaluate whether this refinancing that the plaintiff believed was necessary for the defendant to repay the $25,000 loan would be financially feasible or economically onerous for the defendant. Furthermore, the defendant only requested to borrow $20,000 and the defendant was misled about the total costs of the transaction ultimately presented to him which involved an $80,000 loan. The court credits the defendant's testimony and finds that the plaintiff never informed him that the total cost for the loan would exceed the $4,000 to $5,000 range estimated by the plaintiff. In particular, the plaintiff did not inform the defendant that the plaintiff would charge a finder's fee for the refinancing, that would be added to the origination and loan processing fees incurred as part of the initial advance.

Moreover, the plaintiff failed to offer any evidence explaining why the transaction was structured so that this refinancing was even necessary. The court also credits the defendant's testimony that time was not of the essence in acquiring the loan, and therefore, there was adequate time to locate a lender to provide a loan with installment terms. The court finds that the reasonable implication from the evidence is that the transaction was structured by the plaintiff for its own benefit in order for it to acquire an origination fee, a loan processing fee, as well as a finder's fee, all of which the plaintiff could not have demanded as part of a single loan transaction.

In response to the plaintiff's arguments, the court does not find the existence of unclean hands solely because the annual percentage rate was high or misstated, or solely because the plaintiff failed to thoroughly investigate the borrower's income or ability to pay. In the instant case, the totality of the circumstances precludes the court from finding that the plaintiff's conduct was "fair, equitable and honest." Under these particular circumstances, where the borrower was unsophisticated, was misled, and was unquestionably unable to comply with the terms of the note, the plaintiff has attempted to take advantage of the debtor in order to charge arbitrarily high fees as part of a transaction structured by the plaintiff precisely for this purpose. The court's enforcement of this loan according to its terms would involve the court in this unfair transaction in a manner that would run afoul of the unclean hands doctrine.

II

Unconscionability

In the first, fifth, seventh and eighth special defenses the defendant claims that relief should not be afforded to the plaintiff because the loan transaction was unconscionable. The defendant alleges that the fees and rate of interest were unreasonably high, the plaintiff knew that the balloon payment could not be paid, and the transaction as a whole was onerous and one-sided. "Unconscionability generally requires a demonstration of an absence of meaningful choice on the part of one of the parties together with contract terms which are unreasonably favorable to the other party." Although the courts generally do not find contracts unconscionable where the parties are business persons, the question of unconscionability must be decided on the particular facts and circumstances of the individual case.

In the eleventh special defense, the defendant alleges unconscionability based on a claim that the plaintiff paid taxes owed on the mortgage property solely in order to reap the benefit of the high interest rate of the note. The defendant offered no evidence to support this claim and has indicated in his post-trial memorandum that this defense is being abandoned.

"There are two elements of unconscionability: unfair surprise and oppression. The element of unfair surprise has frequently been termed ... as 'procedural unconscionability' and is implicated by bargaining improprieties in the contract formation process. The element of oppression has been termed 'substantive unconscionability' and is implicated by overly harsh contract terms. The basic test is whether, in light of the general commercial background and the commercial needs of the particular trade or case, the clauses involved are so one-sided as to be unconscionable under the circumstances existing at the time of the making of the contract."

Similar to the previous discussion regarding unjust enrichment, although this was a commercial loan, the evidence nevertheless establishes that the transaction as a whole was unconscionable. The up-front fees were arbitrarily high and the design of the transaction was unreasonably favorable to the plaintiff thus evidencing substantive unconscionability. The defendant believed that he was involved in a $25,000 loan transaction that would be transformed into an installment loan in order for the debt to be repaid. However, the refinancing package presented to him did not involve a simple change of the $25,000 debt into an installment loan. As previously stated, the defendant was misled into a transaction in which he would receive a net advance of $58,721.25 after paying up-front costs totaling $21,278.75.

This transaction involves "unfair surprise" and implicates "bargaining improprieties in the contract formation process" because when the note matured and the defendant needed the means to repay the loan as expressly contemplated by the parties, he was presented with a refinancing that involved a loan amount and closing fees that were high, unexplained and unanticipated. He could either accept the refinancing terms as presented or be exposed to the consequences of the existing default. Such a circumstance involves a restriction of meaningful choice that is characteristic of procedural unconscionability as described in the case law.

In summary, the court relies on the following findings to conclude that the circumstances as a whole establish that the transaction was unconscionable: the defendant was unsophisticated and unrepresented by legal counsel; he was financially unable to comply with the terms of the $25,000 note and this fact was known by the plaintiff when the loan was extended; he was misled about the total, up-front expenses of the transaction, believing that they would be between the $4,000 and $5,000 estimate as represented by the plaintiff; he was not informed until the second closing that the loan amount would increase from $25,000 to $80,000; and he was not informed about the additional fees and expenses associated with the refinancing until he attended this closing. The transaction was unreasonably designed to benefit the plaintiff and created an absence of meaningful choice on the part of the defendant.

The court is mindful that because of the consequences of such findings, findings of unjust enrichment and unconscionability should be carefully made and reserved for only those cases where the facts fully warrant. Moreover, as is typical in such cases, the court cannot say that the defendant is entirely "blameless" because he has received a loan which he has failed to repay. Nevertheless, in the context of this case, Justice Berdon's quote is particularly applicable here: "It does not seem too much to say that one who voluntarily extends credit by disregarding a known risk, or risks which could be discovered by a reasonable effort, should bear the loss when loss occurs."

On the basis of the court's findings that the plaintiff acted with unclean hands and engaged in an unconscionable transaction, the court further concludes that the plaintiff's conduct was unfair, oppressive and unscrupulous in violation of CUTPA. In light of the court's disposition of the special defenses, the only damages sought by the defendant for the plaintiff's CUTPA violation are attorney fees. Based on the evidence, a review of the file, and the defendant's affidavits of attorney fees, the court applies a $150 hourly rate and awards to the defendant attorney fees of $6,750, the court finding this amount reasonable under the circumstances.

CONCLUSION

Therefore, for the foregoing reasons, the court enters judgment in favor of the defendant, John Pluchino and against the plaintiff, Monetary Funding Group, Inc., on the complaint and counterclaim. On the counterclaim, the court awards the defendant $6,750, plus costs.

Case Questions

1. What were the defenses raised by the defendant, John Pluchino, in this case?
2. What was the actual APR on the loan?
3. What is the doctrine of "unclean hands"?
4. How does the court define "predatory lending"?
5. What rationale does the court offer to find that the lender was unconscionable?

Chapter Summary

Predatory lending consists of the use of aggressive sales tactics, the assessment of unnecessary fees and surcharges all in an attempt to gouge the consumer for as much profit as the unscrupulous lender can pull in. Predatory lenders generally target low to middle income individuals who often have blemished credit histories. The effect of predatory lending is that money that would ordinarily find its way into the consumer's pocket is drained away as profit for the lender. Predatory lending schemes often result in the gradual draining away of the consumer's equity in his or her home as well as frequent foreclosures. Other questionable lending practices include payday lending, tax refund loans and rent-to-own schemes. These questionable lending practices assess high interest rates for short-term loans and that results in the consumer spending a great deal more than he or she should have.

Web Sites

- Freddie Mac
  http://www.freddiemac.com
- Center for Responsible Lending
  http://www.responsiblelending.org/
- HUD—Don't be a victim of loan fraud
  http://www.hud.gov/offices/hsg/sfh/buying/loanfraud.cfm
- Government Accounting Office—Challenges Presented by Predatory Lending
  http://www.gao.gov/new.items/d04280.pdf

Key Terms

Predatory lending

Sub-prime borrower

Yield spread premium

Review Questions

1. What is predatory lending?
2. What are some of the methods that predatory lenders use to attract borrowers
3. What are the consequences of predatory lending for the consumer and for the U.S. economy?
4. What disadvantages do overdraft loan programs offer to consumers?

5. What are payday loans and how do they work?

6. Why can payday loans charge much higher interest rates than conventional loans?

7. Explain tax refund loans.

8. What are rent-to-own contracts?

9. What are car title loans?

10. What is an unconscionable contract?

11. What stance have national secondary mortgage market providers, such as Freddie Mac, taken against predatory lenders?

12. What are some methods that consumers can use to avoid loan fraud?

13. What are prepayment penalties?

14. What are the loan payments?

15. What groups are commonly the targets of predatory lenders?

16. In the last few years, there has been a world-wide financial crisis. What information can you locate to explain how this crisis was created?

Chapter 8

Fair Credit Reporting

Chapter Objectives

- Explain the importance of credit reports
- Describe the reasons for the creation of the Fair Credit Reporting Act
- List and explain the provisions under FCRA improving accuracy of credit reports
- Describe who can be provided with a copy of the consumer's credit report
- Explain how a consumer can dispute information on a credit report

I. Introduction

Credit is the real currency of our economy. Those with good credit enjoy opportunities to borrow money, obtain credit cards, loans, personal items, mortgages and many of the material goods that we associate with the "good life." On the other hand, individuals with bad credit histories find that they have few, if any, opportunities to obtain those same items. Credit histories have become even more important in recent years, with credit scores determining not only interest rates on credit cards, but also insurance rates and many other hidden factors.

A. Importance of Good Credit

No one who has ever applied for a mortgage or a car loan would doubt the importance of a good credit history. Lenders of all kinds evaluate credit reports in order to determine if a particular consumer is a risk for nonpayment of a loan. Lenders have learned, over the decades, that individuals with a history of late payments or other bad debts are far more likely to default on future loans than individuals who have consistently paid their bills on time and have no bad debts at all. In earlier times, when consumers and lenders might have actually lived in the same community and individuals might even know each other, poor credit history might not have been such a problem. When there were personal relationships between consumers and lenders, even individuals with poor credit would still attempt to avoid default on their loans. But, in modern times, the chances that a consumer might actually know someone who works for a loan company or a bank, or even that they might be located in the same state, are extremely small. As a result, lenders have come to rely more and more on credit reports as a way of evaluating risk.

> *Getting to the Essentials:*   Good credit is absolutely essential to obtaining credit
> cards, car loans and mortgages.

B. Calculating a Credit Score

A **credit score** is calculated based on a consumer's credit history. These days, a credit history boils down to a single number. Equifax, for instance, refers to this number as a "Beacon" score. This score helps lenders by simplifying the credit evaluation process and giving them a clear indication as to whether or not they should loan money to a particular consumer.

> **Credit score:** A score compiled by a consumer reporting agency, based on positive and negative information in a credit report.

The credit score can range from 300 to 900. Generally, the lower the number, the greater the risk to the lender. There are many different scoring methods used by the major and minor consumer reporting agencies, but many of them are based in whole or in part on the Fair Isaac Corporation system, also known as FICO. The Fair Isaac Corporation is an independent firm that develops software used by lenders, banks and other stations to help automate credit reviews to make them faster to evaluate and less subjective.

The calculations involved in coming up with a credit score vary depending on the credit reporting agency, but most of them follow a similar format. The exact method used to calculate credit scores is considered proprietary information by the major credit reporting agencies, so it is virtually impossible to get the formula used. However, there are some features about the credit score that are widely known. For instance, approximately 30% to 40% of the credit score is based on an individual consumer's payment history. An individual with a long history of late payments will have a lower score, while an individual with few or no late payments scores higher in this category. Approximately 30% of the credit score is based on outstanding debt or debt-equity ratio. Here the scoring is based on the extent of debts held by the consumer. The more money that a consumer owes on mortgages and car loans, the lower the overall score. 10% to 15% of the credit score is based on the length of time that a consumer has had a credit history. The shorter the history, the lower the score. 5% to 15% of the credit score is based on the number of inquiries made by potential lenders. Generally speaking, numerous inquiries indicate a person is applying for credit. However, there could be other reasons for credit inquiries, which is why the percentage for this particular category is so low. Approximately 10% of the credit score is based on the number of credit accounts the consumer has. The idea here is that someone with more credit cards might intentionally max them out in a financial crisis and thus incur a great amount of debt. Other factors that go into calculating a credit score include unpaid, outstanding debts, tax liens, bankruptcies and civil judgments. How each of these entries factors into the ultimate credit score varies depending on the credit reporting agency. Individuals with low credit scores may not qualify for credit at all, or, if they do, they can only obtain it at high interest rates. On the other hand, consumers with high credit scores generally qualify for the best deals from all types of creditors.

Lenders can also review individual credit reports to get a better idea about a particular consumer's payment history, bad debts and other negative entries. They can also see any positive entries on the report that might mitigate any of the bad information.

> *Getting to the Essentials:*   Most credit reporting agencies issue a credit score that provides a shorthand references for a consumer's credit history.

C. Credit Reports

Throughout this chapter, we will use the terms "**consumer report**" and "credit report" interchangeably. The Fair Credit Reporting Act uses the term "consumer report" to refer to a report that evaluates an individual consumer's credit history. However, most other sources call this a credit report. For the purposes of clarity, we will use the term credit report throughout this text, except where it appears in excerpts from the Fair Credit Reporting Act.

Consumer report: Also known as a credit report; it lists a consumer's prior credit transactions, including charge accounts, loans and other financial data.

II. Fair Credit Reporting Act

Like other federal actions, the Fair Credit Reporting Act 15 U.S.C.A. § 1681, was created in response to consumer complaints about the way that credit histories were maintained and the information disseminated to businesses and others. As part of the enabling legislation, the U.S. Congress made specific findings, including:

- Inaccurate reports hurt both the banking system and public confidence
- An elaborate system had developed over time for investigating and evaluating credit worthiness
- Credit reporting agencies have come to play a vital role in the American economy, and
- These credit reporting agencies must carry out their duties in a way that guarantees fairness and accuracy

> *Getting to the Essentials:*   The Fair Credit Reporting Act was created to provide guidelines evaluating and releasing consumer credit histories.

A. Consumer Reports under FCRA

The Fair Credit Reporting Act places strict limitations on the preparation and dissemination of credit reports. Before we can discuss those limitations, we must first address what types of transactions are not covered under FCRA.

1. Exclusions under FCRA

As far as FCRA is concerned, consumer reports (credit reports) only apply in specific situations. When individuals deal with one another on a non-business footing, this is not a transaction that falls under the jurisdiction of the Fair Credit Reporting Act. FCRA also does not classify a consumer report as any report that simply focuses on a series of transactions between the consumer and a particular creditor. It also exempts communications between creditors and consumers.

The Fair Credit Reporting Act focuses on the consumer's credit transactions with a series of creditors and makes reports based on payment history, outstanding balances, unpaid balances and any other relevant information.

Example 8-1

Maria and John entered into an agreement last year for John to purchase Maria's car. John agreed to pay $150 every month for 12 months. On the last payment, Maria would sign over the title to John. Is this a transaction that will appear on John's credit report?

Answer: No. Credit reports do not record private agreements, only those involving consumers and companies.

2. Investigative Consumer Report

FCRA also includes provisions for "investigative consumer reports." An investigative consumer report refers to any report that focuses on the consumer's character, general reputation or personal characteristics. They include background investigation, interrogations of friends and coworkers and are not what we normally would refer to as a "credit report." As long as these reports do not contain credit information, they do not fall under the jurisdiction of FCRA. No form of credit report is permitted to release a consumer's medical information, whether as a part of a standard credit report or in the context of an investigative consumer report.

3. Consumer Reporting Agencies under FCRA

Under the Fair Credit Reporting Act, a **consumer reporting agency** refers to any person or company that, for a fee, assembles and evaluates consumer credit information and provides it to third parties.

Consumer reporting agency: An agency that compiles data on individual consumers and issues credit histories on demand.

B. The Major Credit Reporting Agencies in the United States

In the United States, there are three major consumer reporting agencies, as well as dozens of regional reporting agencies. The "big three" consist of:

- Equifax
- TransUnion
- Experian

1. *Equifax*

Equifax has been in the credit reporting business for decades. Originally founded in 1899, the company has become one of the leaders in providing data on consumers, businesses and industries. It employs over 5000 people scattered across 13 countries and has annual revenues of $2 billion.

2. *TransUnion*

TransUnion originally came into existence as a railcar leasing operation, working with railroad carriers. It eventually expanded into business data and now is one of the three top players in the United States. TransUnion was one of the first credit reporting agencies to provide online access to credit reports. It operates through 250 credit bureaus in major metropolitan areas in every state. It also has offices on five continents.

3. *Experian*

Experian employs more than 4500 people in America and has annual sales revenue of $1.3 billion. It maintains credit information on over 215 million United States consumers.

> ***Getting to the Essentials:*** There are three major agencies United States: Equifax, TransUnion and Experian, as well as numerous smaller reporting agencies scattered across the country.

III. Purposes of Credit Reports Under FCRA

One of the primary purposes for creating the Fair Credit Reporting Act was to limit the organizations that could receive a copy of a consumer's credit report. All credit reports contain sensitive information, and in the days of identity theft, a credit report has everything a potential criminal needs to use another person's accounts. But credit reports also contain information that can be potentially embarrassing to consumers, from outstanding debts to bankruptcies. As a result, FCRA imposes strict limitations on who can receive a copy of a particular consumer's credit report.

A. Furnishing Credit Reports to Others

Part of the income that credit reporting agencies derive comes from charging fees to companies and organizations that want to see a particular person's credit history. Because the credit reporting agencies have a vested interest in making these reports available to as many people as possible, and thus generate more fees, FCRA imposes strict limitations on who is allowed to request a consumer's credit report. These individuals and organizations include:

- Courts
- Creditors

- Employers
- Governmental agencies
- Companies who wish to evaluate a consumer for an offer of credit

1. Courts

Judges have the power to order a copy of an individual consumer's credit report in certain circumstances. For instance, the issue of a person's ability to pay alimony, child support and other court-ordered fees can often be answered by resorting to a copy of the person's credit report. Courts are not allowed to review a person's credit report under any circumstances. Instead, they are limited to issues surrounding a person's ability to pay judgments and other assessments. Although in common legal practice, this method is seldom used by judges.

Example 8-2

Carlos has filed suit against Miranda, alleging that she was negligent when she failed to stop for a red light and smashed her car into his. He'd like to know if Miranda has any assets that might satisfy a judgment, should he win the case. Can Carlos obtain a copy of Miranda's credit report?

Answer: No. Although there is a lawsuit involved, the parties are not permitted to order copies of their opponent's credit histories. Only judges may do that, and only in very limited circumstances, such as child support or divorce cases.

2. Creditors

Potential creditors have the right to review a consumer's report as a condition of extending credit or offering loans. If a company plans on offering credit, then the consumer expressly authorizes the creditor to review his or her credit report as a condition of applying for the loan.

> *Getting to the Essentials:*   In most situations, a consumer must give consent before a credit report can be released.

Figure 8-1. Permissible Purposes of Consumer Reports.

A creditor may review a credit report when it:

"(A) intends to use the information in connection with a credit transaction involving the consumer on whom the information is to be furnished and involving the extension of credit to, or review or collection of an account of, the consumer."[1]

---

3. Employers

Employers can make review of an applicant's credit report a condition of employment. In such a situation, the employer must obtain the applicant's consent to review the credit report. Employers are not permitted to simply pull up the credit reports of all of their employees. (For an example of employer and credit reports, see this chapter's case excerpt).

---

1. 15 U.S.C. § 1681b.

Figure 8-2. Disclosing Credit Reports to Employers.[2]

(A) In general. Except as provided in subparagraph (B), a person may not procure a consumer report, or cause a consumer report to be procured, for employment purposes with respect to any consumer, unless—

(i) a clear and conspicuous disclosure has been made in writing to the consumer at any time before the report is procured or caused to be procured, in a document that consists solely of the disclosure, that a consumer report may be obtained for employment purposes; and

(ii) the consumer has authorized in writing (which authorization may be made on the document referred to in clause (i)) the procurement of the report by that person.

Example 8-3

Mario has worked for ABC Interiors, Inc., for five years. Recently, Mario's supervisor has noticed that Mario seems distracted and nervous. He has also been getting a lot of telephone calls on the job. Although there is no policy about receiving personal telephone calls, Mario's supervisor is worried that Mario's financial problems have begun affecting his job. The company is worried that if Mario files for bankruptcy, or has some other legal action filed against him, he may quit. When Mario first joined the company, he signed a typical employment contract. Can the company order a copy of Mario's credit history in order to determine the current state of his financial affairs?

Answer: No. The company could only obtain a copy of Mario's credit history if it obtained Mario's permission or made it a condition of employment when he was first hired. Typical employment contracts do not contain provisions waiving the employee's rights to privacy.

4. Governmental Agencies

In certain situations, governmental agencies are permitted to review credit reports. For instance, child support enforcement agencies are allowed to order copies of credit reports to evaluate a parent's ability to pay child support payments.[3] This also applies to the Social Security Administration and other state-supported agencies to help them set up awards or to investigate a consumer's past income. Agencies that issue licenses to applicants, such as alcohol permits, also have the right to request a copy of the consumer's credit report as a condition of receiving special licensure or permissions.

a. Law Enforcement

In cases involving investigations of crime involving national security issues, U.S. governmental agencies can review a consumer's credit report and these agencies are under no obligation to reveal that fact to the consumer if there is a chance that the notification would result in

- Endangerment to the life or security of a person
- Cause the consumer to flee the jurisdiction
- Result in the destruction of evidence

---

2. 15 U.S.C. § 1681.
3. § 1681b(4).

- Result in intimidation of witnesses
- Jeopardize or delay an investigation

5. Companies That Issue Offers of Credit or Insurance

In certain situations, a company can review a consumer's credit report without the consumer's permission. A company can review a credit report when it intends to make an offer of credit or insurance coverage to a consumer. These are the offers many of us receive in the mail, sometimes on a daily basis. Letters offering credit cards at favorable terms, including "pre-approval" almost invariably involve a company which has reviewed hundreds, if not thousands of accounts, for consumers who fit their profile. When companies request this information, they may only receive:

- The consumer's name and address
- An identification number that helps to identify the consumer later
- Any other information that is not specific to previous accounts

---

Figure 8-3. Reviewing Credit Reports without the Consumer's Permission.[4]

(B) (i) the transaction consists of a firm offer of credit or insurance;

(ii) the consumer reporting agency has complied with subsection (e); and

(iii) there is not in effect an election by the consumer, made in accordance with subsection (e), to have the consumer's name and address excluded from lists of names provided by the agency pursuant to this paragraph.

(2) Limits on information received under paragraph (1)(B). A person may receive pursuant to paragraph (1)(B) only

(A) the name and address of a consumer;

(B) an identifier that is not unique to the consumer and that is used by the person solely for the purpose of verifying the identity of the consumer; and

(C) other information pertaining to a consumer that does not identify the relationship or experience of the consumer with respect to a particular creditor or other entity.

---

a. Opt Out Provisions

Under FCRA, consumers are permitted to file requests that their names not be released to companies sending out blanket offers of credit or insurance coverage. Similar to the National Do Not Call Registry, when a consumer files the appropriate form with consumer reporting agencies, his or her name cannot be released to companies advertising special deals.

B. Consumer Disclosures

When a consumer's credit report is requested, consumer reporting agencies must notify the consumer, unless the request falls into one of the exceptions set out above. Employers who request credit reports as a condition of employment must do so in clear and

---

4. 15 U.S.C. § 1681.

conspicuous language. In fact, disclosures are the rule when it comes to the various ways that credit reports can be used. Even credit reporting agencies must make disclosures to consumers.

1. Inquiries

The first, and most obvious, form of disclosure is revealing to the consumer when a company has requested a copy of the consumer's credit report.

2. Denials of Credit

The second type of disclosure comes when the consumer applies for credit or a loan and is denied because of information contained in the credit report. In that event, the consumer is entitled to receive a free copy of the report. In addition to a copy of the report, a consumer also has the right to request disclosure of the information in his or her file.

C. Disclosing File Contents to Consumers

Under the Fair Credit Reporting Act, a consumer has the right to all information contained in his or her file, except the actual credit scores or "risk predictors" which involve propriety calculations on the part of the individual consumer reporting agencies.

The consumer can request identification on the sources of the information used to prepare the report, including the name of each person or company that requested a copy of the credit report.[5] Consumers can also request information on dates, original payees and amounts of any checks resulting in adverse notices in their credit report and a record of all credit inquiries by others.

When the consumer reporting agency provides this information, it must also include a summary of the consumer's rights under FCRA.

1. Summary of Consumer Rights

When credit reporting agencies provide information to consumers, they must also include a summary of their rights in connection with the Fair Credit Reporting Act. These rights include:

- A brief description of FCRA
- An explanation of how the consumer can exercise his or her rights under FCRA
- A list of all federal agencies responsible for enforcing FCRA
- A statement that the consumer may have additional rights under state law
- A statement that the credit reporting agency is not required to remove accurate information from a credit report, even if it is damaging to the consumer
- Toll free telephone numbers, with personnel accessible during regular business hours who can answer consumer questions
- Information about disputing information on credit reports

---

5. 15 U.S.C.A. § 1681g.

D. Disputing Credit Report Entries

When a consumer believes that there is inaccurate information on his or her credit report, the consumer has the right to **dispute** the entry. The consumer reporting agency must provide a form that allows consumers to dispute information contained in the credit report. Once a dispute is filed, the agency must respond by conducting an investigation into the claims raised by the consumer. The agency is not allowed to charge the consumer to conduct the investigation.

Dispute: A consumer's challenge of information contained in a credit report.

Figure 8-4. Procedure in Case of Disputed Accuracy.

(a) Reinvestigations of disputed information.

(1) Reinvestigation required.

(A) In general. If the completeness or accuracy of any item of information contained in a consumer's file at a consumer reporting agency is disputed by the consumer and the consumer notifies the agency directly of such dispute, the agency shall reinvestigate free of charge and record the current status of the disputed information, or delete the item from the file in accordance with paragraph (5), before the end of the 30-day period beginning on the date on which the agency receives the notice of the dispute from the consumer.[6]

If the agency is unable to verify the accuracy of the information that forms the basis of the consumer's dispute, then it must remove the disputed item from the credit report.

Figure 8-5. Significance of Consumer Dispute on Credit Report.

Once the consumer files a dispute, the credit reporting agency must:

- Reinvestigate the report free of charge
- Within 30 days of consumer's dispute:
  - Re-verify information as accurate or
  - Delete the contested item

Getting to the Essentials: Consumers have the right to dispute what they believe to be inaccurate information on their credit reports.

Example 8-4

Maria recently received a copy of her credit report and noticed an entry of "bad debt" on an account that she knows was paid in full. She disputes the entry on March 30. On May 1, the credit company reports that it is still investigating the dispute and refuses to remove the entry, stating that 30 business days have not elapsed since she filed her dispute. Is Maria legally entitled to have the entry removed?

Answer: Yes. More than 30 days have passed since she disputed the entry. There is no provision stating that the time must exclude weekends or holidays. Therefore, she is entitled to have the entry removed.

---

6. 15 U.S.C.A. § 1681i.

1. Frivolous or Irrelevant Disputes

In recent years, some individuals and "credit repair" companies have attempted to use the provisions of FCRA to remove accurate, but negative, information from credit reports. The scheme works like this: the consumer has negative entries on his or her credit report that are legitimate. However, these legitimate entries are causing the consumer to have a low credit score. The consumer disputes this accurate information numerous times, hoping that at some point, the credit reporting agency, or the original company, will grow tried of responding to these frivolous claims. When either fails to respond within the 30 day period mandated under FCRA, then the item must be removed from the consumer's credit report. However, the Fair Credit Reporting Act has addressed this technique by creating an exception for frivolous or irrelevant disputes.

Under the provisions of 15 U.S.C.A. § 1681i, a credit reporting agency may terminate any reinvestigation of a disputed item if it determines that the dispute is frivolous or irrelevant. Grounds for making this determination include repeated disputes of accurate information or the failure of the consumer to provide sufficient information to investigate the dispute in the first place.

2. Notice of Reinvestigation

When a reinvestigation is initiated, the consumer must receive a written report of the investigation of the disputed item, including the:

- Results of the reinvestigation
- Reasons for agency's determination that the disputed item is accurate
- Basis of the information used to investigate the disputed item
- Consideration of the consumer information received about the disputed item

3. Statement of Dispute

If the consumer disagrees with the results of the investigation into the disputed item, he or she may file a brief statement about the item that must be included with the negative entry on the credit report. The statements are limited to no more than 100 words. Consumers can use this provision to explain unusual aspects of a particular item or explain important facts about the entry.

4. Deleting Contested Information

If the credit reporting agency discovers that reported information is inaccurate, or that it cannot be verified, it must notify the consumer that the disputed information will be deleted from the consumer's credit report. Future credit reports cannot contain the information.

E. Items That May Not be Reported in Credit Reports

The Fair Credit Reporting Act also has specific provisions for items that cannot appear in credit reports or that must be removed after the passage of time. Medical information cannot appear in a credit report. Among the items that must be deleted over time are:

- Bankruptcy cases more than 10 years old
- Civil suits or judgments more than 7 years old
- Paid tax liens more than 7 years old
- Accounts placed for collection more than 7 years old
- Any adverse information more than 7 years old. Section 605.[7]

Some information may remain on a credit report forever, including records of criminal convictions.

F. Ensuring Accuracy of Credit Reports under FCRA

15 U.S.C. § 1681e of the Fair Credit Reporting Act, requires that consumer reporting agencies must take steps to ensure the accuracy of the reports that they prepare. These procedures include the requirement that the agencies take reasonable steps to verify the identity and purpose of the companies requesting copies of credit reports. The companies take precautions to confirm that credit report requests are not being used to carry out illegal purposes, such as identity theft or credit card fraud. They must also demonstrate internal policies designed to show that their reports are based on accurate information.

G. Obtaining Copies of Credit Reports

When a consumer wishes to obtain a copy of his or her credit report, the credit reporting agency is permitted to charge the consumer for the copy. New legislation gives every consumer the opportunity to obtain one free copy of a credit report each year. If a consumer wants additional copies, he or she must pay for them. The Fair Credit Reporting Act limits the charges for the reports to $8 per report.[8]

1. Free Reports

A consumer is now entitled to receive one free copy of his or her credit report each year. Consumers who have been denied credit based on a credit report are also entitled to receive a free copy of their credit reports.

IV. Enforcing the Provisions of FCRA

When a credit reporting agency violates the provisions of the Fair Credit Reporting Act, there are two different ways to sanction them. The first involves filing a complaint

---

7. 15 U.S.C.A. § 1681c.
8. 15 U.S.C.A. § 1681j.

with the Federal Trade Commission; the second involves bringing a civil suit against the credit reporting agency or other offending party.

A. Administrative Enforcement

The Federal Trade Commission has the authority to investigate and bring civil sanctions against any company that violates the provisions of the Fair Credit Reporting Act. The FTC has the power to fine offending companies or take any of a number of other actions to ensure that companies cease and desist from unlawful practices under FCRA.

Figure 8-6. Administrative Enforcement of FCRA.

Compliance with the requirements imposed under this title shall be enforced under the Federal Trade Commission Act (15 U.S.C. §§ 41 et seq.) by the Federal Trade Commission with respect to consumer reporting agencies.[9]

B. Civil Suits by Consumers

Like many other consumer protection statutes, FCRA also provides a second avenue of approach in situations where companies engage in unlawful practices. Consumers are authorized to bring civil suits against companies. These suits are identical to any other type of civil suit, except that the consumer has specific limitations on the types of damages that he or she can request. Under FCRA, consumers are limited to actual, or out of pocket losses, plus additional damages, ranging $100 to $1000 per violation. See Figure 8-7. We will discuss consumer civil actions in greater detail in Chapter 10.

> *Getting to the Essentials:*   There are two methods of enforcing the Fair Credit Reporting Act: administrative action and individual civil suits.

Figure 8-7. Civil Liability for Willful Noncompliance with FCRA.

(a) In general. Any person who willfully fails to comply with any requirement imposed under this title with respect to any consumer is liable to that consumer in an amount equal to the sum of

(1)(A) any actual damages sustained by the consumer as a result of the failure or damages of not less than $100 and not more than $1,000; or

(B) in the case of liability of a natural person for obtaining a consumer report under false pretenses or knowingly without a permissible purpose, actual damages sustained by the consumer as a result of the failure or $1,000, whichever is greater;

(2) such amount of punitive damages as the court may allow[10]

Figure 8-8. Jurisdiction of Courts for Violations of FCRA.

An action to enforce any liability created under this title may be brought in any appropriate United States district court without regard to the amount in controversy, or in any other court

---

9. 15 U.S.C. § 1681s.
10. 15 U.S.C.A. § 1681n.

of competent jurisdiction, within two years from the date on which the liability arises, except that where a defendant has materially and willfully misrepresented any information required under this title to be disclosed to an individual and the information so misrepresented is material to the establishment of the defendant's liability to that individual under this title, the action may be brought at any time within two years after discovery by the individual of the misrepresentation.[11]

Case Excerpt

Is it a violation of FCRA for a prospective employer to review an applicant's credit history without telling him it is a condition of employment?

Comeaux v. Brown & Williamson Tobacco Co., 915 F.2d 1264 (C.A.9 (Cal.),1990)

Before SNEED, FARRIS and FERNANDEZ, Circuit Judges.

SNEED, Circuit Judge:

Karon Comeaux (Comeaux) filed suit against Brown & Williamson Tobacco Corporation (B & W), alleging that B & W had reneged upon its promise of employment to Comeaux. He asserted six causes of action arising out of B & W's failure to employ him and three causes of action arising out of a credit check B & W performed during the course of the litigation. He appeals the district court's grant of summary judgment in favor of B & W. We affirm in part and reverse and remand in part.

I. FACTS AND PROCEEDINGS BELOW

In July 1987, plaintiff-appellant Comeaux applied for a position as a sales representative with defendant-appellee B & W. He alleges that after several interviews with B & W, the company's hiring manager told him orally that he was hired: "We are making you an offer.... Mr. Watratz ... gave me the okay to go ahead and hire you, but you have to take a physical and we have to wait on the rest of the paperwork to come down." Comeaux asserts that the hiring manager stated that the offer of employment was contingent upon his moving "within five minutes of his first sales stop in Fremont 'as soon as possible.'" In addition, his start date was to be around August 18 and he was to give his then-current employer one week's notice.

Comeaux passed the physical examination, gave notice to his then-current employer, moved with his new wife from San Jose to Fremont, and stood ready to report for work on August 18. On August 18, a B & W manager named Littleton called Comeaux. Littleton said that Comeaux's start date would be delayed, but that there were no problems with Comeaux's employment status.

B & W ran a credit check on Comeaux on August 19, 1987. It does not dispute that it never informed Comeaux that a credit check would be performed and that the findings of the report could affect Comeaux's employment with the company. Furthermore, B & W does not dispute that it violated its own internal policy by failing to inform Comeaux about the credit check and its role in B & W's employment decisions.

---

11. 15 U.S.C. § 1681p.

The credit report revealed that Comeaux had a poor credit history, but it did not indicate that he had filed for protection under Chapter 13 of the Bankruptcy Code. Comeaux states that on August 21, Littleton called him and said: "'They are rejecting your employment. They are not going to be able to go through with everything because of a past credit history, your past credit history.'" Apparently Comeaux asked Littleton whether Comeaux's Chapter 13 bankruptcy was at issue. Allegedly, Littleton then indicated he did not know, since he was not privy to the report, but then stated: "'Bankruptcy or not, it probably wouldn't even matter.'"

On August 25, Comeaux spoke with Paul Watratz, the individual he perceived as having the authority to hire and fire in this case. In the conversation, Watratz confirmed B & W's position regarding Comeaux's employment status. Watratz told Comeaux that B & W had previously found that some sales representatives had mishandled their contingency funds. Reportedly, he said to Comeaux: "If that happened here you could not seek protection under Chapter 13."

Comeaux filed suit against B & W in the California Superior Court in Alameda County on December 15, 1987. B & W had the case removed to federal district court in the Northern District of California. During discovery, Comeaux learned that B & W had checked his credit again in the midst of the litigation.

It is undisputed that B & W requested that Trans Union Credit Information Company (Trans Union), a credit bureau with whom it had an ongoing relationship, check Comeaux's credit again in February 1988. It is also now undisputed that the purpose for which B & W intended to use and did use the credit report was to assist it in preparing its defense of this action. The contract between B & W and Trans Union, signed in November 1986, indicates that the parties are governed by the Federal Credit Reporting Act, 15 U.S.C. § 1681 et seq. (1988) (FCRA); the contract also sets out the exclusive circumstances under which credit reports may be obtained. Deposition testimony of Donna B. Higdon, a B & W employee, revealed that B & W stated in its request to Trans Union for the February 1988 credit report that it sought the report for employment purposes. In her deposition, Darlene Edlin, the employee of B & W who signed the original contract with Trans Union, and who instructed Donna Higdon to order the February 1988 credit report, stated that B & W was not considering Comeaux for employment at the time it ordered that report from Trans Union.

Therefore, in May 1988, Comeaux amended his complaint, ultimately alleging the following nine causes of action: (1) breach of covenant of good faith and fair dealing; (2) termination in violation of the nondiscrimination provision of the Bankruptcy Code; (3) breach of contract; (4) promissory estoppel; (5) wrongful termination in violation of public policy, arising out of the alleged violation of the bankruptcy laws; (6) loss of consortium; (7) invasion of privacy by the February 1988 credit check; (8) willful violation of the FCRA through the February 1988 credit check; and (9) negligent violation of the FCRA through the February 1988 credit check.

In November 1988, B & W moved for summary judgment, asserting that: (1) Comeaux's employment contract with B & W was terminable at will; therefore, there was no breach of the covenant of good faith and fair dealing or of contract as a matter of law; (2) Comeaux's performance was bargained for and that there could thus be no promissory estoppel; (3) B & W had no knowledge of Comeaux's bankruptcy before rendering its employment decision, so it therefore could not have violated 11 U.S.C. § 525(b); (4) B & W violated no public policy as a matter of law, and therefore did not wrongfully terminate Comeaux in violation of public policy; (5) Comeaux did not allege any injury as a consequence of B & W's conduct sufficient to disturb the marital relationship and thus did not cause Mrs. Comeaux's asserted loss of consortium; (6) B & W did not invade Comeaux's privacy because it did not publish the information concerning him; and (7) B & W did not obtain a "consumer report" as defined by the FCRA, which means that it did not violate that Act willfully or negligently.

At a hearing on January 12, 1989, the district court granted partial summary judgment for B & W, issuing a written order on February 15, 1989. Specifically, the judge adopted the reasoning urged by B & W on all claims except the breach of covenant, breach of contract, and FCRA claims. It denied summary judgment as to these claims, ruling that genuine issues of fact material to the remaining claims existed and refuting B & W's claim that the February 1988 report was not a "consumer report."

On March 2, 1989, B & W filed a second motion for summary judgment. On April 3, 1989, the district court granted summary judgment for B & W on the remaining claims. Comeaux appeals the district court's judgment on all claims except the sixth cause of action: loss of consortium. Furthermore, he appeals the district court's refusal to grant him costs under Fed.R.Civ.P. 37(c). This court has appellate jurisdiction under 28 U.S.C. § 1291 (1988).

In their appellate briefs and before the district court, the parties focused on the first of the three provisions and therefore focused on whether B & W failed to employ Comeaux solely because Comeaux had filed for bankruptcy. Comeaux failed to show that B & W knew of the bankruptcy prior to August 21, the date on which B & W informed Comeaux that it would not employ him because of his credit history. Comeaux alleges, however, that B & W did not "finalize" its decision not to hire him until several days later, at which time it clearly knew that Comeaux had filed for bankruptcy. Although there may be a genuine issue as to when B & W's decision not to employ Comeaux was finalized, the resolution of that issue is not material. Comeaux has failed to show that his bankruptcy status was the sole reason B & W decided not to employ him.

In order to maintain a cause of action under section 525(b), a plaintiff must show that one of the reasons for discharge enumerated in section 525(b) provided the sole reason for termination. See, e.g., Laracuente v. Chase Manhattan Bank, 891 F.2d 17, 23 (1st Cir.1989); Stockhouse v. Hines Motor Supply (Wyoming), Inc., 75 B.R. 83, 85, 2 Indiv.Empl.Rts.Cas. (BNA) 487, 488 (D.Wyo.1987). In the instant case, even if B & W had made its final employment decision after it learned of the bankruptcy, B & W told Comeaux before it knew of the Chapter 13 filing that it would not hire him because of his credit history. Thus, knowledge of the bankruptcy was clearly not the sole factor influencing B & W. Therefore; summary judgment for B & W was proper on this claim.

B. Wrongful Termination as Against Public Policy

Comeaux alleges that his termination violated public policy because it offended the policies underlying the Bankruptcy Code. Wrongful termination as against public policy is a California tort cause of action. See Foley v. Interactive Data Corp., 47 Cal.3d 654, 665, 254 Cal.Rptr. 211, 214, 765 P.2d 373, 376 (1988); Tameny v. Atlantic Richfield Co., 27 Cal.3d 167, 178, 164 Cal.Rptr. 839, 846, 610 P.2d 1330, 1336–37 (1980). Comeaux bases this claim on the presumed violation of the Bankruptcy Code. In light of our conclusion that B & W did not violate the Bankruptcy

Code and Comeaux's failure to offer any theory of wrongful termination in violation of public policy other than that grounded in section 525(b), we affirm the district court's grant of summary judgment to B & W on this claim.

C. Breach of Contract

The manner in which the contractual relationship between B & W and Comeaux evolved is somewhat uncertain. Putting the best face on the facts from the standpoint of the plaintiffs, the evolution was as follows. At the time Comeaux applied for his position with B & W, he signed an employment application that included the following language:

It is agreed and understood that by assigning me work with such salary as may be incident thereto, that this application shall constitute the terms of the contract of employment and that the relation between me and the Corporation shall be a hiring at will, terminable at any time by either of the parties thereto.

Subsequently, he was asked to interview with B & W. Several weeks after signing the employment application, B & W offered Comeaux future employment. In the phone conversation in which the offer was tendered, B & W set forth additional terms. The company promised to assign Comeaux work and salary on or about August 18, 1987, if he met the following conditions: (1) taking a physical examination; (2) resigning his then-current job with at least one week's notice; and (3) moving his place of residence to Fremont "as soon as possible."

Comeaux satisfied all of the conditions set forth by B & W. He shifted his position to his detriment in reliance on B & W's promise to assign him work and a salary on or about August 18. But B & W breached its agreement with Comeaux because it never assigned Comeaux work and salary. B & W cannot argue that it had no obligation to assign Comeaux work and a salary on the basis that Comeaux's ultimate employment would be governed by an at-will term in the contract. See Filcek v. Norris Schmid, Inc., 401 N.W.2d 318, 319, 156 Mich.App. 80, 84 (Ct.App.1986) (existence of at-will employment contract does not bar breach of contract action where prospective employer repudiates agreement before employee started employment and after she resigned prior job). We find that, because B & W never assigned Comeaux work and a salary, the parties never reached the point in time when the writing would begin to govern termination of the relationship. Therefore, whether or not Comeaux's ultimate employment would have been at will is immaterial to our analysis of whether the contract was breached before Comeaux's employment began.

On the facts we have assumed, B & W violated its own internal policy by failing to inform Comeaux that his future employment was contingent upon the results of a credit check. If B & W had been forthright with Comeaux, Comeaux could have decided whether to accept B & W's offer on the terms B & W set forth or to attempt to negotiate more favorable terms. Yet B & W deprived Comeaux of the opportunity to make an informed decision prior to accepting the offer and shifting his position to his detriment. All along, unbeknownst to Comeaux, there existed a "hidden" contractual term that had not been disclosed, bargained-for, or agreed-upon. A party may not protect itself from liability under a contract by asserting that a heretofore hidden term is somehow part of the agreement. Comeaux reasonably thought he had bargained for and obtained an opportunity to begin work if he met the explicit conditions set forth by B & W. We would, under these assumptions, hold that B & W is liable to Comeaux for those damages Comeaux incurred in reliance on B & W's promise of employment.

In California, employment is presumed to be "at will," and an employee can be fired without good cause, unless there exists an express or implied contract that restricts the employer's right to terminate the employee. Foley v. Interactive Data Corp., 47 Cal.3d 654, 665, 254 Cal.Rptr. 211, 214, 765 P.2d 373, 376 (1988). Specifically, in California, a for-cause contract exists where: (1) "the parties agreed, expressly or impliedly, that the employee could be terminated only for good cause," or (2) "the contract was supported by consideration independent of the services to be performed by the employee for his prospective employer." Rabago-Alvarez v. Dart Indus., Inc., 55 Cal.App.3d 91, 96, 127 Cal.Rptr. 222, 225 (Ct.App.1976). See Pugh v. See's Candies, Inc., 116 Cal.App.3d 311, 326, 171 Cal.Rptr. 917, 925 (Ct.App.1981).

Neither condition was met here. First, Comeaux failed to show that the writing, which explicitly states that the employment relationship is terminable at will, was superseded by an implied termination-only-for-cause agreement. Second, Comeaux failed to show that the contract was supported by independent consideration. Therefore Comeaux, under the facts we have assumed, is due only reliance damages.

We reverse the district court's grant of summary judgment as to the breach of contract claim because under not unreasonable assumptions with regard to the facts Comeaux would be entitled to recover reliance damages. On remand, the court should assess such damages provided Comeaux establishes the facts we have assumed by a preponderance of the evidence.

IV. CLAIMS ARISING OUT OF THE FEBRUARY 1988 CREDIT CHECK

A. Willful and Negligent Violation of 15 U.S.C. § 1681

In its February 15, 1989 order, the district court held that "the February credit Report is a 'consumer report' as defined by the FCRA" and it denied B & W's summary judgment motion as to the claims of willful and negligent violation of the FCRA. Then on April 3, 1989, it granted summary judgment to B & W on these claims, holding that, although the February 1988 credit report was a "consumer report," the report's use was not within the reach of the FCRA because the report had been used for a "business purpose," not a "consumer purpose."

The district court correctly found that the February 1988 report is a "consumer report" under the FCRA. However, the court erred in concluding that using the report for a "business purpose," removes it from the reach of the FCRA.

The FCRA, 15 U.S.C. § 1681 (1988), provides for civil liability and criminal penalties for those who do not comply with the Act. Sections 1681n and 1681o, respectively, make consumer reporting agencies and users liable for willful or negligent noncompliance with "any requirement imposed" under the Act. Section 1681q provides a criminal penalty for "knowingly and willfully obtaining information on a consumer from a consumer reporting agency under false pretenses." 15 U.S.C. § 1681q. We held in Hansen v. Morgan, 582 F.2d 1214, 1221 (9th Cir.1978), that "§ 1681q states an explicit 'requirement imposed under this subchapter the FCRA.' Noncompliance with § 1681q thereby forms a basis of civil liability under § 1681n." Hansen's construction has been adopted by the other circuits addressing this question.

B & W told Trans Union that it wanted the February 1988 credit report on Comeaux "for employment purposes." The record before us establishes that this statement was false, even though B & W claimed at one stage in the litigation that it was true. Thus,

B & W requested the report under false pretenses, thereby violating section 1681q and providing Comeaux with a cause of action under section 1681n or section 1681o.

B & W argues, however, that its receipt and use of the February 1988 credit report is not governed by the FCRA, which only regulates "consumer reports." It claims that the report was not a consumer report because it sought the report for a non-consumer purpose. The term "consumer report" is defined in section 1681a(d). The plain language of section 1681a(d) reveals that a credit report will be construed as a "consumer report" under the FCRA if the credit bureau providing the information expects the user to use the report for a purpose permissible under the FCRA, without regard to the ultimate purpose to which the report is actually put. Thus, if the user of the report led the agency preparing the credit report to believe, either through commission or omission, that the report was to be used for a consumer purpose such as for an employment purpose, the report is a consumer report within the meaning of the FCRA.

B & W's construction of the statute would render meaningless the FCRA's goal of allowing the release of credit reports for certain purposes only. See, e. g., St. Paul Guardian Ins., 884 F.2d at 884–85 (holding that such an interpretation of the FCRA is "illogical," "untenable," "contrary to congressional intent," and "creates irreconcilable conflicts between FCRA's statutory provisions"). B & W's construction also would render section 1681q meaningless by allowing those who request reports under false pretenses, stating a permissible purpose, to be exempt from section 1681q by using reports for a non-permissible purpose. Id. at 884; Kennedy, 747 F.2d at 369. The district court's conclusion that a report can be a "consumer report" under the FCRA, but not governed by the FCRA because it is for some non-consumer purpose, has no basis in the law of this or any other circuit. The law of this circuit, as well as that of almost all other circuits that have addressed the question, supports the following proposition: If a consumer reporting agency provides a report based on a reasonable expectation that the report will be put to a use permissible under the FCRA, then that report is a "consumer report" under the FCRA and the ultimate use to which the report is actually put is irrelevant to the question of whether the FCRA governs the report's use and the user's conduct.

B & W relies heavily on Mende v. Dun & Bradstreet, Inc., 670 F.2d 129 (9th Cir.1982) to support its position. This case interpreted the California Consumer Credit Reporting Agencies Act, not the FCRA. Even so, it supports Comeaux's position, not B & W's. Referring to similar language in the two acts, the court found dispositive that the defendant was not a consumer reporting agency. Id. at 133–34. The defendant agency had not prepared consumer reports since 1974 and "required that its subscribers sign an agreement that they will use reports on businesses only as a basis for credit to businesses in their capacities as such." Id. at 132. Furthermore, in Mende, "there was no evidence that the reports were used for any other purpose other than their intended purpose as commercial credit reports." Id. at 133. Thus, in contrast to the instant case, the credit agency in Mende was not a consumer reporting agency. Therefore, the Mende court's holding that its defendant was not governed by the FCRA is inapposite.

The district court, therefore, erred in granting B & W's motion for summary judgment. Furthermore, Comeaux's case for relief under section 1681 is so strong that the only genuine issue of material fact is whether B & W's noncompliance with section 1681 was willful. At the minimum, the conduct was negligent. We remand these claims to the district court for a determination of the nature of B & W's noncompliance and the fixing of damages.

VI. CONCLUSION

We hereby affirm in part and reverse and remand in part the district court's grant of summary judgment to B & W. We affirm the district court's grant of summary judgment to B & W on the claims of violation of the Bankruptcy Code, wrongful termination as against public policy, and invasion of privacy. We reverse the district court's grant of summary judgment on the FCRA claims and the breach of contract claim as it relates to the contract arising from Comeaux's acceptance of B & W's telephonic offer, and remand for further proceedings consistent with this opinion. We also reverse and remand the covenant of good faith and fair dealing and promissory estoppel claims for the limited purpose set forth in the opinion. The appellee is to bear the costs of this appeal.

AFFIRMED IN PART; REVERSED AND REMANDED IN PART.

Case Questions

1. Did the company in this case ever inform Comeaux that it was running a credit check on him prior to employing him?

2. What three issues are raised on appeal in this case?

3. Does it help the company that Comeaux's employment was "at will?" Why or why not?

4. How does the court rule on Comeaux's claim of a violation of 15 U.S.C. § 1681?

5. Explain the court's reasoning in its determination that B&W was negligent in the way that it obtained Comeaux's credit report.

Chapter Summary

Having a good credit history is one of the most important things that a consumer can possess. The difference between good credit and bad credit is the difference between being able to qualify for mortgages, loans and credit cards and not having access to any of these items. The Fair Credit Reporting Act was established in recognition of the importance that credit reports play in the lives of everyday consumers. Under the provisions of Fair Credit Reporting Act, credit reports must be maintained in a fair and accurate manner. The FCRA controls who can receive a copy of the consumer's credit report as well as the information that appears on the report. When a report contains inaccurate information, a consumer can dispute the negative entry. Disputes must be investigated by the credit reporting agency, and if it is unable to verify the information, the negative entry must be removed. Credit reporting agencies are under no obligation to investigate disputes by consumers that are deemed to be frivolous or irrelevant. Consumers are entitled to receive a free copy of their credit report when they are denied credit and also under new legislation that allows them one copy of their credit reports free of charge each year.

Web Sites

- Fair Isaac Corporation
  http://www.fairisaac.com
- Experian
  http://www.experian.com
- TransUnion
  http://www.transunion.com
- Equifax
  http://www.equifax.com

Key Terms

Credit score   Consumer reporting agency

Consumer report   Dispute

Review Questions

1. Why did Congress create the Fair Credit Reporting Act?

2. What is a credit report?

3. Why is a good credit report so important?

4. What are the three largest credit reporting agencies in the United States?

5. Other than businesses, who may receive a copy of the consumer's credit report?

6. Is law enforcement entitled to credit reports for individuals involved in national security investigations? Explain your answer.

7. Do credit reports contain medical information? Why or why not?

8. Provide a sample of some negative information that must be removed from a credit report after the passage of time.

9. What disclosures must credit reporting agencies make to consumers?

10. Credit reporting agencies must provide a summary of consumer rights. What does this mean?

11. Is a consumer entitled to dispute information on a credit report? Explain.

12. When a consumer disputes information on a credit report, what action must the credit reporting agency take?

13. What is the rule when a consumer's dispute is deemed to be frivolous or irrelevant?

14. What is the result when the credit reporting agency cannot confirm the accuracy of information on the credit report?

15. When can a consumer receive a free copy of his or her credit report?

Chapter 9

Fair Debt Collection Practices

Chapter Objectives

- Explain the reasons for the creation of the Fair Debt Collection Practices Act
- Describe the persons and organizations that fall under the jurisdiction of the Fair Debt Collection Practices Act
- Explain the limitations on debt collectors under the act
- Describe the remedies available to debtors under the Fair Debt Collection Practices Act
- Describe the enforcement provisions under the act

I. The Fair Debt Collection Practices Act

The Fair Debt Collection Practices Act was enacted in 1977 as a direct response to consumer complaints about abusive and misleading debt collection practices. Created as a subchapter in the much larger Consumer Credit Protection Act, found in Title 15 of the United States Code, the Fair Debt Collection Practices Act is found in 15 § 1692. In creating the Act, the U.S. Congress made specific findings of widespread "abuse, deceptive and unfair debt collection practices by debt collectors." 15 U.S.C.A. § 1692(a). Congress also found that these abusive practices were injuring the American economy by contributing to bankruptcies, "marital instability, to the loss of jobs, and to the invasions of individual privacy." Congress also found that the existing legislation was inadequate to meet the needs of consumers. The Fair Debt Collection Practices Act was designed to stop abusive and deceptive practices by debt collectors. It also provides some guidelines for actions by debt collectors that are considered to be appropriate.

Prior to the creation of Fair Debt Collection Practices Act, debt collectors relied on a wide variety of practices to obtain money from debtors. They would threaten to bring legal actions, including criminal charges, and sometimes resort to threats and other practices designed to annoy, embarrass or wear down a debtor.

> *Getting to the Essentials:* *The Fair Debt Collection Practices Act was created as a means to prevent abusive practices by debt collectors.*

II. Jurisdiction under Fair Debt Collection Practices Act

The act applies to credit transactions involving any obligation where a consumer must pay money for personal, family or household purposes.[1] Fair Debt Collection Practices Act applies to people who are in the business of collecting debts from others, not to creditors or creditors' employees. The act provides definitions that help clear up exactly who qualifies as a creditor, consumer and debt collector.

A. Who Is Covered under Fair Debt Collection Practices Act?

Under the act, a "consumer" is any person who is obligated to pay a debt. The act only applies to natural persons, not corporations or other business entities. "Creditors" are persons or businesses who extend credit or to whom a debt is owed. Finally, "debt collector" is a person or business, separate from the creditor, that is in the business of collecting debts for others. There is an important distinction, under the act, between creditors and debt collectors. The provisions of the Fair Debt Collection Practices Act only apply to debt collectors. Later, when we discuss prohibited practices and the information that debt collectors must provide to consumers, we will see that these provisions do not apply to creditors.

> **Consumer:** Under the Fair Debt Collection Practices Act a person who owes a debt for a personal, family or household purpose.
>
> **Creditor:** A person or business who extends credit or loans money to a consumer.
>
> **Debt collector:** A person or company, separate from the creditor, that is in the business of collecting outstanding debts from consumers.

1. Fair Debt Collection Practices Act Does Not Apply to Actual Creditors

The theory behind the act is that the greatest potential for abuse would come from bill collectors who had no incentive to maintain good relations with the consumer and therefore had a greater tendency to engage in abusive practices in order to collect money. Creditors, on the other hand, have other pressures that would make them tend to use less confrontational methods to get paid. Consider Example 9-1.

Example 9-1

Acme Furniture extended a line of credit to Bob. When Bob failed to pay on his loan, the president of Acme Furniture contacted Bob and asked about the outstanding debt payment. Is the president covered under the Fair Debt Collection Practices Act?

---

1. 1692(a)(5).

Answer: No. The act only applies to people who are in the business of collecting debts for others. It does not govern the person to whom the debt is owed. Acme Furniture does not fall under the jurisdiction of the act.

2. Defining "Debt Collectors" under the Act

Under the act, a debt collector is a person or organization who is in the regular business of collecting debts owed to other people. This category can include debt collection agencies, attorneys and others who represent clients. It does not include the person to whom the debt is owed. The definition also includes some other provisions, such as:

- Use of the postal service to contact consumers
- Any creditor who uses a name other than his own to collect a debt
    - Including any officers or employees of the creditor acting under another name

Under these provisions, a person qualifies as a debt collector whenever he or she works for a debt collection agency, or works directly for a creditor, but under a different name. For instance, when a creditor has a debt collection department under another name, it falls under the jurisdiction of the Fair Debt Collection Practices Act.

3. Defining "Debt" under the Act

The act defines debt in broad terms as any obligation arising under personal, family or household purposes. Courts have interpreted this language to refer to virtually any obligation to pay taken on by a consumer.[2] Courts have further refined this definition to include any transaction where a consumer is offered or extended the right to money, property, insurance or other services.[3] Under this definition, all of the following would qualify as debts under Fair Debt Collection Practices Act:

- Trash collection fees imposed by city or county
- Credit cards
- Automobile liability insurance premium
- Dishonored checks for personal, family or household goods
- Homeowner association fees
- Medical bills
- Car repair bills

Although the courts' definition of "debt" under the act would seem to be very broad, there are limits. For instance, all of the following have been ruled not to constitute debts under the Fair Debt Collection Practices Act and therefore would not bind debt collectors to its limitations:

- Collection of city water and sewer charges owed by businesses
- Residential mortgages
- Debts owed for business transactions
- Child support

---

2. *Berndt v. Fairfield Resorts, Inc.*, 337 F. Supp. 2d 1120 (W.D. Wis., 2004).
3. *Adams v. Law Offices of Stuckert & Yates*, 92 F. Supp. 521 (E.D. Pa., 1996).

- Property settlement under divorce action
- Business loans, even when made between friends
- Motor vehicle impoundment fees
- Fines for criminal violations
- Personal property taxes
- Civil damages

III. Communications between Debt Collectors and Consumers

The Fair Debt Collection Practices Act places strict limitations on the nature of the communications between consumers and debt collectors. These restrictions include how debt collectors can locate consumers, what information they must relate to consumers and restrictions on what debt collectors can say to third parties.

A. Locating Consumers

According to 1692b, debt collectors have the right to attempt to locate a consumer in order to request payment on a debt, but there is only so much information that the debt collector can give to a person in order to discover this information. Under the Fair Debt Collection Practices Act's, "Acquisition of location information" provision, a debt collector can communicate with third parties to locate the consumer, but:

- The debt collector must identify himself or herself and confirm that the debt collector is trying to locate the consumer
- If expressly asked, the debt collector must identify his or her employer or client
- The debt collector is specifically prohibited from telling third parties that the consumer owes a debt
- The debt collector cannot contact the same third party more than once seeking this information, unless the debt collector has reason to believe that the third party has come into new information
- The debt collector cannot communicate by post card
- The debt collector cannot use any language or symbol indicating that it is attempting to collect a debt
- If the debt collector knows that the consumer is represented by an attorney, they must limit communications to the attorney and not the consumer

1. Communicating with the Consumer

Debt collectors can communicate with consumers as long as they follow the rules set out in the Fair Debt Collection Practices Act. They are allowed to contact the consumer in any of the following ways:

- by mail
- by telephone
- by telegram
- by fax

Debt collectors face other limitations in contacting consumers. For one thing, they must not attempt to contact the consumer at 'inconvenient' times of the day or night. Under 15 U.S.C.A. § 1692c, an inconvenient time is any period outside of 8 a.m. to 9 p.m. Any communication falling outside of that time period is considered to be a violation of Fair Debt Collection Practices Act.

> *Getting to the Essentials:*   Under the Fair Debt Collection Practices Act, debt collectors are only permitted to contact consumers during convenient times (between 8 a.m. and 9 p.m.)

a. Calling the Consumer at Work

Debt collectors can call consumers at their workplace, but only if they have no prior information that the employer has a policy against such calls. If the debt collector learns of this policy, then the debt collector cannot contact the consumer at his or her workplace.

Example 9-2

Maria works at a local manufacturing plant. Her shift begins at 8 p.m. and runs until 4 a.m. the next day. RST Debt Collectors contacts Maria at her work at 8:55 p.m. to discuss her outstanding debt to a local furniture company. Maria tells the company that she cannot discuss personal matters on company time. The RST representative tells Maria that she can either talk about the debt now, or they will call her home at 11 a.m., when Maria is trying to sleep. Is this a violation of Fair Debt Collection Practices Act?

Answer: Yes. Once the representative is informed that the consumer cannot discuss the debt at work, the debt collector is not allowed to try to find some way around that policy in order to collect a debt.

What about the debt collector's "statement" that he will call Maria at home at 11 a.m., when she is trying to sleep?

Answer: Without more, there is no violation of Fair Debt Collection Practices Act. If Maria specifically states that she wishes to have no further communication with the debt collector, and he calls anyway, that would be a violation. However, simply calling at 11 a.m. is not considered to be an inconvenient time, even if it happens to be the time when Maria is sleeping.

Once the debt collector has contacted the consumer and discussed the outstanding debt, the debt collector is free to contact the consumer again. However, debt collectors cannot engage in harassment or abusive practices. They are also prohibited from contacting third parties to discuss the consumer's debt situation. As we have already seen, the debt collector can attempt to locate the consumer by speaking with others, but cannot disclose that the matter concerns at outstanding debt. The debt collector can only discuss the consumer's debt with a third party when:

- The consumer has given the debt collector express permission to do so, or
- The consumer is represented by an attorney

b. Attorney Representation

The rules about communicating with the consumer's attorney are straightforward. When the debt collector learns that the consumer has an attorney, he or she can only communicate with the attorney from that point onward. The debt collector is no longer permitted to discuss the case with the consumer.

c. Validating the Debt

Within five days of the initial communication, the debt collector must send the consumer a written notice setting out the following:

- The amount of the debt
- The name of the creditor to whom the debt is owed
- A statement that unless the consumer disputes the amount within 30 days of receipt of the notice, the debt will be considered valid
- A statement that if the consumer disputes any part of the debt, the debt collector will present verification of the debt

d. The Unsophisticated Consumer Test

When it comes to evaluating the communications between debt collectors and consumers, courts follow the so-called "**unsophisticated consumer test.**" This test, sometimes referred to as the "least sophisticated consumer" test, was developed by courts as an objective test to apply to communications between debt collectors and consumers. Under this test, any ambiguities or misstatements of the law are construed against the debt collector, not the consumer. Because Congress specifically mentions the rights of consumers and the widespread abuses in its justification for creating the Fair Debt Collection Practices Act, courts reasoned that all consumers from the most gullible to the most perceptive should be protected as much as possible. The unsophisticated consumer test becomes an issue when we discuss false or misleading statements by debt collectors.

> **Unsophisticated consumer test:** An objective test created by the court system to evaluate the quality of the communication to the consumer; it calls for clear and cogent communications, with no misrepresentations or false statements.

e. Ceasing Communication

The Fair Debt Collection Practices Act also includes a provision that permits a consumer to halt all communications with the debt collector. See Figure 9-1. When the consumer makes this request in writing, the debt collector must honor the request. The debt collector is permitted one last communication that informs the consumer that the debt collector will make no further contact with the consumer, but that the debt collector intends to follow other legal remedies to collect the debt. The most common remedy would be to bring a civil suit seeking the balance of the debt.

Figure 9-1. Ceasing Communication.

If a consumer notifies a debt collector in writing that the consumer refuses to pay a debt or that the consumer wishes the debt collector to cease further communication with the consumer, the debt collector shall not communicate further with the consumer with respect to such debt, except—

(1) to advise the consumer that the debt collector's further efforts are being terminated;

(2) to notify the consumer that the debt collector or creditor may invoke specified remedies which are ordinarily invoked by such debt collector or creditor; or

(3) where applicable, to notify the consumer that the debt collector or creditor intends to invoke a specified remedy.

If such notice from the consumer is made by mail, notification shall be complete upon receipt.[4]

Getting to the Essentials: Once a debtor tells a debt collector to stop communicating with him or her, the debt collector must oblige.

IV. Activities under Fair Debt Collection Practices Act

Now that we know who and what is governed under the Fair Debt Collection Practices Act, we will turn our attention to the actions that are permitted under the act. We will also examine actions that violate the act.

A. Permissible Actions under Fair Debt Collection Practices Act

Debt collectors are permitted to bring any lawful action against a consumer who fails to pay a debt. Lawful actions include:

- Reporting the failure to pay to a credit reporting agency
- Bringing suit to collect the outstanding debt
- Seeking mandatory arbitration

B. Prohibited Actions under Fair Debt Collection Practices Act

We have already seen that there are several specific actions that are prohibited under the act, including contacting consumers at inconvenient times and contacting the consumer after being requested to cease all communication. However, the Fair Debt Collection Practices Act also lists some particular actions that are not permissible, including:

---

4. 15 U.S.C.A. § 1692c.

- Harassment
- False statements
- Misrepresentations
- Unfair or deceptive practices

1. Harassment

Under the Fair Debt Collection Practices Act, debt collectors are not permitted to engage in harassing tactics in order to compel consumers to pay their debts. Harassment includes the use of threats or violence in order to collect money. It also includes publishing a list of "deadbeat" customers and the use of obscene or profane language or repeated telephone calls designed to annoy or embarrass the consumer. For an example of allegations of profane language as harassment under Fair Debt Collection Practices Act, see this chapter's case excerpt.

Figure 9-2. Harassment or Abuse FDCPA.

A debt collector may not engage in any conduct the natural consequence of which is to harass, oppress, or abuse any person in connection with the collection of a debt. Without limiting the general application of the foregoing, the following conduct is a violation of this section:

(1) The use or threat of use of violence or other criminal means to harm the physical person, reputation, or property of any person.

(2) The use of obscene or profane language or language the natural consequence of which is to abuse the hearer or reader.

(3) The publication of a list of consumers who allegedly refuse to pay debts, except to a consumer reporting agency or to persons meeting the requirements of section 1681a(f) or 1681b(3) of this title.

(4) The advertisement for sale of any debt to coerce payment of the debt.

(5) Causing a telephone to ring or engaging any person in telephone conversation repeatedly or continuously with intent to annoy, abuse, or harass any person at the called number.

(6) Except as provided in section 1692b of this title, the placement of telephone calls without meaningful disclosure of the caller's identity.[5]

---

2. False Statements

Debt collectors are prohibited from using false statements in their attempts to obtain money from debtors. They cannot, for example, claim to be attorneys or government officials. They cannot attempt to convince the consumer that he or she is committing a crime by failing to pay the debt. They also cannot:

- State that they work directly for credit bureaus
- Exaggerate the amount owed
- Include fees and surcharges not permitted under FDCPA

---

5. 15 U.S.C.A. § 1692d.

- State that paperwork sent to the consumer constitute legally binding documents, when they do not

- Encourage debtors to sign blank documents

3. *Misrepresentations*

Debt collectors are not permitted to use misrepresentations of the law in order to compel payment. Misrepresentations include statements that the consumer's home or personal belongings will be seized in order to satisfy the debt or that the consumer's salary will be garnished in order to pay the outstanding amount. FDCPA also prohibits debt collectors from claiming that they intend to bring lawsuits against the consumer when they have no such intention. Debt collectors are prohibited from misleading the consumer about the amount, character or legal status of the debt. For instance, a debt collector must inform the consumer that the statute of limitations on collecting a particular debt has passed. Debt collectors cannot tell consumers that they will be assessed fees and surcharges that are not permissible under the law.

Figure 9-3. False or Misleading Representations.

A debt collector may not use any false, deceptive, or misleading representation or means in connection with the collection of any debt. Without limiting the general application of the foregoing, the following conduct is a violation of this section:

(1) The false representation or implication that the debt collector is vouched for, bonded by, or affiliated with the United States or any State, including the use of any badge, uniform, or facsimile thereof.

(2) The false representation of—

(A) the character, amount, or legal status of any debt; or

(B) any services rendered or compensation which may be lawfully received by any debt collector for the collection of a debt.

(3) The false representation or implication that any individual is an attorney or that any communication is from an attorney.

(4) The representation or implication that nonpayment of any debt will result in the arrest or imprisonment of any person or the seizure, garnishment, attachment, or sale of any property or wages of any person unless such action is lawful and the debt collector or creditor intends to take such action.

(5) The threat to take any action that cannot legally be taken or that is not intended to be taken.

(6) The false representation or implication that a sale, referral, or other transfer of any interest in a debt shall cause the consumer to—

(A) lose any claim or defense to payment of the debt; or

(B) become subject to any practice prohibited by this subchapter.

(7) The false representation or implication that the consumer committed any crime or other conduct in order to disgrace the consumer.

(8) Communicating or threatening to communicate to any person credit information which is known or which should be known to be false, including the failure to communicate that a disputed debt is disputed.

(9) The use or distribution of any written communication which simulates or is falsely represented to be a document authorized, issued, or approved by any court, official, or agency

of the United States or any State, or which creates a false impression as to its source, authorization, or approval.

(10) The use of any false representation or deceptive means to collect or attempt to collect any debt or to obtain information concerning a consumer.

(11) The failure to disclose in the initial written communication with the consumer and, in addition, if the initial communication with the consumer is oral, in that initial oral communication, that the debt collector is attempting to collect a debt and that any information obtained will be used for that purpose, and the failure to disclose in subsequent communications that the communication is from a debt collector, except that this paragraph shall not apply to a formal pleading made in connection with a legal action.

(12) The false representation or implication that accounts have been turned over to innocent purchasers for value.

(13) The false representation or implication that documents are legal process.

(14) The use of any business, company, or organization name other than the true name of the debt collector's business, company, or organization.

(15) The false representation or implication that documents are not legal process forms or do not require action by the consumer.

(16) The false representation or implication that a debt collector operates or is employed by a consumer reporting agency as defined by section 1681a(f) of this title.[6]

4. Unfair Practices

In addition to prohibiting practices such as threats or the use of profanity in collecting debts, the FDCPA also outlaws unfair practices. Among such practices specifically mentioned in the statute include:

- Collecting amounts in addition to the actual debt
- Accepting postdated checks and depositing before the date
- Threatening criminal prosecution when no criminal jurisdiction exists
- Using 900 numbers and other telephone charges to collect money from a consumer without his or her knowledge
- Threatening to take judicial action when none is contemplated

Figure 9-4. Unfair Practices.

A debt collector may not use unfair or unconscionable means to collect or attempt to collect any debt. Without limiting the general application of the foregoing, the following conduct is a violation of this section:

(1) The collection of any amount (including any interest, fee, charge, or expense incidental to the principal obligation) unless such amount is expressly authorized by the agreement creating the debt or permitted by law.

(2) The acceptance by a debt collector from any person of a check or other payment instrument postdated by more than five days unless such person is notified in writing of the debt collector's intent to deposit such check or instrument not more than ten nor less than three business days prior to such deposit.

(3) The solicitation by a debt collector of any postdated check or other postdated payment instrument for the purpose of threatening or instituting criminal prosecution.

---

6. 15 U.S.C.A. § 1692e.

(4) Depositing or threatening to deposit any postdated check or other postdated payment instrument prior to the date on such check or instrument.

(5) Causing charges to be made to any person for communications by concealment of the true purpose of the communication. Such charges include, but are not limited to, collect telephone calls and telegram fees.

(6) Taking or threatening to take any nonjudicial action to effect dispossession or disablement of property if—

(A) there is no present right to possession of the property claimed as collateral through an enforceable security interest;

(B) there is no present intention to take possession of the property; or

(C) the property is exempt by law from such dispossession or disablement.

(7) Communicating with a consumer regarding a debt by post card.

(8) Using any language or symbol, other than the debt collector's address, on any envelope when communicating with a consumer by use of the mails or by telegram, except that a debt collector may use his business name if such name does not indicate that he is in the debt collection business.[7]

Getting to the Essentials: The Federal Trade Commission has authority to enforce the provisions of the Fair Debt Collection Practices Act

V. Enforcing the Provisions of Fair Debt Collection Practices Act

The Fair Debt Collection Practices Act can be enforced in two different ways: individual actions by consumers and administrative actions by the Federal Trade Commission. Under 15 USC § 1692k, a consumer can bring an action against a debt collector who violates any of the provisions of Fair Debt Collection Practices Act. If successful, the consumer is entitled to any actual damages sustained by the actions of the debt collector plus an additional assessment of $1000. The consumer may also be entitled to attorney's fees. It is up to the court to determine the severity of the infraction and to make awards commensurate with the severity. See Figure 9-5.

Figure 9-5. Federal Trade Commission Rule § 813. Civil Liability.[8]

(a) Except as otherwise provided by this section, any debt collector who fails to comply with any provision of this title with respect to any person is liable to such person in an amount equal to the sum of—

(1) any actual damage sustained by such person as a result of such failure;

(2) (A) in the case of any action by an individual, such additional damages as the court may allow, but not exceeding $1,000.

The Federal Trade Commission also has the power to bring actions against debt collectors who violate the provisions of FDCPA. The nature of the action brought by the

---

7. 15 U.S.C.A. § 1692f.
8. 15 U.S.C.A. § 1692k.

FTC resembles an unfair or deceptive trade practices action. The Federal Trade Commission has the power to enforce its findings by sanctions and other civil liability.[9]

Case Excerpt

Use of profane language in collecting debts.

Horkey v. J.V.D.B. & Associates, Inc., 333 F.3d 769 (7th Cir. 2003)

MANION, Circuit Judge.

Chris Romero, an employee of J.V.D.B. & Associates, Inc., a debt collection agency, attempted by telephone to collect a client's debt from Amanda Horkey while she was at work. Horkey asked him to give her a number she could call from her home. When he refused she hung up. Romero made a second call and left a profane message with Horkey's coworker. Horkey sued under the Fair Debt Collection Practices Act. J.V.D.B. appeals from the district court's entry of summary judgment in favor of Horkey, the denial of its motion for attorney's fees, and the awarding of statutory and compensatory damages in Horkey's favor. For the reasons set forth below, we affirm in all respects.

I.

J.V.D.B. is a debt collection agency whose employee, identifying himself as Chris Romero, telephoned Amanda Horkey at her place of employment at least twice on January 9, 2001. In the first call, Romero demanded immediate payment of a debt of $817.00. Horkey told Romero that she could not talk to him at work and that she could call him back from her home and arrange a payment schedule. Romero, however, refused to end the conversation, so Horkey hung up on him. Shortly thereafter, Romero called back and spoke with Horkey's coworker, Jimmie Scholes. When Scholes told Romero that Horkey was away from the office and asked if Romero wished to leave a message, Romero told Scholes to "tell Amanda to quit being such a (expletive) bitch," and Romero then hung up the telephone. Scholes passed on the message to Horkey. Shortly after that, Horkey received a third telephone call, but the caller hung up when she answered.

Horkey brought suit under the Fair Debt Collection Practices Act (FDCPA), 15 U.S.C. § 1692 et seq. She alleged the following claims: (1) a violation of § 1692c(a)(3)'s prohibition on contacting the consumer at work in contravention of the employer's policy against such communication; (2) a violation of § 1692c(b)'s limits on contacting a third party about the consumer's debt; (3) a violation of § 1692d's prohibition of obscene or profane language; and (4) a violation of § 1692g's requirement of a validation notice. On January 4, 2002, the district court granted summary judgment in Horkey's favor on all claims except for her § 1692c(b) allegation. In later proceedings, the district court granted J.V.D.B.'s motion for summary judgment as to § 1692c(b) (third-party contact), but denied J.V.D.B.'s motion for attorney's fees pursuant to § 1692k(a)(3), which allows a defendant to recover sanctions for an action brought

---

9. 15 U.S.C.A. § 1692l.

in bad faith and for the purpose of harassment. Ultimately, after a bench trial on the issue of damages, the district court awarded Horkey $1,000 in statutory and $350.00 in actual damages. J.V.D.B. appeals summary judgment as to Horkey's claims under § 1692c(a)(3) and § 1692d, the district court's denial of its motion for attorney's fees, and the district court's award of statutory and actual damages.

II.

This court reviews the district court's grant of summary judgment de novo, construing all facts in favor of J.V.D.B., the nonmoving party. Rogers v. City of Chicago, 320 F.3d 748, 752 (7th Cir.2003). Summary judgment is proper when the "pleadings, depositions, answers to interrogatories, and admissions on file, together with the affidavits, if any, show that there is no genuine issue as to any material fact and that the moving party is entitled to a judgment as a matter of law." Fed.R.Civ.P. 56(c). Thus, "summary judgment is appropriate if, on the record as a whole, a rational trier of fact could not find for the non-moving party." Rogers, 320 F.3d at 752.

The first issue on appeal is whether summary judgment in Horkey's favor was appropriate as to § 1692c(a)(3), which provides that without the prior consent of the consumer given directly to the debt collector or the express permission of a court of competent jurisdiction, a debt collector may not communicate with a consumer in connection with the collection of any debt ... at the consumer's place of employment if the debt collector knows or has reason to know that the consumer's employer prohibits the consumer from receiving such communication.

J.V.D.B. did not have Horkey's prior consent or a court's express permission to communicate with her at work, so the dispositive question is whether it knew or had reason to know that Horkey's employer prohibited such communication.

The only evidence to which Horkey points in support of the district court's conclusion, as a matter of law, that J.V.D.B. knew or should have known that her employer prohibited her from receiving calls from debt collectors is her statement to Romero that she could not talk to him at work and her request for a number she could call from her home. As Horkey paraphrased her protest in her affidavit, she "told Romero that (she) could not talk to him at work and asked him to give (her) his telephone number so that (she) could call him back from (her) home to set up a payment schedule." J.V.D.B. argues that this statement is susceptible to various interpretations and that Romero therefore was in no position to know that Horkey's employer prohibited her from receiving debt-related communication at work. The salient question is whether Horkey's statement was clear enough that, as a matter of law, J.V.D.B. knew or had reason to know that Horkey's employer prohibited her from receiving Romero's call at work.

We agree with the district court that it was. Horkey informed Romero that she could not discuss her debt while at work, and J.V.D.B. presents no evidence that Horkey's employer did allow her to take debt-related calls. Therefore we conclude that in this instance Romero had reason to know that Horkey's employer prohibited her from receiving communications related to debt collection while at work. See United States v. Central Adjustment Bureau, Inc., 667 F. Supp. 370, 388 (N.D.Tex.1986), aff'd as modified, 823 F.2d 880 (5th Cir.1987) (holding that, after the consumer wrote the debt collector and "requested in writing that he not call her at work," further calls violated § 1692c(a)(3)).

It is true, as J.V.D.B. argues, that saying "I cannot talk with you at work" could conceivably be understood to mean something other than "my employer forbids me from talking with you at work." It could, for example, mean "I do not wish to talk with you at work" or "I am too busy to talk with you at work." But this observation does not create an issue of material fact because, as we observed in Gammon v. GC Servs. Ltd. P'Ship, 27 F.3d 1254 (7th Cir.1994), the FDCPA exists to protect the unsophisticated consumer. Id. at 1257. Unsophisticated consumers, whatever else may be said about them, cannot be expected to assert their § 1692c(a)(3) rights in legally precise phrases. It is therefore enough to put debt collectors on notice under § 1692c(a)(3) when a consumer states in plain English that she cannot speak to the debt collector at work. That is what Horkey did. Without evidence that J.V.D.B. knew, contrary to Horkey's assertion, that her employer did not prohibit her from taking debt-related calls at work, she is entitled to summary judgment on her § 1692c(a)(3) claim.

We now turn to Horkey's claim under § 1692d. Section 1692d provides that "a debt collector may not engage in any conduct the natural consequence of which is to harass, oppress, or abuse any person in connection with the collection of a debt." 15 U.S.C. § 1692d. Section 1692d(2), which is the specific subsection upon which the district court granted summary judgment, further provides that "the use of obscene or profane language or language the natural consequence of which is to abuse the hearer or reader" is a violation of this section. Id. The uncontested evidence is that, within minutes after Horkey told Romero that she could not discuss the debt while at work, Romero called again and left a message with Horkey's coworker, Jimmie Scholes, asking Scholes to "tell Amanda to stop being such a (expletive) bitch." In an attempt to sidestep what would otherwise be a clear violation, J.V.D.B. asserts that Romero's message "was not spoken in connection with a debt collection nor was it meant to abuse the hearer or reader." Each half of this statement is preposterous.

To state the obvious, Romero's message was "in connection with the collection of a debt" because the undisputed evidence is that Romero called Horkey's workplace for only one reason: to collect a debt. In that context, when he told Horkey (via Scholes) to "stop being such a (expletive) bitch," Romero was not offering general advice about how Horkey could improve her disposition. He was telling her, crudely but specifically, to be more receptive to his entreaties regarding the debt. No other interpretation of the facts is reasonable and thus, as a matter of law, Romero's message to Horkey was "in connection with the collection of a debt."

J.V.D.B.'s assertion that Romero's message was not intended to abuse the hearer likewise fails. J.V.D.B. points to no evidence in the record regarding Romero's intent, which is just as well, because Romero's intent is irrelevant. What is determinative is whether "the natural consequence of" Romero's obscenity-laced message was to "abuse the hearer." 15 U.S.C. § 1692d(2). We need not examine the varying meanings of the words employed to determine that, in the context used, they were abusive as a matter of law. Unequivocally they were. We therefore affirm summary judgment as to Horkey's claim under § 1692d(2).

J.V.D.B. also points out that Romero "never spoke to" Horkey during his second call, apparently insinuating that there can be no liability under § 1692d(2) where the offending language is routed through an intermediary as opposed to being spoken directly to the consumer. Had the same message been left on Horkey's voicemail, a violation would be conclusive. This is worse because a third person received and relayed the statement. But because J.V.D.B. fails to develop this argument on appeal, the issue is waived.

Next, we consider J.V.D.B.'s third argument, that the district court erred in denying its motion for attorney's fees pursuant to § 1692k(a)(3), which allows a defendant to collect reasonable attorney's fees "on a finding by the court that an action under this section was brought in bad faith and for the purpose of harassment." We review the district court's finding on the issue of bad faith for clear error. Swanson v. Southern Or. Credit Serv., Inc., 869 F.2d 1222, 1229 (9th Cir.1988). We review the ultimate grant or denial of attorney's fees under § 1692k(a)(3) for an abuse of discretion. Zagorski v. Midwest Billing Servs., Inc., 128 F.3d 1164, 1166 (7th Cir.1997). J.V.D.B. contends that Horkey violated § 1692k(a)(3) by bringing a meritless claim under § 1692c(b). Section 1692c(b) states that

> except as provided in section 1692b of this title, without the prior consent of the consumer given directly to the debt collector, or the express permission of a court of competent jurisdiction, or as reasonably necessary to effectuate a post-judgment judicial remedy, a debt collector may not communicate, in connection with the collection of any debt, with any person other than the consumer, his attorney, a consumer reporting agency if otherwise permitted by law, the creditor, the attorney of the creditor, or the attorney of the debt collector.

The district court denied summary judgment in Horkey's favor as to § 1692c(b) because it found that there was no evidence that Romero discussed Horkey's debt with Scholes; i.e., in the district court's estimation, Romero's call to Scholes was not "in connection with any debt" and was thus not actionable under § 1692c(b). Instead, reasoned the court below, Romero's conversation with Scholes "was merely limited to inquiring as to (Horkey's) whereabouts and entailed the use of inappropriate, profane language." Nonetheless, the district court denied J.V.D.B.'s motion for attorney's fees as to this issue because it reasoned that the message Romero left with Scholes "could be construed as sort of in context relating to" the debt that Romero was attempting to collect from Horkey. This is a generous assessment of the foul conversation Romero had with Scholes. But because all of the evidence points to the conclusion that Romero's only reason for calling Horkey's workplace was to collect a debt, we share the district court's assessment of the situation insofar as it held that a reasonable lawyer could have argued from these facts that Romero's abusive conversation with Scholes was in connection with a debt and therefore triggered liability under § 1692c(b).

We also affirm the denial of J.V.D.B.'s § 1692k(a)(3) motion on an alternate ground. For J.V.D.B. to prevail, it would have to establish that Horkey's "action" was brought in bad faith and for harassing purposes. 15 U.S.C. § 1692k(a)(3). An "action" "in its usual legal sense means a lawsuit brought in a court." Black's Law Dictionary 28 (6th ed.1990). Thus, J.V.D.B. must show that Horkey's entire lawsuit, and not just her claim under § 1692c(b), was brought in bad faith and to harass J.V.D.B. Although we have not had occasion to delineate what constitutes a lawsuit brought in bad faith and for the purpose of harassment under § 1692k(a)(3), we are confident that no sound concept of such a suit could encompass an action in which the plaintiff wins summary judgment on three of her four asserted claims and has a colorable argument as to the claim on which she ultimately did not prevail. The district court was, accordingly, correct to deny J.V.D.B.'s motion for attorney's fees under § 1692k(a)(3). We cannot fathom how it could have done otherwise. In fact, at this juncture any bad-faith accusations would more appropriately be directed at J.V.B.D. for appealing the denial of its attorney's fees, but that issue is not before us.

Finally, we address J.V.D.B.'s appeal as to the $1,000 in statutory damages and $350.00 in actual damages. J.V.D.B. predicates its success on the issue of damages on our reversing summary judgment. Because we affirm summary judgment in all respects, J.V.D.B.'s appeal as to damages fails.

III.

For the reasons set forth above, we affirm in all respects.

Case Questions

1. Explain the basic facts of this case.
2. What damages did Horkey receive at the end of the bench trial?
3. According to the court, did Horkey sufficiently communicate to Romero that she was not permitted to discuss financial issues while she was at work?
4. How does the "unsophisticated consumer" test figure in the discussion of work-related calls?
5. What does the court rule on the question of the use of profanity as harassment under FDCPA?

Chapter Summary

The Fair Debt Collection Practices Act was created in 1977 as a direct response to the complaints about unfair and abusive debt collection practices. Under the act, debt collectors have specific limitations placed on the tactics and techniques that they can use to collect debts for their clients. The Fair Debt Collection Practices Act does not govern creditors. Instead, it polices debt collection agencies. Under the act, debt collectors must inform debtors about the amount of money that they owe, the name of the organization to whom the consumer owes this money and any other features of the debt. Debt collectors are prohibited from engaging in abusive or harassing techniques in order to obtain payment. Debt collectors cannot engage in false and misleading statements to compel consumers to pay. If the consumer notifies the debt collection agency in writing, requesting no further communication, this request must be honored by the debt collector. When a consumer challenges debt collection practices under the Fair Debt Collection Practices Act, this does not result in the erasure of the debt. Instead, the act authorizes specific sanctions against debt collectors who engage in unlawful practices. Individual consumers and the Federal Trade Commission can bring actions against debt collectors who violate the provisions of the Fair Debt Collection Practices Act.

Web Sites

- Federal Trade Commission—full text of the Fair Debt Collection Practices Act http://www.ftc.gov/bcp/edu/pubs/consumer/credit/cre27.pdf

- Fair Debt Collection Practices Act Links
  http://www.ftc.gov/os/statutes/fdcpajump.htm
- Federal Citizen Information Center
  http://www.pueblo.gsa.gov/cic_text/money/fair-debt/fair-dbt.htm

Key Terms

Consumer   Debt collector

Creditor   Unsophisticated consumer test

Review Questions

1. Why was it necessary to create the Fair Debt Collection Practices Act?

2. What persons and organizations are governed under the ac?

3. Who qualifies as a "debt collector" under the Fair Debt Collection Practices Act?

4. List and describe the methods that collectors can use to communicate with debtors.

5. Are creditors governed by the Fair Debt Collection Practices Act? Explain your answer.

6. What types of debts are governed under the act?

7. Under what circumstances can a debtor ask a debt collector to stop communicating with him or her?

8. Can attorneys act as debt collectors? Explain your answer.

9. What is the "unsophisticated consumer rule?"

10. What are some examples of harassment as defined by the Fair Debt Collection Practices Act?

11. What types of misrepresentations are considered to be illegal under the act?

12. Provide examples of false statements as that term is defined under the act.

13. Explain how the Fair Debt Collection Practices Act is enforced against debt collectors who violate its provisions.

14. Explain the legal principles from this chapter's case excerpt.

15. What are some examples of transactions that are not considered to be "debts" under the Fair Debt Collection Practices Act?

Chapter 10

Remedies Available to the Consumer

Chapter Objectives

- Explain the basic phases of a civil action
- Describe the differences between mediation and arbitration
- Displaying equitable remedies
- List and describe monetary damages
- Explain how damages are assessed in consumer protection cases

I. Introduction to Consumer Remedies

Throughout this book, we have referred to the fact that most federal and state statutes concerning consumer protection have two-part remedies. One remedy is to bring administrative action against the wrongdoer. In those circumstances, the Federal Trade Commission, on the federal level, or some state agency, pursues individuals and companies that have violated consumer protection laws. But there is almost always a second option: consumer civil action. Almost all federal and state consumer protection laws give consumers the right to bring civil suits on their own behalf. This two-part approach has several distinct advantages. It increases the likelihood that companies that violate consumer protection laws will be sanctioned, either by governmental action or in the judgment awarded in civil suits. Companies are also more likely to conform to the statutes, knowing that they can be sanctioned in either way. In this chapter, we will examine the process of bringing a civil action, first by the general concepts and procedures in civil cases and then addressing the specifics of consumer protection acts. We will also discuss the differences between monetary damages and equitable remedies.

II. An Overview of the American Legal System

When a consumer decides to bring an action against a company, the procedure followed is the same, whether it is a violation of the Fair Credit Reporting Act, the Truth in Lending Act, or any of the other consumer protection statutes we have discussed in this text. A civil suit follows the same course, whether it is a simple action between individuals or a class action complaint against a large, multi-national corporation. Before we can discuss the details of these suits, we must first address a more fundamental question involving the terminology used in civil cases.

A. Terminology in Civil Cases

When a consumer decides to sue a company for a violation of a consumer protection act, the consumer is referred to as a **plaintiff**. The person or company sued is referred to as the **defendant**. The plaintiff files a complaint against a defendant. The complaint contains the plaintiff's factual allegations about the wrong allegedly committed by the defendant. The complaint must be physically served on the defendant. Companies often appoint agents for service of process. These agents are the legally appointed representatives of companies and a plaintiff must serve a copy of the complaint on the agent in order to initiate the lawsuit.

Once served, the defendant responds with an answer. The answer contains denials of the allegations raised by the plaintiff and any contentions raised by the defendant against the plaintiff.

Getting to the Essentials:	Civil cases use specific terminology to refer to the pleadings and parties

Plaintiff: The party who files suit by bringing a complaint, which alleges that the defendant has wronged the plaintiff in some way.

Defendant: The party against whom the complaint is brought.

Complaint: The pleading setting out the plaintiff's allegations against the defendant.

Answer: The pleading filed by the defendant that denies the allegations in the complaint and raises any allegations against the plaintiff.

Example 10-1

Carlos obtained a credit card last year and has not been paying the minimum monthly payment. The credit card company has brought a civil action against him for nonpayment. Who is the plaintiff and who is the defendant in this case?

Answer: Carlos is the defendant because the credit card has brought a civil action against him. The credit card company is the plaintiff.

B. Discovery

Discovery is the process that both parties use to learn facts about the allegations raised by the other party. Civil cases have a wide variety of methods that parties can use to investigate the contentions raised by the other party. These methods include:

- Depositions
- Interrogatories
- Request for production of documents

Discovery: The exchange of information between the parties in a lawsuit.

1. Depositions

A **deposition** is a face-to-face session between the attorneys in the case and a witness. Once the witness is sworn in, the attorneys may question the witness about any issues involved in the case. Depositions occur long before the trial is ever set. There is no judge present during a deposition. If the attorneys have any objections about questions raised, they may reserve them for discussion during trial. The questions and answers are transcribed by a court reporter. Later, the court reporter will produce a transcript of the session that both sides in the case can refer to in order to prefer for trial. In civil cases, the transcript can be used in place of live testimony, should the witness become unavailable. Deposition transcripts can also be used to contradict the live testimony of a witness.

Deposition: Oral questions of a witness, taken under oath, by an attorney.

2. Interrogatories

Unlike depositions, **interrogatories** are written questions that are sent between the plaintiff and defendant in a civil case. The parties must respond in writing to each question posed. Interrogatories serve an important function in helping to pin down important points in the parties' version of the case. The answers to interrogatories are submitted under oath.

Interrogatories: Written questions posed by one party to another.

3. Requests for Production of Documents

In addition to depositions and interrogatories, parties are also permitted to serve **requests for production of documents** on each other. These requests can demand that one party send the other copies of photographs, reports, studies or almost any other writing that a party might rely on in presenting its case. When served with a request for production of documents, the party must respond or the judge will impose sanctions against that party.

Request for production of documents: A discovery method that demands copies of any document that a party might rely on in presenting its case at trial.

Getting to the Essentials:	There are several different methods of gaining information from the other side in a civil case, including depositions, interrogatories and requests for production of documents.

Example 10-2

Maria has filed suit against DEF Company for violation of a federal consumer protection action. Her suit is brought in federal court and she has recently required the president of DEF Co., to answer written questions. Are these interrogatories or depositions?

Answer: They are interrogatories. Because the questions were posed in writing, they meet the requirements of interrogatories, not depositions.

4. The Significance of Completing the Discovery Process

When the parties complete the discovery phase, the case is ready for trial. Most jurisdictions have rules that limit the discovery phase to six months, but parties are free to request an extension of that time period. In some cases, discovery can last for years. When the process finally comes to an end, the trial judge will schedule the case for trial.

C. Civil Trials

Civil trials proceed in the same fashion, no matter what the allegations raised by the parties. At the beginning of the trial, a jury is selected from residents of the area. The plaintiff bears the burden of proving the allegations in the complaint and therefore the plaintiff presents his or her case first.

Presenting a case is something that we have all seen portrayed on television and in movies. However, these fictional accounts often take considerable liberties with the actual trial process. A party proves his or her allegations in one of two ways: witness testimony and evidence. Witnesses must testify for the plaintiff in order to prove the factual allegations that are raised in the complaint. The plaintiff can also present evidence to prove these allegations. In a consumer protection case, the plaintiff will often take the stand and testify about his or her dealings with the defendant. The plaintiff may also present evidence in the form of written communications with the defendant including contracts or any other documents that help to prove the allegations in the complaint. Each witness will be cross-examined by the defendant's attorney as the case for the plaintiff proceeds. When the plaintiff has presented all of his or her evidence and witnesses, the defendant has the opportunity to do the same. The case for the defense proceeds in exactly the same way as the plaintiff's. The defense presents witness testimony and evidence to deny the allegations that are raised in the complaint.

When the case is over, the judge instructs the jury on the applicable law and then sends the jury to the jury room where they will consider the witness testimony and evidence they have seen and reach a determination. The jurors are secluded from all outside influence and given the opportunity to discuss the case. When they reach a decision about which side they believe presented the more believable case, they present their decision as a **verdict**.

> *Getting to the Essentials:*   Civil trials follow the same procedure, regardless of the allegations.

Verdict: The jury's conclusion about the facts in a trial.

1. Verdicts in Civil Cases

In a civil case, the jury's verdict is usually presented as "We, the jury, find for the plaintiff" or "We, the jury, find for the defendant." Verdicts in civil cases have nothing to do with guilt or innocence. Instead, the jurors determine liability. If the jurors believe that the plaintiff has proven his or her case, then they will reach a verdict finding the defendant **liable** to the plaintiff. Once they have determined liability, the jurors then move on the issue of damages. If they find that the defendant is liable, they must determine the extent of the defendant's monetary liability to the plaintiff. The money award is referred to as damages, discussed later in this chapter.

> **Liable:** A determination that one party has some obligation to another party, usually in the form of monetary payments

> *Getting to the Essentials:*   Civil cases do not determine guilt or innocence; they determine liability.

D. Appeals in Civil Cases

Losers in civil trials have the right to appeal. The appeal may be based on the party's claim that the jury acted contrary to the evidence or that the judge made some error during the trial. Appeals can drag on for years, as parties take the case to higher courts. Some consumer civil actions have gone as high as the U.S. Supreme Court, although most are settled before they ever reach that court.

E. Settlement

When a case is settled, it means that the parties have reached an agreement that terminates the case. A case may settle at any time during the litigation, either before, during or even after trial while the case is on appeal. A settlement almost always involves payment of money from one side to the other in exchange for dismissing the claim. Cases that are dismissed through settlement cannot be brought back at a later time.

> **Settlement:** A negotiated closure of the issues in a civil trial that ends the litigation.

III. Arbitration & Mediation

The vast majority of civil cases never reach trial. Some are settled by voluntarily actions by the parties, but many other are diverted to arbitration before the case ever reaches a courtroom. Many consumer lending agreements contain provisions requiring arbitration of any issues between the parties.

A. Arbitration

When a case is submitted to **arbitration,** a third party resolves the differences between the parties. Mandatory arbitration clauses are now standard in agreements as diverse as credit card agreements and automobile loans. Many of these agreements not only require arbitration, but also mandate that the arbitration must be held in the lender's home state, not the consumer's. (For an example of an arbitration agreement, see this chapter's case excerpt). Mandatory arbitration requires the parties to submit their differences to an arbitrator who makes a final determination of the issues. When a case is submitted to mandatory arbitration, the parties cannot seek a civil trial if they are dissatisfied with the result. That is not the case with mediation.

> *Getting to the Essentials:*   Arbitration avoids a civil trial by forcing the parties to accept the decision of a neutral, third party.

Arbitration: A process that avoids a civil trial by requiring parties to submit their differences to a neutral third party for disposition.

B. Mediation

When a case is mediated, a third party works with the parties to help them reach a mutually acceptable agreement. Unlike arbitrators, who can enforce their decisions on both parties, mediators let the parties reach their own agreements. Most consumer agreements do not contain provisions for mediation. If the parties cannot reach an agreement through mediation, they can still bring their claims in a civil court.

Mediation: The process of working out disagreements by having a neutral, third party who works with the parties to reach a mutually acceptable agreement.

IV. Equitable Remedies

U.S. Courts must have the power to make binding judgments on the parties involved in the litigation. This authority is referred to as jurisdiction. There are several different types of jurisdiction, including personal jurisdiction (power to make binding judgments on the parties) and subject matter jurisdiction (power to hear the issues involved in the case), among others. If a trial court has the appropriate jurisdiction, a judge can enter a wide range of orders on the parties involved in the case and can enforce these judgments through its many powers. One of the most interesting powers possessed by a trial court is its equity power.

Jurisdiction: A court's power to enter orders binding persons involved or to entertain the subjects litigated between the parties.

Equity is the power of a court to order individuals to do, or refrain from doing, certain actions. In consumer protection litigation, there are times when a party does not want monetary damages. Instead, the party would simply like the party to be ordered to stop doing a certain action. In other circumstances, the party might want the court to force the other party to honor a contractual obligation. When a party makes any of these requests, it is asking the court to use its equity powers. A trial court can exercise its equity power to order any of the following:

- Injunction
- Specific performance
- Rescission
- Reformation

> *Getting to the Essentials:* Courts have broad equity powers; they can order parties to stop certain actions, or to perform specific actions.

Equity: A trial court's power to order individuals to take certain actions; it arises from the court's authority to enforce fairness and justice.

A. Injunction

An **injunction** is a court's order that prohibits an individual or a company from taking a specific action. Temporary restraining orders are a good example of an injunction. In a temporary restraining order (TRO), a court orders a party to cease doing a specific action for ten days. At the conclusion of that period, the court will bring the parties together to make further findings.

Injunction: A court order prohibiting an individual or company from taking a specific action.

A request for an injunction is common in consumer protection cases. A consumer might request an injunction to prevent a company from continuing to charge fees or from taking steps to foreclose or repossess property.

B. Specific Performance

In cases where the parties have entered into a contract and one party wants the other to abide by that agreement, the issue will involve an order of **specific performance**. When a court enters an order of specific performance, it orders a party to carry out the action agreed on in the contract. For instance, a party may have agreed to make regular monthly payments on a loan. The lender might request specific performance by the consumer to continue making the payments. The consumer might counter that the contract was invalid and request a court to invalidate the contract. In such a situation, a court that sided with the lender might enter an order directing the consumer to specifically perform the terms agreed in the contract and continue to make payments.

Specific performance: A court order requiring a party to abide by the terms of a contract.

What happens when a court orders a party to specifically perform and the party refuses? The court may use its contempt powers to compel performance. For instance, a court could order that a party who fails to abide by its rules could be fined for every day that it fails to carry out the court's order. The court might also order that the party be arrested and held in jail temporarily until a hearing date can be set to consider the issues. With these kinds of powers at the court's command, most parties who receive court orders obey them.

C. Rescission

Another equitable remedy that a party may seek in consumer protection cases is an order of **rescission**. Rescission is a court order that cancels or voids the contract and attempts to place the parties into the positions that they were before the contract was ever negotiated. An order of rescission voids the legal consequences of the contract and also orders the parties to return any property or money paid to date. Rescission is an order often sought by consumers against companies that the consumer alleges has violated state or federal consumer protection laws. Many states impose strict limits on a court's power to order rescission by limiting it to cases where the consumer can prove actual fraud, duress or some other impropriety.

Rescission: Canceling or voiding a contract.

D. Reformation

When a party requests **reformation**, the party is actually requesting the court to change the terms of the contract to what that party claims was the original intention of the parties. A party might claim that although a contract states one thing, the understanding of the parties was something entirely different. Although reformation is a valid remedy, it is rarely seen in consumer protection cases because most states follow a "duty to read" position on contracts.

Reformation: A court order conforming the written portion of a contract to the oral understanding of the parties.

1. "Duty to Read"

The so-called "duty to read" is actually a duty imposed on all parties to written contracts. In states that follow this model, when a person signs a contract he or she is deemed to have read every provision. When the party signs the contract, he or she is not simply affixing a signature, he or she is actually agreeing to every clause in the contract. This prevents a party from later claiming that a particular provision or clause was never discussed by the parties and the consumer did not know that that clause was in the contract. Although "duty to read" makes sense from a legal standpoint, it has sometimes resulted in harsh rulings against consumers. As a result, many states have passed rules requiring particularly important contract provisions to be in larger type than other provisions. This is an attempt to do with away with the "small print" phenomenon of inserting consumer waivers and the surrender of other rights in tiny print buried deep in the contract.

Example 10-3

Maria has requested that the court order the defendant in her case, DEF Co., to stop calling her at home to request payment on her outstanding bill and to cancel the contract. What types of equitable remedies are these?

Answer: Injunction and rescission. An injunction is a court order that prohibits a party from taking a specific action, such as to stop calling a party to collect on a bill. Rescission is the cancellation of a contract.

V. Monetary Damages

Equitable remedies are only one type of relief that plaintiffs may seek in consumer protection cases. The other type is monetary **damages**, commonly referred to simply as damages.

Damages refer to the monetary, property, or personal losses suffered by the plaintiff. The point of an award of damages is to restore the plaintiff to the condition he or she was in prior to the loss, when that is possible. However, damages also play a second role: they are often seen as a way of punishing the defendant for conduct, or making an example of the defendant for others in the industry. Damages come in three broad categories, including:

* Compensatory damages
* Punitive Damages
* Nominal damages

Damages: A general term for an order requiring monetary payment by one party to another.

> *Getting to the Essentials:*   Damages are an award of money that must be paid by one party to another.

A. Compensatory Damages

Compensatory damages are designed to restore the plaintiff to his or her original condition, or to reimburse the plaintiff for out of pocket expenses. When a court awards compensatory damages, it orders the defendant to make a monetary payment to the plaintiff in a specific amount. Plaintiffs must prove the exact amount of their out of pocket expenses in order to receive this award.

In consumer protection cases, compensatory damages are often limited to out of pocket expenses directly tied to the defendant-company's actions. If the plaintiff had to pay for another car, obtained a new loan at a higher interest rate or had other expenses tied to improper actions by the defendant, these would all qualify as compensatory damages.

1. Calculating Monetary Damage Awards

When courts consider the final amount to award in a consumer protection case, the court is guided by a relatively simple principle: the plaintiff should receive whatever amount it takes to put the plaintiff back on the same footing he or she was in prior to entering into the contract. Consumer protection cases have important considerations for courts because many of the state and federal statutes place specific limitations on what qualifies as compensatory damages. Consider Figure 10-1, which provides an overview of the damages that can be awarded for the topic we discussed in Chapter 8. For the damages for violating the Fair Debt Collection Practices Act, see Figure 10-1.

Figure 10-1. Damages for Violation of Fair Credit Reporting Act.[1]

(a) In general. Any person who willfully fails to comply with any requirement imposed under this title with respect to any consumer is liable to that consumer in an amount equal to the sum of

(1)(A) any actual damages sustained by the consumer as a result of the failure or damages of not less than $100 and not more than $1,000; or

(B) in the case of liability of a natural person for obtaining a consumer report under false pretenses or knowingly without a permissible purpose, actual damages sustained by the consumer as a result of the failure or $1,000, whichever is greater;

(2) such amount of punitive damages as the court may allow; and

(3) in the case of any successful action to enforce any liability under this section, the costs of the action together with reasonable attorney's fees as determined by the court.

Figure 10-2. Damages for Violation of Fair Debt Collection Practices Act.[2]

(a) Amount of damages

Except as otherwise provided by this section, any debt collector who fails to comply with any provision of this subchapter with respect to any person is liable to such person in an amount equal to the sum of—

(1) any actual damage sustained by such person as a result of such failure;

(2)(A) in the case of any action by an individual, such additional damages as the court may allow, but not exceeding $1,000; or

(B) in the case of a class action, (i) such amount for each named plaintiff as could be recovered under subparagraph (A), and (ii) such amount as the court may allow for all other class members, without regard to a minimum individual recovery, not to exceed the lesser of $500,000 or 1 per centum of the net worth of the debt collector; and

(3) in the case of any successful action to enforce the foregoing liability, the costs of the action, together with a reasonable attorney's fee as determined by the court. On a finding by the court that an action under this section was brought in bad faith and for the purpose of harassment, the court may award to the defendant attorney's fees reasonable in relation to the work expended and costs.

(b) Factors considered by court

In determining the amount of liability in any action under subsection (a) of this section, the court shall consider, among other relevant factors—

(1) in any individual action under subsection (a)(2)(A) of this section, the frequency and persistence of noncompliance by the debt collector, the nature of such noncompliance, and the extent to which such noncompliance was intentional; or

(2) in any class action under subsection (a)(2)(B) of this section, the frequency and persistence of noncompliance by the debt collector, the nature of such noncompliance, the resources of the debt collector, the number of persons adversely affected, and the extent to which the debt collector's noncompliance was intentional.

---

    1. 15 U.S.C. § 1681n.
    2. 15 U.S.C. § 1681o.

> *Getting to the Essentials:*   Most federal and state consumer protection laws contain limitations on the available damages to consumers.

As you can see in both Figures 10-1 and 10-2, federal legislation has specifically addressed the issue of damages. When a consumer brings an action under the Fair Credit Reporting Act, he or she will receive at least $100 for compensatory damages and no more than $1000. The consumer may also be entitled to punitive damages. Under the Fair Debt Collection Practices Act, the consumer is limited to total damages of no more than $1000. For class actions under the same act, the maximum amount is $500,000. These types of limitations are common in all consumer protection statutes. Legislators are faced with two competing interests in such cases: on one hand, they want to penalize companies that engage in unfair practices; on the other hand, they do not want to open the floodgates of litigation to consumers who see a chance to get rich off relatively minor infractions. Limiting the maximum possible damages in such cases is one way to strike a balance between these interests.

2. Consequential Damages

Consequential damages are often included in discussions of compensatory damages, but they actually fall into a different category. Consequential damages are those losses specifically tied to a particular contract breach. We can differentiate between compensatory damages and consequential damages by saying that compensatory damages are out of pocket expenses tied to breach of contract by a party, while consequential damages are those losses that will come from the failure to perform under the contract. A party might have specific losses because of the paperwork and other inconveniences brought about by a contract breach, but consequential damages refer to the profits that would have come from the contract. Future payments, interest charges and other benefits are examples of consequential damages. In consumer protection cases, companies often counter claim against a consumer for consequential damages, saying that they have lost future revenues by the consumer's failure to make payments on the loan.

Figure 10-3. Final damage awards in contract trials, 2001.[3]

Table 6. Final award amounts for civil jury and bench contract trials with plaintiff winners in State courts in the Nation's 75 largest counties, 2001

Case type	Final amount awarded to plaintiff winners			Percent of trials with final awards --	
	Number	Total	Median	Over $250,000	$1 million or more
Jury trials[a]	964	$1,769,033,000	$81,000	27.9%	10.7%
Fraud	174	$653,154,000	$87,000	33.3%	20.1%
Seller plaintiff	194	67,816,000	68,000	20.9	7.9
Buyer plaintiff	278	98,538,000	62,000	25.1	7.3
Mortgage foreclosure	--	--	--	--	--
Employment discrimination	66	44,616,000	218,000	43.6	16.0
Other employment dispute	105	257,999,000	83,000	28.8	7.4

3. Contract Trials and Verdicts in Large Counties, 2001. Bureau of Justice Statistics, U.S. Department of Justice.

Rental/lease	40	13,375,000	81,000	21.5	9.0
Tortious interference	47	575,307,000	117,000	48.1	12.3
Partnership dispute	15	51,610,000	90,000	41.6	15.7
Subrogation	26	1,248,000	8,000	--	--
Other or unknown contract	19	5,370,000	77,000	22.5	14.9
Bench trials	1,381	$272,226,000	$30,000	10.9%	1.9%
Fraud	179	$115,173,000	$61,000	28.0%	4.6%
Seller plaintiff	724	96,873,000	29,000	7.8	1.6
Buyer plaintiff	198	31,772,000	16,000	6.9	1.4
Mortgage foreclosure	13	2,731,000	70,000	13.6	13.6
Employment discrimination	7	297,000	40,000	--	--
Other employment dispute	54	7,754,000	58,000	15.4	--
Rental/lease	136	10,737,000	14,000	9.0	0.7
Tortious interference	33	4,274,000	44,000	8.7	--
Partnership dispute	3	851,000	191,000	**	--
Subrogation	15	786,000	28,000	12.3	--
Other or unknown contract	20	977,000	5,000	6.6	--

Note: Data for final awards in jury contract trials were available for 99.1% of all jury plaintiff winners.

Data for final awards in bench contract trials were available for 99.0% of all bench plaintiff winners.

Final amount awarded includes both compensatory (reduced for contributory negligence), fees and costs, and punitive damage awards. Award data were rounded to the nearest thousand.

--No cases recorded.

**Too few cases to obtain statistically reliable data.

aDoes not include jury trials that involved trials with a directed verdict, judgments notwithstanding the verdict, and jury trials for defaulted defendants.

3. Liquidated Damages

In some cases, the parties can agree in advance about the amount of damages that will be awarded in the event that a contract is not fully performed. These are referred to as liquidated damages. Within certain limitations, the parties are free to negotiate any terms and payments that they like. However, in consumer protection cases, liquidated damages are often a contested issue. Liquidated damage clauses assume that the parties have equal bargaining power and are able to negotiate favorable terms. This is extremely rare in consumer-creditor relations where the terms are presented on a "take it or leave it" basis. As a result, courts have been reluctant to uphold liquidated damage provisions in consumer contracts.

B. Punitive Damages

The topic of **punitive damages** is actually mentioned in several federal consumer protection statutes. An award of punitive damages is the court's way of punishing the defendant for some action. These damages are awarded in addition to any compensatory damages and are designed to punish the defendant for particular actions. A court might award punitive damages against a debt collector that uses obviously illegal practices to obtain fees or a company that routinely flouts other consumer protection statutes.

Punitive damages: Monetary awards assessed against a defendant designed to punish the defendant for behavior and to set an example for other similarly situated defendants.

Figure 10-4. Punitive Damages Awarded to Plaintiff Winners.[4]

Table 7. Punitive damages awarded to plaintiff winners in contract jury and bench trials in the Nation's 75 largest counties, 2001

Case type	Jury trials awarded punitive damages	Bench trials awarded punitive damages	Punitive damages awarded to plaintiff winners in jury and bench contract trials Median damages awarded		Number of trials with punitive damages of $1 million or more —	
			Jury	Bench	Jury	Bench
Contract cases	98	39	$111,000	$46,000	18	--
Fraud	27	32	$100,000	$52,000	5	--
Seller plaintiff	5	4	4,000	5,000	--	--
Buyer plaintiff	15	1	275,000	82,000*	3	--
Mortgage foreclosure	--	--	--	--	--	--
Employment discrimination	13	--	606,000	--	5	--
Other employment dispute	16	--	151,000	--	1	--
Rental/lease	9	--	15,000	--	2	--
Tortious interference	8	1	92,000	10,000*	1	--
Partnership dispute	4	--	186,000	--	1	--
Subrogation	--	--	--	--	--	--
Other or unknown contract	1	1	500*	1,000*	--	--

Note: Data for punitive damage awards in jury contract trials were available for 99.5% of all jury plaintiff winners.

Data for punitive damage awards in bench contract trials were available for 100.0% of all bench plaintiff winners.

Not shown are jury trials that involve trials with a directed verdict, judgments notwithstanding the verdict, and jury trials for defaulted defendants. These cases accounted for 1 punitive damage verdict with a plaintiff winner.

In this study, cases are classified by the primary case type, though many cases involve multiple claims (that is, contract and tort). Under laws in almost all States, only tort claims qualify for punitive damages.

If contract cases involved punitive damages, it involved a related tort claim.

Detail may not sum to total because of rounding.

--No cases recorded.

*Not median but the actual amount awarded.

C. Nominal Damages

In a technical sense, any violation, no matter how small, justifies an award of damages. However, courts are not as hyper-technical as they are often portrayed in the media. For minor infractions, courts will usually not award any damages, or if they do, they award nominal damages. Nominal damages are an award of a small or token amount to a plaintiff who has proved a technical, but not serious violation. An award of less than $100 is usually seen as nominal damages.

---

4. Civil Trial Cases and Verdicts in Large Counties, 2001. Bureau of Justice Statistics, U.S. Department of Justice.

VI. Complaining to Federal, State and Private Organizations

The Federal Trade Commission provides a forum for consumers to file complaints about companies. It provides an online complaint form where consumers can fill out information about the company, the action and submit it to the FTC in an encrypted format. The Federal Trade Commission does not act as a prosecutor for individual complaints. Instead, it acts on behalf of the government to bring actions against companies that have a history of engaging in abusive practices. Consumers who want individual redress must still resort to civil actions.

A. Complaints to Local Better Business Bureau

In addition to filing complaints with the FTC, consumers can also file complaints with local branches of the Better Business Bureau. This agency has no enforcement powers, but can often take action behind the scenes to work out agreements with local businesses and consumers.

B. Using the Media

For consumers who want to go beyond the conventional format of bringing a civil suit or complaining to the FTC, there are other alternatives. They can engage in letter writing campaigns, stage protests, write letters to the editor, or try to use the power of the media to help.

1. TV and Newspaper "Crusaders"

In recent years, some television and print media have appointed themselves consumer watchdogs by creating programs that allow individuals to complain about particular businesses. These media outlets will often publish unflattering stories about a particular business and attempt to resolve an issue on behalf of a consumer through the power of the press. Many of these programs tend to disappear after a short period, but when one is active in an area, that can often be quite effective for individual consumers who manage to catch the media's attention.

Case Excerpt

When are arbitration clauses excessive?

DeGraziano v. Verizon Communications, Inc., 325 F.Supp.2d 238 (E.D.N.Y.,2004)

MEMORANDUM OF DECISION AND ORDER

SPATT, District Judge.

Joanne Degraziano ("Degraziano" or the "plaintiff") commenced this action against Verizon Communications, Inc. ("Verizon Communications"), Cellco Partnership d/b/a Verizon Wireless ("Verizon Wireless"), Vodafone Group, PLC ("Vodafone"), Bank of America, N.A. (U.S.A.), Bank of America Corporation, Discover Bank, Discover Financial Services, Inc. and Morgan Stanley Dean Witter and Company (the "defendants") alleging various violations of the Fair Credit Reporting Act (the "FCRA"), 15 U.S.C. 1681, et seq. On March 30, 2004 a stipulation was filed with the Court dismissing the claims against the defendants Bank of America, N.A. (USA) and Bank of America Corporation with prejudice.

Presently before the Court is a motion by the defendants Verizon Communications and Verizon Wireless (the "moving defendants") to (1) dismiss the first and second causes of actions and compel arbitration of those claims; and (2) dismiss the third and fourth causes of action pursuant to Rule 12(b)(6) of the Federal Rules of Civil Procedure ("Fed. R. Civ.P.") for failure to state a claim.

I. BACKGROUND

A. As to the Motion to Compel Arbitration of the First and Second Causes of Action

The following facts are taken from the complaint and from the Declaration of Jeffrey Nason, the Supervisor, Customer Satisfaction for the Northeast Area of Verizon Wireless, sworn to on December 8, 2003, and are undisputed unless otherwise noted.

On or about May 4, 1998, the plaintiff began receiving wireless telephone services from Verizon Wireless. As a precondition of receiving such services, the plaintiff agreed to a Cellular Services Agreement (the "CSA"). Among its terms and conditions, the CSA includes an arbitration clause which states:

Independent Arbitration. INSTEAD OF SUING IN COURT, YOU'RE AGREEING TO ARBITRATE DISPUTES ARISING OUT OF OR RELATED TO THIS OR PRIOR AGREEMENTS. THIS AGREEMENT INVOLVES COMMERCE AND THE FEDERAL ARBITRATION ACT APPLIES TO IT. ARBITRATION ISN'T THE SAME AS COURT. THE RULES ARE DIFFERENT AND THERE'S NO JUDGE AND JURY. YOU AND WE ARE WAIVING RIGHTS TO PARTICIPATE IN CLASS ACTIONS, INCLUDING PUTATIVE CLASS ACTIONS BEGUN BY OTHERS PRIOR TO THIS AGREEMENT, SO READ THIS CAREFULLY. THIS AGREEMENT AFFECTS RIGHTS YOU MIGHT OTHERWISE HAVE IN SUCH ACTIONS THAT ARE CURRENTLY PENDING AGAINST U.S. OR OUR PREDECESSORS IN WHICH YOU MIGHT BE A POTENTIAL CLASS MEMBER. (We each retain our rights to complain to any regulatory agency or commission.) YOU AND WE EACH AGREE THAT, TO THE FULLEST EXTENT PROVIDED BY LAW: (1) ANY CONTROVERSY OR CLAIM ARISING OUT OF OR RELATING TO THIS AGREEMENT, OR TO ANY PRIOR AGREEMENT FOR CELLULAR SERVICE WITH U.S. OR, ANY OF OUR AFFILIATES OR PREDECESSORS IN INTEREST, OR TO ANY PRODUCT OR SERVICE PROVIDED UNDER OR IN CONNECTION WITH THIS AGREEMENT OR SUCH A PRIOR AGREEMENT, WILL BE SETTLED BY INDEPENDENT ARBITRATION

INVOLVING A NEUTRAL ARBITRATOR AND ADMINISTERED BY THE AMER-
ICAN ARBITRATION ASSOCIATION ("AAA") UNDER WIRELESS INDUSTRY
ARBITRATION ("WIA") RULES, AS MODIFIED BY THIS AGREEMENT. WIA
RULES AND FEE INFORMATION ARE AVAILABLE FROM U.S. OR THE AAA; (2)
EVEN IF APPLICABLE LAW PERMITS CLASS ACTIONS OR CLASS ARBITRA-
TIONS, YOU WAIVE ANY RIGHT TO PURSUE ON A CLASS BASIS ANY SUCH
CONTROVERSY OR CLAIM AGAINST US, OR ANY OF OUR AFFILIATES OR
PREDECESSORS IN INTEREST, AND WE WAIVE ANY RIGHT TO PURSUE ON
A CLASS BASIS ANY SUCH CONTROVERSY OR CLAIM AGAINST YOU....

At some point in time the plaintiff was unable to pay her monthly bills for monies
owed to, among other entities, Verizon Wireless. During 2001, the plaintiff entered
into a debt reduction program with the Daly Law Center to arrange settlements on
her debts. In February 2002, Verizon Wireless provided a report to Asset Manage-
ment Outsourcing Recoveries, Inc. ("AMO Recoveries") in which Verizon Wireless reported that the plaintiff's account was in collection with an outstanding balance of
$681.97.

The Daly Law Center, on behalf of the plaintiff, and AMO Recoveries, on behalf
of Verizon Wireless, settled the outstanding balance for $340.49. Along with a letter
dated February 20, 2002, the Daly Law Center submitted a check in the amount of
$340.49 to AMO with a request that AMO report to the credit/consumer reporting
agencies that the outstanding balance was resolved. The plaintiff alleges that Verizon
Wireless failed to inform the credit/consumer reporting agencies that the outstanding balance was satisfied.

Thereafter, the plaintiff was unable to secure financing for the purchase of a motor
vehicle allegedly due to her credit history. The plaintiff asserts two causes of action
against Verizon Wireless: (1) that by failing to make any updates and/or reports to the
credit/consumer reporting agencies since February 2002 or by implementing proper
policies, procedures or controls, Verizon Wireless has knowingly and in bad faith
breached the duties imposed on it by the FCRA; and (2) that by failing to make any
updates and/or reports to the credit/consumer reporting agencies since February
2002 or by implementing proper policies, procedures or controls, Verizon Wireless
has negligently breached the duties imposed on it by the FCRA. For these alleged violations of law the plaintiff seeks compensatory damages for "humiliation," actual
financial damages, and punitive damages.

B. As to the Motion to Dismiss

As indicated above, Verizon Communications moves to dismiss the third and fourth
causes of action pursuant to Rule 12(b)(6) for failure to state a claim. For purposes
of this motion, the relevant facts are taken from the complaint and accepted as true.

The plaintiff alleges that Verizon Communications and Vodafone are the two parent companies of Verizon Wireless, holding a 56% and 44% ownership interest, respectively.

The third cause of action alleges that because these parent companies enjoy complete ownership of Verizon Wireless they "play the part of the 'master' with the role of
the 'servant/agent' being played by Verizon Wireless." As such, the plaintiff alleges that
liability for the intentional and negligent failure of Verizon Wireless to comply with
the FCRA extends to Verizon Communications and to Vodafone. The complaint further alleges that it was the responsibility of Verizon Communications and Vodafone

to establish quality and managerial controls and policies to ensure that Verizon Wireless did not violate and laws in the performance of its duties on behalf of its "masters." The fourth cause of action seeks to pierce the corporate veil of Verizon Wireless and impose liability on Verizon Communications and Vodafone. In particular, the plaintiff claims that Verizon Communications and Vodafone are responsible for any and all illegal actions taken by Verizon Wireless because of (1) their complete "dominion and control" over Verizon Wireless, (2) "the closeness of the relationship" between Verizon Wireless and its parent companies, (3) the fact that all assets and liabilities of the company are reflected on the balance sheets of its parent companies, and (4) as parent companies, Verizon Communications and Vodafone failed to fulfill their duty of establishing managerial or quality policies, procedures, or controls to ensure that Verizon Wireless did not violate any laws in the performance of its duties.

II. DISCUSSION

A. As to the Motion to Compel Arbitration

Under the Federal Arbitration Act (the "FAA"), written provisions to arbitrate controversies included in any contract affecting interstate commerce "shall be valid, irrevocable and enforceable, save upon such grounds as exist under law or equity for the revocation of any contract." 9 U.S.C. § 2. There is a well-settled federal policy encouraging arbitration of disputes where a contract so provides. Because of this strong federal preference for arbitration as a dispute resolution procedure, any doubts concerning whether there has been a waiver of the right to arbitrate must be resolved in favor of arbitration.

Before a district court may compel arbitration, it "must first determine two threshold issues that are governed by state rather than federal law: (1) Did the parties enter into a contractually valid arbitration agreement? and (2) If so, does the parties' dispute fall within the scope of the arbitration agreement?"

Here, it is undisputed that the parties entered into the CSA containing the following arbitration provision:

Independent Arbitration. INSTEAD OF SUING IN COURT, YOU'RE AGREEING TO ARBITRATE DISPUTES ARISING OUT OF OR RELATED TO THIS OR PRIOR AGREEMENTS. . . .

Thus, the contractual agreement to arbitrate is valid. Furthermore, the claims alleged in the first and second causes of action fall within the scope of this arbitration provision. The clause in this case which states that Verizon Wireless and the plaintiff agree to "arbitrate disputes arising out of or related to this or prior agreements ..." is the "paradigm of a broad clause." In the Court's view, the plaintiff's claims that Verizon Wireless violated the FCRA arise out of and are related to the CSA. As such, the plaintiff's claims are "presumptively arbitrable." As the party opposing arbitration, the plaintiff has the burden of proving that the claims are not subject to arbitration.

The plaintiff advances numerous arguments in support of her contention that the first and second causes of action are not arbitrable. Although none of these contentions have merit, to complete the record, the Court will address these arguments.

First, the plaintiff contends that Verizon Wireless "waived its rights to arbitrate and the right cannot be revived." A party may waive its right to arbitration by expressly indicating that it wishes to resolve its claims before a court, or by impliedly waiving its right to enforce a contractual arbitration clause by "engaging in protracted litigation that results in prejudice to the opposing party." Based on the record submitted to the Court there is no indication that Verizon Wireless expressly waived its right to arbitrate.

The plaintiff contends that Verizon Wireless waived the right to arbitrate by placing the plaintiff's account for collection with AMO Recoveries. However, the plaintiff provides no legal support for this proposition. In any event, the Court finds that Verizon Wireless did not waive its right to arbitration by engaging in "protracted litigation." This determination is fact specific. Factors to consider include: (1) the time elapsed from the commencement of litigation to the request for arbitration; (2) the amount of any litigation (including exchanges of pleadings, any substantive motions, and discovery); and (3) proof of prejudice, including taking advantage of pre-trial discovery not available in arbitration, and expense.

Applying this analytical framework, the Court finds that (1) the lapse in time between the commencement of litigation and the demand for arbitration was brief as less than two months passed between the service of the complaint and Verizon Wireless's demand for arbitration, (2) because Verizon Wireless's motion to compel arbitration was served in lieu of an answer, the parties did not engage in meaningful litigation, and (3) the plaintiff has not indicated that she has been prejudiced in any way.

Next, the plaintiff argues that the letter from AMO, in which it was agreed that a discounted sum would be accepted in satisfaction of the money owing, coupled with a letter from the Daly Law Center enclosing a check for the settlement amount constituted an "accord and satisfaction and thus a new contract between the parties" which negated the arbitration provision. The Court disagrees.

"A party seeking to establish an accord and satisfaction must demonstrate that there was a disputed or unliquidated claim between the parties which they mutually resolved through a new contract discharging all or part of their obligations under the original contract." There is no evidence that remotely indicates that a new contract was created by the acceptance of a reduced payment or that the plaintiff and Verizon Wireless discharged their obligations under the CSA.

In any event, the issue of whether there was an accord and satisfaction negating an arbitration provision is one to be determined by the arbitrators and not the Court. Thus, even if meritorious, this issue is not for the Court to decide.

In addition, the plaintiff contends that compelling arbitration of alleged violations of the FCRA is improper because doing so would force the plaintiff to "waive her rights under the FCRA and all protections afforded to her by law." This contention is also misplaced. It is well-settled that statutory rights may be arbitrated "so long as the prospective litigant effectively may vindicate his or her statutory cause of action in the arbitral forum." The plaintiff has not explained why her claims cannot be advanced through arbitration.

Finally, the Court notes that the remaining arguments, namely that "the defendant concedes the inapplicability of the arbitration clause" and that the "defendants' motion qualifies as a motion for summary judgment and fails to meet the standards for such a decision" are patently without merit.

Accordingly, the motion by Verizon Wireless to compel arbitration of the first and second causes of action is granted.

III. CONCLUSION

Based on the foregoing, it is hereby

ORDERED, that the motion by Verizon Wireless to compel arbitration of the first and second causes of action is GRANTED; and it is further

SO ORDERED.

Case Questions

1. What is the main point of contention in this case?

2. Does Federal law encourage or discourage the use of arbitration clauses in contracts?

3. Does the principle of "accord and satisfaction" negate the arbitration clause? Why or why not?

4. Can parties waive statutory rights through an arbitration clause?

Chapter Summary

A civil case is brought by a plaintiff against a defendant. A civil case is based on the plaintiff's contention that the defendant has committed some wrongdoing that has resulted in property or financial loss. Most consumer protection laws give individual consumers a cause of action against companies and individuals who violate those laws. When a consumer brings a complaint, he or she is referred to as a plaintiff. The party who is sued is labeled a defendant. Once a complaint has been filed, the defendant must file an answer, which denies the allegations of the complaint. Discovery is the process through which the parties in a civil case learn facts about the contentions of the parties. Parties can conduct depositions, which are oral questions of witnesses in the case. Interrogatories, on the other hand, are written questions posed to parties in a civil action. Many consumer protection cases end in arbitration because of clauses inserted in credit offers. Arbitration is a method to bypass civil cases by submitting the issues to a neutral, third party for resolution.

Civil cases can end in a variety of ways, either by settlement or by the decisions of an arbitrator. In any event, the parties must consider the potential for damages and equitable remedies. An equitable remedy is a court's order compelling a party to take a particular action. Damages, on the other hand, are monetary payments made by one party to another. In consumer protection cases, there may be issues of consequential damages, which are financial losses directly tied to the actions of the parties. Liquidated damages are clauses included in credit and loan contracts where the parties agree, in advance, to the amount of damages. In addition to bringing civil suits, consumers can also complain to the Federal Trade Commission, state agencies and even invoke the power of the press to redress specific problems.

Web Sites

- Federal Trade Commission
  http://www.ftc.gov
- State of Connecticut Department of Consumer Protection
  http://www.ct.gov/dcp/site/default.asp
- New York State Consumer Protection Board
  http://www.consumer.state.ny.us/

Key Terms

Plaintiff	Settlement
Defendant	Arbitration
Complaint	Mediation
Answer	Jurisdiction
Discovery	Equity
Deposition	Injunction
Interrogatories	Specific performance
Request for production of documents	Rescission
Verdict	Reformation
Liable	Damages
Punitive damages	

Review Questions

1. What terms describe the parties in a civil case?
2. What are the possible jury verdicts in a civil case?
3. What is an injunction?
4. What is specific performance?
5. What are compensatory damages?
6. What are liquidated damages?
7. What are consequential damages?
8. What limits are placed on the award of damages in typical consumer protection cases?
9. What is discovery in civil cases?
10. What is the difference between interrogatories and depositions?

11. Explain jurisdiction.

12. How is mediation different than arbitration?

13. Explain the court's decision in this chapter's case excerpt.

14. How can consumers use the "power of the press" to redress wrongs?

15. Does the FTC prosecute cases on behalf of individual consumers? Explain your answer.

Chapter 11

When the Contract Is Invalid

Chapter Objectives

- Explain how a consumer contract can be voided by reason of the consumer's capacity
- Describe contracts that are unenforceable because of illegality or public policy reasons
- Explain the concepts of duress and coercion and the impact that they have on consumer contracts
- Describe the doctrine of promissory estoppel
- Explain accord and satisfaction

I. Contracts That Are Invalid because of the Consumer's Status

In this chapter, we will address the legal issues involved in creating a wide variety of consumer credit arrangements. Whether it is a credit card agreement or car loan, almost all consumer protection issues boil down to the issue of contract law. In a credit card agreement, for instance, we have all of the elements of a contractual agreement. One party agrees to do something for the other party. In this case, the credit card company agrees to extend credit for purchases and cash advances and to charge an interest rate on the money involved. The consumer agrees to pay regular monthly payments and any other fees that form part of the agreement. This is a contract. Car loans, mortgages, overdraft protection accounts, checking accounts and a multitude of other consumer issues all revolve around contract law. The fact that they also can involve federal issues, such as Truth in Lending, Real Estate Settlement Procedures Act or Fair Debt Collection Practices simply means that when the parties sue, they have several grounds to allege in their complaints.

Because the basics of contract law are so important to these relationships, we must examine the features of contract law that have a direct bearing on consumer law issues. Typically, the legal elements of a contract consist of:

- Mutual Assent
- Consideration
- Capacity
- Legality

Several of these elements have no real significance to consumer law. Mutual assent, for instance, is the so-called "meeting of the minds" between the parties. This is an element that shows that both parties were in agreement to be bound by a contract. That is usually not an issue in consumer credit arrangements. Both parties realize that they are entering into a contract. The real issue is the fine points of that arrangement, such as hidden fees, costs, and other charges, not the fact that the contract itself actually exists.

We can also say the same thing about consideration. Commonly referred to as "bargained for exchange," consideration is the requirement that both parties to a contract bring something of value to the exchange. Contracts require consideration in order to prove that both parties are actually bound to one another. This, also, is usually not an issue in consumer protection cases. The parties do not dispute that both parties are bound to one another. The question in such cases is just how far those obligations go. We have dispensed with the two first elements of a contract by showing that they have no real significance in consumer credit arrangements. However, that cannot be said of the last two elements. They are both extremely important. For instance, there is the issue of capacity.

A. Capacity

Capacity refers to a party's ability to know and understand the effect of entering into a contract. It also refers to the fact that the party entered into the contract freely and voluntarily. Later in this chapter, we will see that there are challenges to consumer credit agreements that can be based on duress, coercion and undue influence. All of these attack the premise that the consumer entered into the contract willingly. However, before we can address those issues, we must look closely at the element of capacity that refers to a consumer's ability to understand that he or she is entering into a contract.

One of the most important elements of any contract is a showing that both parties had capacity. When dealing with consumer credit issues, this involves proof about only one party: the consumer. Major corporations, such as credit card issuers and lenders, are deemed to have capacity. Businesses do not have the option of stating that they were insane at the time that the contract was created, but consumers can. Capacity, then, is proof that the consumer understood what he or she was doing when the consumer credit agreement was created. If the consumer, or the consumer's family, can show that capacity was absent, the court is authorized to rule the contract null and void.

> **Capacity:** An individual's ability to know and understand the consequences of entering into a legally binding agreement.

Capacity is not the same thing as making good business decisions. In order to show that a consumer lacked capacity, the evidence must show that the consumer was mentally incompetent. A person can be mentally competent and still exercise poor judgment, make terrible choices and even make extremely risky investments and still be considered mentally competent. If this is the standard, then how does a consumer prove that he or she was mentally incompetent at the time that the consumer credit agreement was created? Fortunately, there are some legal standards. A person lacks mental capacity if he or she does not know and understand the legal significance of the action. A person also lacks capacity if he or she falls into one of the categories where legal capacity is presumed. These categories include:

- Minors
- Individuals acting under the influence of alcohol or drugs
- Individuals declared mentally incompetent by a court

> **Getting to the Essentials:**   A consumer credit agreement can be invalidated by showing that the consumer lacked legal capacity.

1. Minors

When a person falls below a certain age level, the law presumes that he or she lacks capacity to enter into a contract. This age varies from state to state, but is usually either 18 or 21 years old. As far as the law is concerned, any individual below this age who enters into a contract is presumed to lack capacity. Contracts entered into with minors are not enforceable.

Example 11-1

Jack finds a credit card application on his parents' bureau and completes it. Although Jack is 12 years old, he puts his age on the credit card application as 21 and even gives himself an annual income of $42,500. The company issues the card and Jack uses it to make purchases. Later, when Jack fails to make payments on the credit card, debt collectors begin calling. Jack's mother informs them that he is 12 years old and even provides a copy of his birth certificate. The company sues anyway, alleging that Jack fraudulently gave his age as 21. How does the court rule?

Answer: The court will dismiss the suit. Jack's age means that he lacks capacity. Therefore the contract is unenforceable, no matter what information Jack provided on the contract.

Minor: A person who is under the age of full legal rights and duties.

> **Getting to the Essentials:**   Minors are presumed to lacked capacity to enter into a contract

a. Advanced Age

Although there is a specific age that creates a legal presumption against capacity, the same rule does not apply on the other end of life. There is no preset limit beyond which a person is presumed to lack capacity because of advanced age. The reason is simple: the elderly show remarkable differences in ability. Some middle aged people may show signs of decreasing abilities, while some octogenarians remain quick witted and wily. As a result, cases involving allegations of incapacity in elderly consumers must be addressed on a case-by-case basis. For an example of such a case, see this chapter's case excerpt.

Figure 11-1. Contract trial plaintiff winners.[1]

Table 4. Contract trial plaintiff winners in State courts in the Nation's 75 largest counties, 2001

Case type	All contract trials[a]		Jury trials[b]		Bench trials	
	Number	Plaintiff winners[c]	Plaintiff Number	winners[c]	Number	Plaintiff winners[c]
Contract cases	3,625	64.8%	1,528	61.6%	2,037	67.8%
Fraud	602	58.3%	273	61.5%	314	56.7%
Seller plaintiff	1,196	76.8	271	70.1	913	78.9
Buyer plaintiff	779	61.5	452	62.6	320	60.9
Mortgage foreclosure	22	72.7	--	--	22	72.7
Employment discrimination	160	43.8	138	45.7	17	41.2
Other employment dispute	282	55.7	163	63.2	108	47.2
Rental/lease	276	64.9	63	63.5	212	65.6
Tortious interference	133	57.9	71	57.7	58	56.9
Partnership dispute	41	46.3	22	68.2	18	16.7
Subrogation	61	67.2	40	50.0	19	100.0
Other or unknown contract	73	56.2	35	54.3	36	55.6

Note: Data on plaintiff winners were available for 99.9% of all contract trials.

Detail may not sum to total because of rounding.

--No cases recorded.

[a]Includes bench and jury trials, trials with a directed verdict, judgments notwithstanding the verdict, and jury trials for defaulted defendants.

[b]Does not include jury trials that involved trials with a directed verdict, judgments notwithstanding the verdict, and jury trials for defaulted defendants.

[c]Excludes bifurcated trials where the plaintiff litigated only the damage claim.

Advanced age is one of the factors that a court can consider in evaluating the consumer's capacity. If the consumer suffers from senile dementia, or physical problems that prevent him or her from knowing and understanding the consequences of entering into a legally binding agreement, then the court can rule the contract void and refuse to enforce it. The same rule applies in situations where a person is under the influence of alcohol or some other drug.

B. Intoxication

Just as a contract with a minor or someone suffering from Alzheimer's disease is voidable, so too is a contract entered into with an intoxicated person. A consumer who signs a consumer agreement under the influence has the right to have the contract ruled null and void. However, the issue in these cases involves actually proving the consumer's sobriety at the time that he or she signed the consumer credit agreement. The consumer may be hard pressed to claim intoxication without any witnesses. However, if the consumer can show intoxication, then the court can void the contract just as if he or she were a minor.

---

1. Contract Trials and Verdicts in Large Counties, 2001. Bureau of Justice Statistics, Selected Findings. Civil Justice Survey of State Courts, 2001. January, 2005.

C. Mental Incompetence

The final category of individuals who cannot enter into legally binding contracts is the mentally incompetent. A court can declare a person mentally incompetent and, after that declaration, he or she cannot enter into contracts. Even if the person does, the contract will be declared void. In the usual scenario, the mentally incompetent person has a guardian appointed to handle the person's business. That does not mean, however, that the person will not complete credit card agreements, enter into loans and do any of a number of activities with companies. After all, when was the last time a credit card company confirmed that an applicant was mentally competent when they received an application? Most companies operate on the assumption that the consumer-applicant is perfectly competent until proven otherwise.

States approach the issue of contracts with the legally insane in different ways. For instance, some jurisdictions follow the rule that such a contract is immediately void, while other jurisdictions state that the contract will be declared void when the issue comes up in litigation.[2] However, in situations where the person has been adjudicated legally insane, most jurisdictions follow the rule that such a contract is absolutely void and unenforceable.[3]

D. Enforceable and Unenforceable Contracts

We have used the term "enforceable" and "unenforceable" several times in this chapter without examining what these terms actually mean. What is the difference between an enforceable contract and unenforceable contract?

An enforceable contract has all requisite legal elements. The parties can use the court system to compel the other party to abide by the terms of an enforceable contract. As we saw in the previous chapter, parties to an enforceable contract can request damage awards and also equitable remedies, such as injunctions and specific performance. Unenforceable contracts are just the opposite. Some legal element is missing and the courts will refuse to enforce the contract's provisions. There are many contracts entered into that are unenforceable, however the parties abide by the terms and the issues in the contract are never brought before a court. In Example 11-1, for instance, if Jack had simply made payments on the credit card bills, the unenforceability of the credit card agreement would never have become an issue. Parties have wide latitude to negotiate terms with one another and they can even carry on with a contract that a court would never enforce. However, when the parties resort to litigation, then enforceability becomes a primary issue. That takes us to the fourth and final element of a legally valid contract: legality.

> *Getting to the Essentials:* An "unenforceable" contract is one that court will not honor.

---

2. *Handley v. Handley*, 172 Kan. 659, 243 P.2d 204 (1952).
3. CJS Contracts § 145.

E. Legality

In order to use the court system to enforce a contract, the parties must show that the contract is legal. When a consumer challenges a credit agreement with a statement that it is in violation of applicable federal law, such as the Truth in Lending Act, the consumer is actually saying that the contract is not legal and therefore the credit company cannot use the court system to order the consumer to abide by its terms.

Legality in contracts is required in order to avoid an uncomfortable and bizarre situation for the court system. If legality were not required, then the court would be called upon to enforce the provisions of a contract that are not legal. Parties would use the legal system to impose illegal contract terms on one another. That situation is untenable and a court will refuse to place itself in that situation. As a result, if the consumer can show that the contract terms violate the law, then the court may rule the contract illegal and therefore unenforceable.

We have already seen examples of illegal contracts throughout this book. For instance, a lender who charges fees and interest rates higher than those permitted under state or federal law is engaging in an illegal contract. Those additional fees and interest rates cannot be enforced through the legal system. When we examined the issues surrounding fair debt collection, we saw other examples of illegal tactics that cannot be enforced through a judge's rulings. However, contract law goes even further than a simple statement that a contract with illegal terms cannot be enforced. Courts also invoke public policy concerns for refusing to impose contract terms.

1. Public Policy

In some situations, a court may refuse to enforce a contract not because it violates the law, but because it violates "public policy." The term encompasses a broad range of activities that may not be strictly illegal, but involve practices that courts do not like to enforce. For instance, contracts can be ruled void for public policy on any of the following grounds:

- The contract forces the consumer to surrender some basic right
- The contract involves excessive charges and fees that essentially destroy a consumer's ability to function
- The contract is unduly burdensome for the consumer

When a court rules that a contract is void for public policy reasons, such as forcing the consumer to surrender a basic right, such as the right to ever bring suit or challenge the creditor's actions, courts will refuse to enforce it. "Void for public policy" is a term that gives courts a great deal of flexibility in forcing companies to abide by more reasonable terms, even when these terms are allowed by the applicable law.

> *Getting to the Essentials:*   Courts may invalidate a contract on public policy grounds, even when the terms are legal.

II. Mistake as Grounds to Void a Contract

A court can rule that a contract is void and therefore unenforceable when the parties can prove **mistake**. However, "mistake" has a specific meaning in contract law that does not apply to other areas of life. In contract law, a mistake is an error about a fact that is shared by both sides. It is not a mistake, for instance, when the consumer signs a credit agreement he or she shouldn't have. Instead, a mistake would be both the consumer and the credit card company believing that an interest rate was at 7% when it was actually at 5%. Because both sides have to share in an error for it to be ruled a mistake, very few consumer contracts can be voided because of this ground.

Mistake: An unintentional error or act by both sides to a contract.

In consumer credit agreements, there are generally three different types of mistakes that can result in a void contract. These include:

- Mistaken description
- Mistaken existence
- Mistaken value

A. Mistaken Description

Mistaken description concerns an issue such as an incorrect interest rate. If both parties have a mistaken belief about a term in the contract, then the court may simply reform the contract to have it reflect the stated belief.

B. Mistaken Existence

Mistaken existence, on the other hand, refers to a mutual mistake about the existence of a critical element to the contract. When the credit card company issues a card in an incorrect company name, for instance, this is a mistake of existence. Because there is no such company in that name, the credit agreement can be ruled null and void.

C. Mistaken Value

Mistaken value concerns a mutual mistake about the value of an item used as collateral or reference in the credit agreement. Suppose, for example, that both the homeowner and the mortgage lender believe that a home is worth $125,000, when it is only worth $100,000. In this example, because both parties share a mistaken belief about the worth of the collateral for the loan, the entire contract may be voided.

Getting to the Essentials:	The defense of mistake is rarely used in consumer credit agreements.

III. Canceling a Contract because of Duress, Coercion or Undue Influence

No person can be compelled into entering into a contract against his or her will. Such a contract is a nullity. If the consumer can show that the credit agreement was created under these situations, then the court can refuse to enforce the contract. There are three basic allegations that a consumer can bring to challenge the contract as unlawful because his or her will was overcome to enter it. They are:

- Duress
- Coercion
- Undue influence

A. Duress

Duress is the application of force, or the threat of force, that causes a person to do something that he or she would not otherwise have done. When a person acts under duress he or she does not act voluntarily. Simply threatening a person with physical violence if he does not sign a contract is an example of duress. Some states have defined duress as any action that overcomes the will of another person and compels agreement to the contract when the person really has no intention of giving it.

Duress: Unlawful pressure on a person to do what he or she would not otherwise have done.

The problem with duress has always been how to apply it in individual cases. When a defendant threatens to kill the consumer if he refuses to sign a contract, the court has no difficulty in ruling that the contract was the product of duress and refusing to enforce it. However, there are very few cases with such obvious violence. Instead, courts are often presented with situations where the issues are cloudier. Is it duress to "suggest" that signing the contract will avoid "trouble?" Consider Example 11-2.

Example 11-2

Maria is home one day when a door-to-door salesman knocks on her door. He urges her to apply for a "signature loan" so that she can fix up her home. The loan is for a total of $5000, but the payments seem high. As she considers the loan paperwork, the salesman continually stares at her. She doesn't like his eyes and feels uncomfortable. She signs the paperwork. Does she have a claim for duress?

Answer: No. Sidestepping the issue of the three-day "cooling off" period required for loans under the Truth in Lending Act, the fact that the man stared at Maria is not enough to qualify as duress. The court will probably enforce this agreement.

When the defendant can show that the consumer exercised his or her own free will, even if the consumer entered into a bad bargain, a claim of duress will almost always fail. Duress also goes to the facts as they occurred at the time that the contract was created. The fact that the creditor later engaged in questionable or even threatening practices does not void the contract, although it may provide grounds for other actions. Some states have gone so far as to create a presumption against duress when the parties can show that the consumer was free to consult with an attorney before signing the agreement. Other states limit the application of duress to situations involving a direct threat of physical harm. As a result, a consumer's claim of duress will usually not succeed in voiding a credit agreement.

> *Getting to the Essentials:*   Duress is the claim that a consumer's will was overcome by force or the threat of force.

Example 11-3

John is in terrible financial trouble and a representative from Stick It To 'Em Lending, Inc., calls him up and offers him a loan. The loan has a very high interest rate, terrible terms and is a generally a bad bargain, but John feels that he has no choice if he is going to attempt to get out of his financial straits. Does John have a claim of duress?

Answer: No. As long as John's financial problems were not caused by Stick It To 'Em Lending, then there is no duress.[4]

B. Coercion

Coercion is the opposite of duress. Instead of physical threats, coercion is mental compulsion, or overcoming a consumer's will through mental tactics. An example of coercion is blackmail, where the party's will is overwhelmed not by violence, but by the threat of potential humiliation or embarrassment. Coercion as a defense to a contract is more successful because there are numerous examples of creditors, debt collectors and others using mental tactics to get money from consumers. Examples of these tactics include the threat of lawsuits or criminal charges, when neither would be appropriate or even possible.

> *Getting to the Essentials:*   Coercion is the claim that the consumer's will was overcome by psychological manipulation.

Coercion: Compulsion through psychological factors that makes a person act against his or her free will.

C. Undue Influence

The third type of defense available to a person who claims that a contract was entered into against his or her will is **undue influence**. If duress is a physical threat and coercion is a mental threat, then undue influence is a violation of trust. The defense of undue influence arises in situations where one person has a position of trust with the consumer and then abuses that trust by involving the consumer in transactions that go against the consumer's interest. Claims of undue influence are often brought against attorneys, family members, caregivers and others who are responsible for the care of the elderly. They abuse this position to enrich themselves at the other's expense. Like contracts produced by duress or coercion, contracts produced through undue influence are unenforceable.

---

4. *French v. Shoemaker*, 81 US 314, 20 L Ed 852 (1871).

Undue Influence: The abuse of a position of trust to overcome a person's will, usually to the benefit of the person exerting the improper control.

IV. Important Legal Doctrines for Consumer Contracts

So far, our discussion about contract law and consumer protection has focused on the issues involved in creating the contract. However, there are several important legal doctrines that may come into play after the contract comes into existence that may prevent the implementation of the contract or actually result in the contract being unenforceable. Some of the most important of these legal doctrines include:

- Promissory estoppel
- Waiver
- Accord and satisfaction
- Caveat Emptor
- Laches

A. Promissory Estoppel

"Estoppel" is a concept that has existed in both the American and English legal systems for centuries. The premise behind estoppel is simple: when person A makes a statement that person B relies upon, A is prevented from denying the truth of his statement. Promissory estoppel is based on the principle that when a person acts in reliance on another person's promise, the other cannot deny that the promise existed. Consider Example 11-4.

Example 11-4

Cash & Carry Auto Loans is in the business of financing used car sales. Victor goes to Cash & Carry and arranges an oral agreement to finance the purchase of a used car that he likes. He makes regular payments on the car for two years. When he makes his last payment, he requests the title to the car. Cash & Carry denies that they had any contract with Victor, but they do thank him for his regular, monthly "donations." Can Victor claim promissory estoppel?

Answer: Yes. Because Victor acted in compliance with a promise, even an oral promise, Cash & Carry is barred, under promissory estoppel, from claiming that the promise ever existed. The company must present the title to the car to Victor.

Courts often invoke the doctrine of promissory estoppel as a way to prevent an injustice to one party. In the situation in Example 11-4, it would be unjust to allow Cash & Carry to accept Victor's money and provide nothing. Faced with this proposition, most courts would rule that Cash & Cash must deliver the title.

Promissory estoppel: A legal doctrine that holds that a person or company is barred from claiming that a promise never existed when another person relied, in good faith, on that promise.

> *Getting to the Essentials:*   A contract that is otherwise unenforceable may
> become enforceable when a party can show that
> promissory estoppel applies.

B. Waiver

The concept of waiver has become important in recent years with creditors and others attempting to insert waiver clauses in their credit agreements. A waiver is the surrender of a right, whether granted by contract or by law. A consumer may be presented with a credit agreement where he or she waives all rights to sue for any violation by the creditor. If such a waiver were upheld, it would essentially give the consumer no power to bring a lawsuit for any infraction by the creditor. As we have already seen, courts would probably rule that such a waiver violated public policy and would refuse to enforce it. But waivers of lesser rights are often upheld. For instance, it is now common for a consumer to waive his or her right to bring a civil action in favor of mandatory arbitration. Courts routinely uphold these civil waivers. A party can waive a right orally, in writing or by action, but in most consumer credit arrangements, the waiver is in writing.

Waiver: A voluntary and intentional abandonment or relinquishment of a right, claim, or privilege.

C. Accord and Satisfaction

Accord and satisfaction is another term with ancient roots. The theory behind accord and satisfaction is that the parties are always free to negotiate new terms with one another, even after the contract has been created. When there is a dispute between the parties, one can invoke the provisions of accord and satisfaction by offering new terms that are accepted by the other. Consider Example 11-5.

Example 11-5

Maria receives a bill from her cellular phone service. She has had numerous discussions with the company about this bill. She has repeatedly stated that the company has charged her for minutes that she never used. Maria believes that the proper total for the bill should be $225, but the company continues to bill her for $432. Maria writes out a check for $225 and writes "accord and satisfaction" on the check. The company cashes the check and then brings action against Maria for the remaining $207. Maria counters that the bill has been paid in full. Who is correct?

Answer: Maria. By writing "accord and satisfaction" on the check, Maria has essentially renegotiated the terms of the contract with the cell phone company. When the company cashed the check, it accepted her terms. The company has lost the right to sue for the balance because of the principle of accord and satisfaction.

Companies are familiar with the concept of accord and satisfaction and routinely refuse to accept payment for less than the full amount of a bill, realizing that they will face the same consequences as the cell phone company did in Example 11-5.

Accord and satisfaction: The renegotiation of a term of a contract, such as an outstanding bill amount by the offer of one party, accepted by the other.

D. Caveat Emptor

We have encountered the phrase, "**caveat emptor**" on several previous occasions. In earlier chapters, we saw that caveat emptor, or "let the buyer beware" was the approach used by most courts in assessing business relations between consumers and companies throughout most of the 18th and 19th centuries. Under this ruling, consumers bear the responsibility of making sure that they get the best deal possible and when they don't, that is their own problem. However, caveat emptor as a legal philosophy has been abandoned in most consumer credit arrangements in favor of a more judicious approach. Courts have realized that creditors and consumers are not on an equal playing field when it comes to negotiating terms. Consumers cannot, for example, offer to change the terms in a credit card agreement. These arrangements are often presented with no option for changes. Because of this, the principle of caveat emptor has been abandoned in the vast majority of consumer protection cases.

Caveat emptor: (Latin), "let the buyer beware;" the legal principle that the consumer bears the burden of negotiating the best terms and if he or she fails to do so, must live with the results.

E. Laches

The final legal doctrine discussed in this chapter concerns laches. This is another ancient doctrine that goes to the actions of the parties involved in contract. Under the doctrine of laches, when a party has a legal right and fails to exercise it, the right is lost. In many ways, the doctrine of laches resembles statutes of limitation. Under a statute of limitation, the government must bring a criminal action against a person charged with the crime within a specific time period after the crime has been committed. If the government fails to do so, then it can never charge the defendant. The doctrine of laches is the corollary to the statute of limitations, applied to contract law. When a party to a contract has the right to sue, for example, and fails to exercise that right within a reasonable period of time, the right to sue is lost forever. Most states set specific time limitations for particular types of contract actions. Consider the situation in Example 11-6.

Example 11-6

ABC Credit Card Company has an action against Carlos for failure to make payments. Two years after failing to receive a regularly scheduled payment by Carlos, ABC Credit Card Company brings an action against him. Carlos counters that under the doctrine of laches, ABC has waived its rights and cannot sue him. Is he correct?

Answer: Yes. In most situations, a company must act within a "reasonable period of time" to bring an action. Although a reasonable period of time varies from case to case, most courts would rule that waiting 24 months to assert a claim is too long and therefore the doctrine of laches prevents ABC from suing Carlos for the outstanding balance.

Laches: Failure or delay in asserting a legal right.

Case Excerpt

How does advanced Alzheimer's disease affect a person's consumer rights?

Estate of Henderson ex rel. Johnson v. Meritage Mortg. Corp., 293 F.Supp.2d 830 (N.D.Ill.,2003)

MEMORANDUM OPINION AND ORDER

CASTILLO, District Judge.

The Estate of Josephine Henderson ("the Estate") filed suit against Meritage Mortgage Corporation ("Meritage") and MDR Mortgage Corporation ("MDR") claiming that the fees assessed for a home-equity loan made to Henderson violated federal and state law. Presently before this Court is Defendants' motion to dismiss the complaint. (R. 12-1, Defs.' Mot. to Dismiss.) Defendants' motion raises two arguments: (1) Plaintiff's complaint fails to state a claim upon which relief can be granted because all claims are barred by the applicable statutes of limitations; and (2) even if the state-law claims are not barred, the Court lacks subject-matter jurisdiction over them. For the reasons provided below, we deny Defendants' motion to dismiss in its entirety.

RELEVANT FACTS

Josephine Henderson died intestate on July 31, 2001. Although vascular disease ultimately caused Henderson's death, other significant conditions noted on her death certificate included dementia. (Id., Ex. A, Certificate of Death.) Her son, Frank Johnson, the independent administrator of the Estate, brings this action on her behalf.

From at least September 1998 until her death in 2001, Henderson "suffered from advanced Alzheimer's disease, dementia and other mental disorders." During this time, Johnson lived with Henderson and observed her on a daily basis. In his sworn affidavit, Johnson noted that by 1998, Henderson could not read, do simple arithmetic, consistently recognize her own son, feed or dress herself, remember the date or use the phone to make calls. Johnson had to warn Henderson about interacting with sales people. He also noted that Henderson "was under the delusion that she had no bills, including water, gas or phone bills, and was incapable of paying them." She put all correspondence and invoices, unopened, in a dining room drawer."

MDR is a mortgage brokerage. Sometime in September 1998, an MDR agent approached Henderson and encouraged her to obtain a home-equity loan to finance home improvements. On October 2, 1998, MDR secured through Meritage, a mortgage lender, a $40,200 home-equity loan for Henderson. Henderson, nearly 83 years old, agreed to make 330 monthly payments of $434.96. At the time of the loan, Henderson owned her home outright and she lived on a monthly income of $946 from Social Security benefits and a widow's pension. Thus, the loan's payment schedule would consume 46% of her monthly income until she was over 110 years old.

The home improvements started sometime in 1998 or early 1999, but were never completed. On September 23, 1999, Resource Baneshares Mortgage Group, Inc., a loan servicing group to whom Meritage transferred the loan, filed a foreclosure complaint against Henderson. Johnson contends that neither he nor Henderson received notice of the foreclosure until Johnson was served with eviction papers on April 9, 2002, almost one year after Henderson's death. Johnson further asserts that he had no knowledge of the home-equity loan until he received notice of the eviction. In August 2002 Johnson searched through his mother's things and discovered materials concerning the home-equity loan. Johnson then enlisted the help of an attorney to obtain copies of the closing papers from Meritage.

Johnson responded to the foreclosure proceedings in the Circuit Court of Cook County by filing a countersuit alleging that neither he nor his mother had notice of the mortgage, foreclosure or sale. On November 21, 2002, his claim was dismissed without prejudice because it was brought by the next of kin rather than by the Estate. Johnson then applied to become the independent administrator of the Estate, which was granted on January 9, 2003. On February 28, 2003, he filed the present complaint.

LEGAL STANDARDS

A motion to dismiss under Federal Rule of Civil Procedure 12(b)(6) tests the sufficiency of the complaint, not the merits of the suit. This Court views all facts alleged in the complaint, as well as any inferences reasonably drawn from those facts, in the light most favorable to the plaintiff. This Court may also review any documents referred to in the complaint. We will grant a motion to dismiss only if it appears beyond doubt that the plaintiff can prove no set of facts entitling him to relief.

ANALYSIS

The Estate alleges that the fees charged to structure the mortgage, as well as the mortgage itself, were illegal and unconscionable. The Estate seeks relief under the Real Estate Settlement Procedures Act ("RESPA"), 12 U.S.C. §§ 2601–2617, the Truth in Lending Act ("TILA"), Pub.L. No. 90-321, 82 Stat. 146 (codified in scattered sections of 15 U.S.C.), the Home Ownership and Equity Protection Act ("HOEPA"), Pub.L. 103–325, 108 Stat. 2190 (codified in scattered sections of 15 U.S.C.), the Fair Housing Act ("FHA"), 42 U.S.C. §§ 3601–3619, the Equal Credit Opportunity Act ("EOCA"), 15 U.S.C. §§ 1691–1691f and section 1981 of the Civil Rights Act, 42 U.S.C. § 1981. The complaint also includes state-law claims of breach of fiduciary duty, inducing breach of fiduciary duty, unjust enrichment and violations of the Illinois Consumer Fraud and Deceptive Business Practices Act ("ICFA"), 815 Ill. Comp. Stat. 505/1–505/12.

Defendants assert that the Estate's claims are barred by the applicable statutes of limitations. Plaintiff's RESPA, TILA and HOEPA claims have one-year statutes of limitations. 12 U.S.C. § 2614; 15 U.S.C. § 1640(e). Plaintiff's ECOA, FHA, and section 1981 claims have two-year statutes of limitations. 15 U.S.C. § 1691e(f); 42 U.S.C. § 3613(a)(1)(A). Plaintiff's ICFA claim has a three-year statute of limitations. 815 Ill. Comp. Stat. 505/10a(e). Defendants assert that all of these statutes of limitations started to run on October 2, 1998, the day that Henderson entered into the mortgage agreement.

The Estate responds that the statutes of limitations have not expired because, under the federal discovery rule, the claims did not accrue on the loan's closing date. The Estate also argues that, even if the statutes of limitations have expired, this Court should equitably toll them. The federal discovery rule, on the one hand, provides that a claim does not accrue, and the statute of limitations does not begin to run, until (1) a "party performs the alleged unlawful act" and (2) "the party bringing a claim discovers an injury resulting from this unlawful act." The equitable tolling doctrine, on the other hand, "permits a plaintiff to avoid the bar of the statute of limitations if despite all due diligence he is unable to obtain vital information bearing on the existence of his claim." Under the equitable tolling doctrine, "the plaintiff is assumed to know that he has been injured, so that the statute of limitations has begun to run; but he cannot obtain information necessary to decide whether the injury is due to wrongdoing and, if so, wrongdoing by the defendant."

Turning to the question of when Plaintiff's claims accrued, it is undisputed that the alleged unlawful act occurred when the loan was consummated, but the parties dispute when Henderson (or her Estate) discovered the resulting injury. Plaintiff alleges that because Henderson suffered from advanced Alzheimer's disease when the loan was consummated, she lacked the mental capacity to discover her injury, and therefore invokes the federal discovery rule to toll the statutes of limitations. Defendants contend that "mental illness, even where rising to the level of insanity, (will not) delay the statute of limitations from running." Ebrahimi v. E.F. Hutton & Co., Inc., 852 F.2d 516, 521 (10th Cir.1988). The Tenth Circuit in Ebrahimi relied in part on a passage in Crawford v. United States, 796 F.2d 924, 927 (7th Cir.1986), stating that "if the running of the statute of limitations depended on what the particular plaintiff actually knew given his mental or other incapacities, the discovery rule would swallow most of the provisions related to tolling, at least for disabilities that affected cognition and were in existence at the time of the accident." However, the next sentence in Crawford states that the Court did not determine "when if ever mental incapacity tolls the administrative statute of limitations."

The Seventh Circuit later addressed this very question in Barnhart v. United States, 884 F.2d 295 (7th Cir.1989). Although the court once again did not affirmatively determine when mental disorders toll statute of limitations, it provided significant guidance on how the question should be answered. In Barnhart, the Seventh Circuit considered whether "an adult with no legal guardian" could rely on the discovery rule to toll the statute of limitations if the adult's mental state "rendered him incapable of 'discovering' the cause of his injury." Barnhart, 884 F.2d at 299. The court ultimately concluded that the plaintiff's mental disorder did not preclude him from discovering his injury because he had filed a timely action against a different defendant and because his mental disorder only eroded or impaired his "desire to proceed with a recognized cause of action." Id. at 299–300. Finally, the court stated that application of the discovery rule in this context should "focus on awareness or ability to comprehend." Id. at 299. The court noted that it was not "foreclosing the possibility that a mental disability preventing a plaintiff from discovering or understanding the cause of an injury (or rendering him or her entirely incapable of bringing a legal action) might toll the statute of limitations in similar cases." Id. at 299–300; see also Miller v. Runyon, 77 F.3d 189, 191 (7th Cir.1996) ("The traditional rule that mental illness tolls a statute of limitations applies only if the illness in fact prevents the sufferer from managing his affairs and thus from understanding his legal rights and acting upon them.")

While both Crawford and Barnhart addressed the application of the discovery rule to the administrative statute of limitations under the Federal Tort Claims Act, the effect of mental disorders on the application of the discovery rule applies generally to all statutes of limitations.

Plaintiff alleges that Henderson could not read, do simple arithmetic, consistently recognize her own son, feed or dress herself, remember the date or use the phone to make calls. Viewing these facts and all reasonable inferences in the light most favorable to Plaintiff, we conclude that Henderson lacked the ability to comprehend her injury and, due to advanced Alzheimer's Disease, to act upon her legal rights. By focusing on Henderson's "awareness or ability to comprehend," as instructed by Barnhart, rather than on what Henderson actually knew, as cautioned against in Crawford, we conclude that Plaintiff's claim accrued, at the earliest, on July 31, 2001, when Henderson died and her claims passed to her Estate. Once her claims passed to her Estate, Henderson's mental disorder was no longer relevant.

We must now determine when the Estate discovered Henderson's claims. The complaint is silent about who was responsible for administering the Estate prior to Johnson's appointment as independent administrator. Drawing all reasonable inferences in favor of the Estate, we assume that the Estate discovered Henderson's claims when Johnson discovered them. There are several dates when Johnson could have discovered Henderson's claims: when the loan closed (October 2, 1998); when construction started on Henderson's home (early 1999); when Johnson learned about the home-equity loan (April 9, 2002); or when Johnson received the loan documents (August 2002). Again, viewing the facts and all reasonable inferences in the light most favorable to Plaintiff, we conclude, at this stage of the proceedings, that Johnson was unaware of Henderson's injury until April 9, 2002. Thus, we conclude for the purposes of the motion to dismiss that the statutes of limitations did not begin to accrue until that date. The present action was filed on February 28, 2003, well within all applicable statutes of limitations, so Plaintiff's claims are not time-barred. Of course, discovery in this case may reveal that the Estate discovered Henderson's injury prior to April 9, 2002, in which case Defendants are free to renew this argument by filing an appropriate motion for summary judgment.

Alternatively, if there was no administrator appointed for Henderson's Estate, the claims may have accrued when Johnson was appointed independent administrator. See Clifford v. United States, 738 F.2d 977, 980 (8th Cir.1984) (holding that the statute of limitations does not start to run until an individual with knowledge of the injury also has the legal right or duty to sue).

The remaining issues before this Court—whether the statute of limitations should be equitably tolled, whether the shorter federal statutes of limitations should apply to Plaintiff's state-law claims and whether this Court has subject-matter jurisdiction over Plaintiff's state-law claims—need not be addressed as we have already found that Plaintiff's claims are not barred by the applicable statutes of limitations.

CONCLUSION

For the reasons stated above, Defendants Meritage Mortgage Corporation and MDR Mortgage Corporation's motion to dismiss is denied in its entirety.

Case Questions

1. Describe Henderson's mental condition before she entered into the agreement with MDR.
2. How much of Henderson's income would her new mortgage payments consume?
3. Explain the court's rationale concerning advanced mental disease and the tolling of the statute of limitations.
4. Are the plaintiff's claims bared by the statute of limitations? Why or why not?

Chapter Summary

In this chapter we have seen that the basic arrangement between a consumer and the creditor is a contract. As a contract, consumer credit agreements must meet some basic requirements. For instance, a consumer must have legal capacity to enter into a contract. Examples of individuals who lack capacity include minors, mentally incompetent individuals and those operating under the influence of alcohol or some other drug. In addition to a showing of capacity, parties to a contract must also show that the contract itself is legal. Contracts that contemplate unlawful terms will not be enforced by the court system. Courts are also empowered to nullify a contract on the grounds of public policy concerns, such as when a credit company insists that a consumer waive important rights in order to obtain financing.

Contracts can also be nullified on the grounds of duress, coercion or undue influence. Duress is a claim of physical threat that overwhelms the consumer's freedom of choice. Coercion is a claim of psychological manipulation to overcome the will of the consumer and force him or her to sign an agreement. Undue influence is the abuse of a position of trust to compel another to enter into a contractual agreement. There are many important court doctrines involved in contract law. Promissory estoppel, for example, is a doctrine that holds that when one party undertakes an obligation under a contract, the other party is prevented from claiming that the promise never existed. Parties are also free to waive important rights as part of a contractual agreement. The doctrine of laches applies to contract law. When a party has a right and fails to use that right, it may be lost forever.

Web Sites

- Find Law.com—contract law overview
  http://www.findlaw.com/01topics/07contracts/
- Commercial and Contract Law
  http://www.hg.org/commerc.html
- Legal Information Institute—Contract Law
  http://topics.law.cornell.edu/wex/contract

Key Terms

Capacity	Promissory estoppel
Minor	Waiver
Mistake	Accord and satisfaction
Duress	Caveat emptor
Coercion	Laches
Undue Influence	

Review Questions

1. What is capacity?
2. What are some examples of individuals who lack capacity to enter into a contract?
3. Who qualifies as a minor?
4. What is the rule about intoxication and contracts?
5. What is the definition of mentally incompetent?
6. What is the difference between an enforceable and an unenforceable contract?
7. Explain the phrase "void for public policy concerns."
8. How does contract law define mistake?
9. Explain duress.
10. Define coercion.
11. What is undue influence?
12. Explain the doctrine of promissory estoppel.
13. What is a waiver?
14. Explain the concept of accord and satisfaction.
15. What is the doctrine of laches?

Glossary

Accord and satisfaction
The renegotiation of a term of a contract, such as an outstanding bill amount by the offer of one party, accepted by the other.

Annual percentage rate
The amount that credit costs a consumer on a yearly basis.

Answer
The pleading filed by the defendant that denies the allegations in the complaint and raises any allegations against the plaintiff.

Arbitration
A process that avoids a civil trial by requiring parties to submit their differences to a neutral third party for disposition.

Attorneys' fees
A court award that requires the losing party to a lawsuit to pay the winning party's legal expenses.

Bait and Switch
A deceptive practice where a merchant blurs a consumer with the promise of one type of goods but ultimately provides inferior goods.

Balance computation method
The method used to calculate interest fees and balances on open-ended credit transactions.

Capacity
An individual's ability to know and understand the consequences of entering into a legally binding agreement.

Causation
A direct connection between one party's actions and the resulting injury to the other party.

Caveat emptor
(Latin), "let the buyer beware;" the legal principle that the consumer bears the burden of negotiating the best terms and if he or she fails to do so, must live with the results.

Clear and convincing evidence

A level of proof higher than mere preponderance of the evidence. In most civil trials preponderance of the evidence is sufficient.

Closed-end credit arrangement

A credit transaction where the terms, including interest rate and amount borrowed are known before the agreement is consummated.

Coercion

Compulsion through psychological factors that makes a person act against his or her free will.

Complaint

The pleading setting out the plaintiff's allegations against the defendant.

Consumer

Under the Fair Debt Collection Practices Act a person who owes a debt for a personal, family or household purpose.

Consumer report

Also known as a credit report; it lists a consumer's prior credit transactions, including charge accounts, loans and other financial data.

Consumer reporting agency

An agency that compiles data on individual consumers and issues credit histories on demand.

Cramming

Adding unauthorized charges to a person's telephone bill.

Credit score

A score compiled by a consumer reporting agency, based on positive and negative information in a credit report.

Creditor

A person or business who extends credit or loans money to a consumer.

Damages

A general term for an order requiring monetary payment by one party to another.

Debt collector

A person or company, separate from the creditor, that is in the business of collecting outstanding debts from consumers.

Defendant

The party against whom the complaint is brought.

Deposition

Oral questions of a witness, taken under oath, by an attorney.

Discovery

The exchange of information between the parties in a lawsuit.

Dispute

A consumer's challenge to information contained in a credit report.

Duress

Unlawful pressure on a person to do what he or she would not otherwise have done.

Equity

A trial court's power to order individuals to take certain actions; it arises from the court's authority to enforce fairness and justice. Also, the difference between what a homeowner owes on his or her home and the market value.

Express warranty

A pledge, promise or assurance made orally or in writing that provides details about a product.

Fiduciary

A person who enjoys a position of trust to another; a person who handles money or property for another.

Fraud

A civil or criminal action based on the defendant's knowing, false statement that an innocent party relied upon to his or her disadvantage.

Injunction

A court order prohibiting an individual or company from taking a specific action.

Interrogatories

Written questions posed by one party to another.

Jurisdiction

A court's power to enter orders binding persons involved or to entertain the subjects litigated between the parties.

Laches

Failure or delay in asserting a legal right.

Lemon law

A state statute that protects automobile consumers by providing them with legal actions against car manufacturers.

Liable

A determination that one party has some obligation to another party, usually in the form of monetary payments.

Market share theory

The premise that in any particular industry, 70% is owned by a small number of companies. When it is impossible to identify a specific manufacturer, courts will assess damages against the companies with the largest market share.

Material fact
A fact that is basic to a contract, one that the parties consider to be an essential ingredient of the negotiations.

Mediation
The process of working out disagreements by having a neutral, third party who works with the parties to reach a mutually acceptable agreement.

Minor
A person who is under the age of full legal rights and duties.

Mistake
An unintentional error or act by both sides to a contract.

Negligent misrepresentation
A statement made by a defendant that the defendant either does not know is truthful or does not care is truthful that induces a party to enter into an agreement.

Open-ended credit
Under the provisions of sub-part B of Regulation Z, a credit arrangement without a fixed term or a fixed amount borrowed.

Parol evidence rule
A rule that prohibits oral testimony to interpret or alter the terms of a written contract.

Passing Off
Presenting inferior products as if they were quality or name brand products.

Payment schedule
A provision of a closed-end credit agreement which shows all payments required under the loan.

Phishing
The process of using email and web sites that appear to be legitimate to gather sensitive information on consumers that can then be used for criminal activities.

Plaintiff
The party who files suit by bringing a complaint, which alleges that the defendant has wronged the plaintiff in some way.

Predatory lending
Using tactics and practices that are not industry standards and that trick or intimidate customers into accepting terms, fees and services that do not benefit them.

Privity
A relationship between two parties that is sufficiently close to establish that each was aware of the legal ramifications of entering into a contractual relationship with one another.

Product liability
A claim brought by a consumer for the harm caused by the manufacture, design, production and marketing of a product without regard to fault. Imposing liability on a manufacturer for producing a defective product.

Promissory estoppel
A legal doctrine that holds that a person or company is barred from claiming that a promise existed when another person relied, in good faith, on that promise.

Proximate cause
An event that immediately precedes the injury and is the natural and direct cause of the injury.

Punitive damages
Monetary awards assessed against a defendant designed to punish the defendant for behavior and to set an example for other similarly situated defendants.

Ratification
The process of confirming and accepting a previous action; a void contract can be ratified after the fact to make it legally enforceable.

Reformation
A court order conforming the written portion of a contract to the oral understanding of the parties.

Regulation Z
Legislation that imposes the provisions of TILA on creditors.

Request for production of documents
A discovery method that demands copies of any document that a party might rely on in presenting its case at trial.

Rescission
Canceling or voiding a contract.

Right of rescission
The consumer's right to cancel the credit arrangement within three business days of consummation.

Security Interest
The pledge of real or personal property as collateral for a loan.

Settlement
A negotiated closure of the issues in a civil trial that ends the litigation.

Skimming
Using a handheld device to illegally copy credit card information.

Specific performance
A court order requiring a party to abide by the terms of a contract.

Strict liability
Liability without regard to fault for particularly dangerous activities.

Sub-prime borrower
 A borrower with poor credit who only qualifies for higher than average interest loans.

Treble damages
 An award of damages three times the amount of the actual damages incurred by a party.

Undue Influence
 The abuse of a position of trust to overcome a person's will, usually to the benefit of the person exerting the improper control.

Unsophisticated consumer test
 An objective test created by the court system to evaluate the quality of the communication to the consumer; it calls for clear and cogent communications, with no misrepresentations or false statements.

Uttering
 To present to another.

Verdict
 The jury's conclusion about the facts in a trial.

Waiver
 A voluntary and intentional abandonment or relinquishment of a right, claim, or privilege.

Warranty
 A promise, assurance or guarantee that a particular fact or condition is true.

Yield spread premium
 A fee paid to a mortgage broker who arranges for a loan that provides an interest rate above the going rate.

Index

Annual percentage rate, 112
Appeals, civil cases, 195
Arbitration and mediation, 195–196
Arbitration clauses, unreasonable, 137

Bait and switch, 24
Balance computation method, credit cards, 113
Balance transfer fees, credit cards, 114
Balloon payments, 142
Better Business Bureau, complaints to, 204
Billing errors, credit cards, 114
Bogus e-mail, example, 88
Breach of duty, 46
Breach of warranty, 45
Bureau of Consumer Protection, 28

Calculating credit score, 152
Calculating damages, 199–200
Car title loans, 141
Causation, 47
Caveat emptor, 23
Caveat emptor, contracts, 224
Charging high interest rates, 133
Civil cases, appeals, 195
Civil cases, completing discovery process, 194
Civil cases, depositions, 193
Civil cases, discovery, 192–194
Civil cases, interrogatories, 193
Civil cases, request for production of documents, 193
Civil cases, settlements, 195
Civil cases, terminology used, 192
Civil trials, 194–195
Civil trials, verdicts, 194–195
Closed-end Credit Agreements, 115–119
Closed-end Credit Agreements, amount financed, 116

Closed-end Credit Agreements, annual percentage rate, 116
Closed-end Credit Agreements, assumption policy, 119
Closed-end Credit Agreements, contract reference, 118–119
Closed-end Credit Agreements, demand feature, 117
Closed-end Credit Agreements, finance charge, 116
Closed-end Credit Agreements, identification of creditor, 116
Closed-end Credit Agreements, insurance and debt cancellation provisions, 118
Closed-end Credit Agreements, itemization of amount financed, 116
Closed-end Credit Agreements, late payments, 117
Closed-end Credit Agreements, payment schedule, 117
Closed-end Credit Agreements, prepayment provisions, 117
Closed-end Credit Agreements, required deposit, 119
Closed-end Credit Agreements, required disclosures, 115
Closed-end Credit Agreements, security interest, 117
Closed-end Credit Agreements, security interest charges, 118
Closed-end Credit Agreements, total of payments, 117
Closed-end Credit Agreements, total sale price, 117
Closed-end Credit Agreements, variable rate, 116
Coercion, canceling contract, 221
Commercial advertisements, limitations on, 34

Communications between debt collectors and consumers, 176–179

Communications between debt collectors and consumers, "unsophisticated consumer test", 178

Communications between debt collectors and consumers, attorney representation, 178

Communications between debt collectors and consumers, calling consumer at work, 177–178

Communications between debt collectors and consumers, ceasing communication, 178–179

Communications between debt collectors and consumers, communicating with consumer, 176–177

Communications between debt collectors and consumers, locating consumers, 176

Communications between debt collectors and consumers, validating debt, 178

Compensatory damages, 199–200

Consequential damages, 201–202

Consumer remedies, 191

Consumer, Magnuson-Moss Warranty Act, 70

Contracts, accord and satisfaction, 223–224

Contracts, accord and satisfaction, 223–224

Contracts, advanced age, 215

Contracts, canceling because of duress, coercion or undue influence, 219–222

Contracts, capacity, 214–215

Contracts, caveat emptor, 224

Contracts, coercion, 221

Contracts, enforceable and unenforceable, 217

Contracts, important legal doctrines, 222–224

Contracts, intoxication, 216

Contracts, invalid because of consumer's status, 213–217

Contracts, laches, 224

Contracts, legality, 218

Contracts, mental incompetence, 217

Contracts, minors, 215

Contracts, mistake, 218–219

Contracts, mistaken description, 219

Contracts, mistaken existence, 219

Contracts, mistaken value, 219

Contracts, promissory estoppel, 222

Contracts, public policy, 218

Contracts, rent to own, 142

Contracts, undue influence, 221–222

Contracts, waiver, 223

Cramming, 91

Credit card theft and fraud, 97–98

Credit cards, 111–115

Credit cards, adjusted balance, 114

Credit cards, annual percentage rate, 112

Credit cards, applications, 111

Credit cards, average daily balance, 113

Credit cards, balance computation method, 113

Credit cards, balance transfer fees, 114

Credit cards, billing errors, 114

Credit cards, cash advance fees, 114

Credit cards, disclosures, 111–114

Credit cards, fees for issuance, 112

Credit cards, grace period, 112

Credit cards, minimum finance charge, 112

Credit cards, over-the-limit fees, 114

Credit cards, previous balance, 114

Credit cards, statement on charge card payments, 114

Credit cards, transaction charges, 112

Credit cards, two cycle average daily balance, 113

Credit repair, 139–140

Credit reporting agencies, 154–155

Credit reports, 153

Credit reports, companies that issue offers a credit, 158

Credit reports, consumer disclosures, 158–159

Credit reports, courts, 156

Credit reports, creditors, 156

Credit reports, deleting contested information, 161

Credit reports, denials of credit, 159

Credit reports, disclosing file contents to consumers, 159

Credit reports, disputing credit report entries, 160

Credit reports, employers, 156–157

Credit reports, ensuring accuracy, 162

Credit reports, frivolous or irrelevant disputes, 161

Credit reports, furnishing to others, 155–158

Credit reports, governmental agencies, 157

Credit reports, inquiries, 159

Credit reports, items that may be not be reported, 161–162

Credit reports, law enforcement, 157

Credit reports, notice of reinvestigation, 161

Credit reports, obtaining copies of, 162

Credit reports, obtaining free copies, 162

Credit reports, opt out provisions, 158

Credit reports, state of dispute, 161

Credit reports, summary of consumer rights, 159

Credit score, calculating, 152

Credit, importance of good, 151

Credit, open-ended, 108–111

Damages, 47–48

Damages, Monetary, 199–202

Debt collector, defined under Fair Debt Collection Practices Act, 175

Debt defined under Fair Debt Collection Practices Act, 175–176

Deceptive practices, 23–25

Deceptive trade practices, common-law remedies, 25

Deceptive trade practices, examples of, 23–24

Deceptive trade practices, federal regulation, 26–29

Deceptive trade practices, state agency investigations, 33

Depositions, civil cases, 193

Disclaimers, warranties, 79

Disclaiming warranties, 67

Do Not Call Registry, 28

Duress, canceling contract, 220–221

Duty, 46

Duty to comply with health and safety regulations in product liability, 56

Duty to read, 198

Duty to test and inspect under product liability, 55

Duty, breach of, 46

E-mail, bogus, 88

Equifax, 155

Equitable remedies, 196–199

Equitable remedies, injunction, 197

Equitable remedies, reformation, 198–199

Equitable remedies, rescission, 198

Equitable remedies, specific performance, 197–198

Equity, stripping, 135–136

Experian, 155

Fair Credit Reporting Act, 153–155

Fair Credit Reporting Act, administrative enforcement, 163

Fair Credit Reporting Act, civil suits, 163–164

Fair Credit Reporting Act, consumer reporting agencies, 154

Fair Credit Reporting Act, consumer reports, 153

Fair Credit Reporting Act, enforcing, 162–164

Fair Credit Reporting Act, exclusions, 153–154

Fair Credit Reporting Act, investigative consumer report, 154

Fair Credit Reporting Act, purposes of credit reports, 155–162

Fair Debt Collection Practices Act, Chapter 9

Fair Debt Collection Practices Act, activities permitted, 179–183

Fair Debt Collection Practices Act, actual creditors, 174–175

Fair Debt Collection Practices Act, debt defined, 175–176

Fair Debt Collection Practices Act, defining "debt collector", 175

Fair Debt Collection Practices Act, enforcement, 183–184

Fair Debt Collection Practices Act, false statements, 180–181

Fair Debt Collection Practices Act, harassment, 180

Fair Debt Collection Practices Act, jurisdiction, 174–176

Fair Debt Collection Practices Act, misrepresentations, 181–182

Fair Debt Collection Practices Act, permissible actions, 179

Fair Debt Collection Practices Act, prohibited acts, 179–183
Fair Debt Collection Practices Act, unfair practices, 182–183
Fair Debt Collection Practices Act, who is covered, 174
Federal Trade Commission, 26–29, 120
Federal Truth in Lending Act, 105–108
Federal Truth in Lending Act, enforcement, 120–122
Federal Truth in Lending, consumer actions, 120
Federal Truth in Lending, continuing obligation of creditors, 108
Federal Truth in Lending, criminal liability, 121
Federal Truth in Lending, Federal Trade Commission, 120
Federal Truth in Lending, finance charges, 107
Federal Truth in Lending, initial disclosures, 107–108
Federal Truth in Lending, preemption of state law, 121–122
Federal Truth in Lending, time of disclosures, 106–107
Financing fees, 133
Fitness for purpose, warranty of, 68
Forgery, 93–95
Forgery, basic elements of, 93–94
Forgery, make, alter or possess a writing, 94
Forgery, uttering and delivering, 94–95
Forgery, without authority, 94
Fraud, 4–9
Fraud, alleging in complaint, 6
Fraud, criminal law and, 7–8
Fraud, limitations on, 6
Fraud, proving, 5–6
Fraud, sales statements, 6

Good and workmanlike performance, warranty of, 68–69
Grace period, credit cards, 112

High pressure sales tactics, 136

Identity theft, 98–99
Implied warranties, 67–69
Implied warranties, Magnuson-Moss Warranty Act, 73

Inherently dangerous objects, 56
Injunctions, 31, 197
Insurance schemes, 140–141
Interest rates, charging high, 133
Internet Fraud, Investigating, 91–93
Internet fraud, jurisdictional issues, 92
Internet scams, 89

Jurisdictional issues, Internet fraud, 92

Laches, contracts, 224
Legal System, overview of, 191-195
Lemon laws, 75
Liquidated damages, 202
Loan churning, 140
Loan flipping, 140
Loans, car title, 141
Loans, payday, 141
Loans, tax refund, 141

Magnuson-Moss Warranty Act, 69–75
Magnuson-Moss Warranty Act, consumer defined, 70
Magnuson-Moss Warranty Act, consumer products, 70
Magnuson-Moss Warranty Act, definitions, 70
Magnuson-Moss Warranty Act, enforcement, 71
Magnuson-Moss Warranty Act, implied warranties, 73
Magnuson-Moss Warranty Act, jurisdiction, 69
Magnuson-Moss Warranty Act, other federal laws, 73
Magnuson-Moss Warranty Act, statements not covered, 72–73
Magnuson-Moss Warranty Act, what is required, 73–74
Magnuson-Moss Warranty Act, written warranties, 71–72
Media, as a source for complaints, 204
Mediation, arbitration and, 195–196
Merchantability, warranty of, 68
Mistake as grounds to void contract, 218-219
Mistaken existence, ground to void contract, 219
Mistaken value, grounds to void contract, 219

Model Uniform Products Liability Act, 54

Monetary damages, 199–202

Monetary damages, compensatory, 199–200

Monetary damages, calculating damages, 199–200

Monetary damages, consequential damages, 201–202

Monetary damages, liquidated damages, 202

Monetary damages, nominal, 203

Monetary damages, punitive damages, 202–203

Negligent misrepresentation, 9–15

Negligent misrepresentation, defenses, 13–15

Negligent misrepresentation, defenses not available, 15

Negligent misrepresentation, elements of, 9–10

Negligent misrepresentation, mistake, 13

Negligent misrepresentation, monetary damages, 10–11

Negligent misrepresentation, opinions, 12

Negligent misrepresentation, pleading, 13

Nominal damages, 203

Notice of rescission, 119–120

Open-ended credit, 108–111

Oral and written warranties, conflicts, 66–67

Overdraft loan programs, 139

Overview of American Legal System, 191–195

Parol evidence rule, 66

Passing off, 24

Payday loans, 141

Payments, balloon, 142

Phishing, 90–91

Pre-payment penalties, 134–135

Predatory lending, 132–136

Predatory lending practices, other, 136–137

Predatory lending, consequences of, 138

Privity, 43–44

Product liability, 41–44

Product liability, arguments for and against, 51

Product liability, basis of lawsuit, 50–51

Product liability, contract law, 45

Product liability, design defect, 52

Product liability, doctrine of, 49–56

Product liability, duty to comply with health and safety regulations, 56

Product liability, duty to test and inspect, 55

Product liability, federal legislation, 54–55

Product liability, finding of fault, 50

Product liability, history of, 42–43

Product liability, inherently dangerous objects, 56

Product liability, manufacturing defect, 52

Product liability, marketing defect, 52

Product liability, plaintiff injured by, 52

Product liability, proving, 51–53

Product liability, proving a defect, 52

Product liability, state statutes, 53

Product liability, tort reform, 56

Product liability, traditional negligent theories, 45–49

Promissory estoppel, 222

Punitive damages, 202–203

Questionable lending practices, other, 138–142

Reformation, 198–199

Regulation Z, 106

Remedies, equitable, 196–199

Rent to own contracts, 142

Reports, credit, 153

Request for production of documents, civil cases, 193

Rescission, 198

Rescission, notice of, 119–120

Rescission, right of, 119–120

Right of Rescission, 119–120

Scams, Internet, 89

Settlements, civil cases, 195

Skimming, 97–98

Specific performance, 197–198

Stripping equity, 135–136

Tax refund loans, 141

Tort reform and product liability, 56

TransUnion, 155

TV and newspaper "crusaders," 204

Undue influence, contracts, 221–222

Unfair and deceptive trade practices, federal legislation, 26–29

Unfair and deceptive trade practices, state law, 29–32

Uniform Commercial Code, 32–33

Uniform Deceptive Trade Practices Act, 29–32

Uniform Deceptive Trade Practices Act, attorneys' fees, 31

Uniform Deceptive Trade Practices Act, exceptions, 30–31

Uniform Deceptive Trade Practices Act, injunctions, 31

Uniform Deceptive Trade Practices Act, remedies, 31–32

Uniform Deceptive Trade Practices Act, treble damages, 32

Waiver, contracts, 223

Warranties, 63–76

Warranties, disclaimers, 79

Warranties, disclaiming, 67

Warranties, express, 65–66

Warranties, history of, 63–65

Warranties, implied, 67–69

Warranties, oral and written, conflicts, 66–67

Warranty actions, state-based, 75

Warranty of fitness for purpose, 68

Warranty of good and workmanlike performance, 68–69

Warranty of merchantability, 68

Warranty, breach of, 45

Written warranties, Magnuson-Moss Warranty Act, 71–72

Yield spread premiums, 137